JESUIT STUDIES

St. Thomas Aquinas
on Analogy

A TEXTUAL ANALYSIS
AND SYSTEMATIC SYNTHESIS

George P. Klubertanz, S.J.

WIPF & STOCK · Eugene, Oregon

Wipf and Stock Publishers
199 W 8th Ave, Suite 3
Eugene, OR 97401

St. Thomas Aquinas on Analogy
A Textual Analysis and Systematic Synthesis
By Klubertanz, George P.
ISBN 13: 978-1-60608-450-2
Publication date 01/07/2009
Previously published by Loyola University Press, 1960

IMPRIMI POTEST: Leo J. Burns, S.J.
                 Provincial of the Wisconsin Province
                 October 3, 1958
IMPRIMATUR: ✠ Albert Cardinal Meyer
                 Archbishop of Chicago
                 April 7, 1960

CONTENTS

This book is a textual study of St. Thomas' doctrine on analogy. It joins a long line of similar studies, each claiming to be an accurate account of St. Thomas' thought on the problem. Such perennial interest in Thomistic analogy is not surprising, for the problem is a central one for Thomistic metaphysics.

Except for a few drastically monistic systems of metaphysics, most philosophies admit that the objects which they know are not all simply and entirely of a piece. They likewise maintain—unlike William James—that plurality as such is unintelligible. To make multiplicity intelligible, there seem to be only a very few alternative methods. In Platonic and Neoplatonic systems, nonbeing, or matter as opposed to being, functions to introduce radical differentiation. Some philosophers speak of appearance; others of evil; some, following Aristotle, find a principle in form and potency; still others make use of the notion of composition.

On the plane of language there are parallel solutions. The primitive forms of logical positivism seemed infatuated with the notion of a perfect language from which all ambiguity would be excluded and in which all errors become impossible—a monism of meaning. Recently it has seemed to many analysts that language is in fact filled with ambiguities and that they could be removed only in very limited areas and at a cost of making language highly abstractionist. In other types of approach appeal is made to an "unknown" (Locke, Spencer), or to a "knowledge by equivocation" (Maimonides); to symbolic knowledge, myth, metaphor, suprarational intuition, and even to completely noncognitive factors such as sentiment, voluntary or "animal" faith.

In the thought of St. Thomas Aquinas, also, the problem of multiplicity is one of the reasons for analogy, and a significant part of what he says about analogy is devoted to *predication*. To this extent, and in this sense, an investigation of analogy is of highly contemporary significance. It can be contended that analogy is more sophisticated and more supple than its corresponding doctrines in other philosophies.

An area of special concern in Thomistic analogy is the problem of our knowledge of God. For a relatively small number of philosophies there is a question whether the existence of God can even be known; that is, whether it is possible for man to come to know anything beyond the range of his sense experience. But this is a question that can arise only under very narrow and limiting suppositions.

The much more perennial problem—and, one is led to suspect, the real one—is the *status* of our knowledge of God. Over against the rationalists and gnostics of all ages there have been the proponents of negative theology. And in all cases the reason urged has been the transcendent perfection of God. Thus there is a tension and a conflict: God is known to exist, He is known to be beyond created perfections, and apparently to know Him better is to realize more and more the inadequacy of our knowledge of Him. But then how can this be called a "knowledge" of Him? How can we know that God is other than all created perfections unless in some way we do know what God is?

Doctrinally, this is a difficult problem, and St. Thomas dealt with it repeatedly. It is at the center of some of his most profound discussions of analogy. Consequently a detailed study of Thomistic analogy is of vital importance today for those many philosophers who are concerned with the meaning of our statements about God.

On the strictly textual side the problem is not only difficult but tantalizing. St. Thomas speaks of analogy in almost every one of his works, in a variety of contexts, yet he nowhere gives a thorough *ex professo* treatment of the problem. Analogy is discussed only within the framework of a specific instance of analogous likeness, only as a reply to a specific objection.[1] St. Thomas left no general treatise on analogy. If the importance of analogy in Thomistic metaphysics explains the large number of previous textual studies, the scattered and partial texts explain in great part the deficiencies and conflicting interpretations of these studies. There is no simple answer to the question: What is St. Thomas' doctrine of analogy? To give even a complicated answer is difficult enough, though this is what this book attempts to do, at least in a preliminary fashion.

Chapter 1, after a sketch of traditional interpretations and recent investigations of Thomistic analogy, outlines the areas which previous studies have not handled satisfactorily and indicates a plan of attack which may yield more reliable results. A major feature of this plan is a printed collection of the texts in which St. Thomas discusses analogy; also included in this collection are a number of texts which illustrate different types of analogy. These printed texts, together with a chronological listing of St. Thomas' writings and an index of the most common analogy terms, are given in their entirety in the Appendix. The remaining chapters of the book are devoted to an analysis of

---

[1] "His texts on the notion of analogy are relatively few, and in each case they are so restrained that we cannot but wonder why the notion has taken on such an importance in the eyes of his commentators" (Etienne Gilson, *The Christian Philosophy of St. Thomas Aquinas*, translated by L. K. Shook, C.S.B., p. 105 [New York: Random House, 1956]). Though the present investigation has uncovered a great number of texts, M. Gilson's comment on their restricted nature remains true.

these texts, and conclude with a doctrinal summary. Shortcomings are inevitable in a work of this nature, but the texts given
in the Appendix should help subsequent research correct and
complete this study.[2]

This book owes its origin to the help of many friends. The
Reverend William L. Wade, S.J., director of the Department of
Philosophy at Saint Louis University, urged its composition and
provided assistance. A number of graduate students, Mr. Robert
Barr, S.J., Sister Thomas Marguerite Flanagan, C.S.J., Mr.
Francis Mininni, S.J., Mr. Denis David Savage, and Miss Rosa
Chua Tiampo, wrote their master's theses under the author's
direction on analogy in various works of St. Thomas. The great-
est contribution was made by Mr. Patrick J. Burns, S.J., who
spent a year as a graduate assistant at Saint Louis University,
rechecking the previous studies, completing the tedious and
painstaking work of reading the *Opera omnia* of St. Thomas,
finding and checking the secondary sources, and cooperating in
the analysis and classification of texts. Without his generous and
competent help this work would have been many more years in
the writing.

---

[2] "The discussion of the meaning of St. Thomas's doctrine on analogy can last as
long as each side can discuss new texts, all authentically Thomistic, to justify
its thesis" (*ibid.*, p. 107).

CHAPTER I

Backgrounds and Problems

This introductory chapter will review the traditional interpretations of St. Thomas' doctrine of analogy, comment on recent contributions, and outline the areas in need of further investigation. Although no formal study of the sources of St. Thomas' doctrine of analogy will be made, the reader is referred to the pioneering work of Hampus Lyttkens on the subject.[1] Lyttkens traces the early mathematical and distributive meanings of *analogia* in Plato and Aristotle, the new role it assumed in Neoplatonic and Augustinian exemplarism, and the *pros hen* equivocity of Aristotle, which reached St. Thomas through Albert[2] and Averroes.[3] The most penetrating study of analogous predication in Aristotle has been made by Joseph Owens, C.Ss.R., although Lyttkens independently reached the

---

[1] Hampus Lyttkens, *The Analogy between God and the World: An Investigation of Its Background and Interpretation of Its Use by Thomas of Aquino*, pp. 15-163. Uppsala: Almqvist and Wiksells, 1952.

[2] *Ibid.*, pp. 153-63.

[3] Lyttkens has not traced the notion of analogy in detail through Averroes. The results of a preliminary examination of Averroes as a source for St. Thomas are not very promising, and the one interesting link found (see Chap. 3, n. 10) may indicate a reason. Lyttkens (p. 77) makes a few remarks on Averroes' analogy doctrine. He also mentions Avicenna on the same page and discusses Pseudo-Dionysius, pp. 87-97. The Neoplatonists treated include Plotinus, Proclus, Porphyry, Philo, Simplicius, Ammonius, and Albinus. Notably absent are Boethius, Scotus Erigena, Avicebron, and the Victorines.

same conclusions.[4] The recent work of Robert J. Henle, S.J.,[5] has superseded the earlier studies of Geiger[6] and Fabro[7] in the limited but crucial area of St. Thomas' handling of Plato and of *Platonici* texts, including those texts which develop the analogy of participation.

The names of three men stand out as commentators on St. Thomas' doctrine of analogy: Cajetan, Sylvester of Ferrara, and Suarez. Most modern literature on the subject can be traced back to one of these early commentators. Their respective positions and the refinements of their modern followers have been adequately sketched by Lyttkens, but for purposes of convenience a résumé of that sketch will be given here.[8] A bibliography has been appended to this book in case the reader wishes to examine the literature himself.

In case some readers are not immediately familiar with the traditional terms and definitions used in Thomistic discussions of analogy, a summary may refresh their memories. In the traditional account terms *(nomina)* are of three kinds: univocal (having the same meaning in all of its uses, as *horse*); equivocal (having different meanings that have no relation to each other, as *dog* said of animal and star); and analogous (having several meanings which are partly the same and partly different or which are related to one another, as *healthy*)..Analogy is the re-

---

[4] See Joseph Owens, C.Ss.R., *The Doctrine of Being in Aristotelian 'Metaphysics,'* pp. 49-63, 328-39 (Toronto: Pontifical Institute of Mediaeval Studies, 1952). Lyttkens discusses Aristotle's *pros hen* equivocity on pp. 52-58.

[5] Robert J. Henle, S.J., *Saint Thomas and Platonism* (The Hague: Nijhoff, 1956). Some of the valuable methodological conclusions of this study are summarized by the author in "Saint Thomas' Methodology in the Treatment of 'Positiones' with Particular Reference to 'Positiones Platonicae,'" *Gregorianum,* XXXVI (1955), 391-409.

[6] L.-B. Geiger, O.P., *La participation dans la philosophie de S. Thomas d'Aquin.* Paris: Vrin, 1942.

[7] C. Fabro, *La nozione metafisica di partecipazione secondo S. Tommaso d'Aquino,* second edition. Milan: Vita e Pensiero, 1950.

[8] Lyttkens, *Analogy,* pp. 205-43.

lationship that an analogous term has to the things of which it is predicated (called *analogates* or *inferiors*), or the relationship among the analogates themselves. The *analogon* is the perfection which is common to all the analogates, in the sense just defined. The analogy of attribution is that analogy in which the analogon is principally or perfectly in one analogate, called the *primary analogate*, and only secondarily (by relation) in the other or secondary analogates. The analogy of proportion is that analogy in which one analogate is directly related to another (A : B). The analogy of proportionality is that analogy in which there is no direct relationship between the analogates themselves; there is instead a relationship within each of the analogates, and these relationships are similar, though all the relata, four in number, are different. Schematically, "A is analogous to B" means "A is composed of two elements, *a* and *x*; likewise, B is composed of two components, *b* and *y*; none of these four terms is similar to any other, but the relationship of *a* to *x* is like that of *b* to *y*— *a* : *x* :: *b* : *y*." Finally, an analogy is called "proper" if the perfection is intrinsic to each of the analogates in question, and "improper" or "extrinsic" if the perfection is present only in one of the analogates.

A. CAJETAN

Most influential of all the commentators on St. Thomas has been the fifteenth-century Thomist, Cardinal Cajetan. Cajetan builds his interpretation of St. Thomas around an early text, in the *Commentary on the Sentences of Peter Lombard*, where St. Thomas speaks of analogy *secundum intentionem et non secundum esse, secundum esse et non secundum intentionem*, and *secundum intentionem et secundum esse*.[9] To these three categories Cajetan reduces all other divisions and distinctions of

---

[9] *I Sent.*, d. 19, q. 5, a. 2 ad 1. Cajetan's position is analyzed by Lyttkens, *Analogy*, pp. 205-15.

analogy found in the text of St. Thomas. Analogy *secundum esse et non secundum intentionem* is treated first. Cajetan calls this the analogy of inequality; a name and its meaning are entirely the same, as *body* means the same whether we are speaking of terrestrial or celestial bodies, but the essence named is of unequal perfection in the two cases. Cajetan claims that this is equally true of all genera with respect to their various species. He concludes by saying that the analogy of inequality is not properly analogy at all, and so rejects it as a mode of analogy. The second of St. Thomas' classes, *secundum intentionem et non secundum esse*, Cajetan calls analogy of attribution, and illustrates with the use of the term *healthy* applied to medicine, urine, and animal. This analogy taken formally (that is, with regard to what is actually signified in this way) is extrinsic; the analogous perfection *(health)* exists properly only in one of the beings about which it is predicated, the primary analogate (the animal, for health). Secondary analogates are denominated from the numerically single perfection of the primary analogate on the basis of the various relations that obtain between them and the primary analogate (cause, goal, exemplar, sign, and so forth; for example, medicine is healthy inasmuch as it is the cause of the animal's health). The analogous concept involved (health) contains distinctly the perfection of the primary analogate, but only indistinctly the relations of the secondary analogates to this perfection in the primary analogate. The expression "analogy of proportion" is not found in Cajetan—naturally enough, because he treats proportion as another word for analogy. All instances of it, however, he reduces to this analogy of attribution. The third of St. Thomas' classes, *secundum intentionem et secundum esse*, Cajetan calls analogy of proportionality, identifying it with the analogy discussed by St. Thomas in his *Quaestiones disputatae de veritate*, second question, eleventh article. The example used by Cajetan is that of vision as used of intellect and sight; for just as understanding makes a thing present to the soul, so does sight to the living body. This type alone is analogy in the proper sense, since only in this type does each of the analogates intrinsically possess the analogous perfection, which is proportionately similar in all analogates. The analogous concept involved in proportionality may be one which perfectly represents the proportion in one analogate and imperfectly represents the proportions belonging to all the others; it may also be one which imperfectly summarizes a number of different proportions but does not express the special proportions peculiar to each analogate. The former clear concept is simply many concepts and only proportionately one; the latter or confused *(con-fused)* concept is simply one and proportionately many.

Cajetan's followers have been numerous.[10] Beginning with the seventeenth-century Thomist, John of St. Thomas, they are all concerned to defend the main positions of Cajetan against opposing schools of interpretation. Most are conscious of certain tensions within their doctrine of analogy: (1) They insist that, although the analogous perfection is found *properly* in only one of the analogates in the analogy of attribution, this does not mean that the secondary analogate possesses no relevant intrinsic perfection at all. (2) They describe the analogous concept involved in the analogy of proportionality now as a *similar relation,* now as a *similar perfection* which is the basis of a similar relationship. (3) They point out many "mixed" analogies, in which the same ontological situation gives rise to two different types of analogous predication. (4) They maintain that the analogates in the analogy of proportionality are mutually independent, not all dependent upon a *primary* analogate as in the analogy of attribution, at least as far as the meaning of the analogous concept is concerned. Textually, Cajetan's fol-

---

[10] The most important of these are discussed by Lyttkens, *Analogy*, pp. 215-25. See the bibliography appended to this book for further information.

lowers have added very little to his work, although a number of special studies have been undertaken to prove that Cajetan's interpretation is faithful to the text of St. Thomas.[11] Unfortunately, these have generally resulted in adding more and more texts of St. Thomas to the prefabricated categories of Cajetan, regardless of how well they fit into those categories. None of Cajetan's followers, for example, has wondered about the textual validity of his basic identification of the analogy *secundum intentionem et secundum esse* with the analogy of proportionality treated in *De veritate*, q. 2, a. 11. Nor has any of them adequately defended Cajetan's reduction of numerous Thomistic statements on analogy to a single category of attribution by extrinsic denomination.

B. SYLVESTER OF FERRARA

Sylvester of Ferrara differs from Cajetan in his interpretation of Thomistic analogy principally by insisting that every analogy includes a first analogate which determines the import of the analogous concept; this is true both in the analogy of attribution and in the analogy of proportionality.[12] Sylvester takes this position on textual grounds: St. Thomas says in his *Summa theologiae* that in *all* analogical predication there is one primary analogate to which the others refer.[13] He attempts to reconcile this statement with St. Thomas' insistence in *De veritate*, q. 2, a. 11 that the analogy of proportionality expresses no direct relationship between the various analogates. He explains that St. Thomas is there merely rejecting the position that a name predicated absolutely of a creature can lead directly to a knowledge of the Creator and be so predicated of Him; that St. Thomas does not intend to exclude a proportional relation-

---

[11] See the works of Feckes, Goergen, Penido, Phelan, and Ramirez listed in the bibliography.

[12] Sylvester of Ferrara's position is discussed by Lyttkens, *Analogy*, pp. 225-28.

[13] *S.T.*, I, q. 13, a. 6, c.

ship between the analogates in such a way that one can be referred to the other as to a first analogate. Sylvester also attempts to reconcile St. Thomas' doctrine of an analogy *unius ad alterum* between creatures and their Creator (found both in the *Summa contra gentiles*[14] and in the *Summa theologiae*[15]) with his denial of an analogy of proportion in *De veritate*, q. 2, a. 11. Proportion must be merely one type of analogy *unius ad alterum*, which is a general designation that includes proportionality as well as proportion. Thus St. Thomas is rejecting only a direct proportion between God and creatures in *De veritate*, q. 2, a. 11, not all analogy of one-to-another, and affirming only one type of analogy of one-to-another (that is, proportionality) in the two *Summae*, not every type covered by this general term.

Sylvester's modern followers have added little to his interpretation.[16] Textually, they have strengthened his position of a first analogate in every analogy by collecting texts in which St. Thomas discusses a relationship of priority and posteriority between analogates.[17] Yet, generally speaking, their textual position is weak. Neither Sylvester nor his followers have justified the reductionism which characterizes his approach to St. Thomas' doctrine on analogy. His preoccupation with reconciling apparently conflicting texts has prevented him from scrutinizing his inadequate basic categories.

C. SUAREZ

Francis Suarez disagrees sharply with Cajetan's doctrine on analogy. The analogy of attribution is not always extrinsic; the

---

[14] *C.G.*, I, cap. 34.

[15] *S.T.*, I, q. 13, a. 5, c.

[16] These are discussed by Lyttkens, *Analogy*, pp. 228-33. The bibliography contains further information.

[17] For example, A. Van Leeuwen, S.J., "L'analogie de l'être. Genèse et contenu du concept d'analogie," *Revue néo-scolastique de philosophie*, XXXIX (1936), 293-320.

analogous perfection may exist properly in all the analogates, not only in the first analogate. This is the case in the analogy between Creator and creature, where an analogous concept designates *abstracte et praecise* the intrinsic perfection common to both analogates.[18] The analogy of proportionality, on the other hand, is not representative of the relation between God and the world. Proportionality for Suarez involves two proportions: one in which the analogous perfection exists perfectly, another in which it exists only by reference or comparison. Proportionality is always to some degree figurative or metaphorical. Since creatures exist in their own intrinsic perfection, this type of analogy cannot be used to describe their relation to God. Textually, Suarez says that St. Thomas teaches an intrinsic analogy of attribution between creatures and their Creator, but no elaborate textual proof is given for this position.

Modern Suarezians have modified some of Suarez's positions on analogy, but no significant textual study has appeared on the relationship between Suarezian and Thomistic analogy. Father Descoqs, having rejected proportionality, tries to show that St. Thomas is not speaking of Cajetan's proportionality in *De veritate*, q. 2, a. 11.[19] Santeler finds both intrinsic and extrinsic attribution in St. Thomas, as well as proportionality.[20] No independent examination of the Thomistic corpus of analogy texts has yet been published by a Suarezian; even when rejecting Cajetan's interpretation, they discuss Thomistic analogy in the light of Cajetan's categories. The preponderance of Cajetan's influence in the systematic elaboration of a theory of analogy is more readily appreciated in those who opposed him. Even when they disagreed, they used his frame of reference.

---

[18] Suarez is discussed by Lyttkens, *Analogy*, pp. 234-41. He agrees (p. 238, n. 9) with those critics who say that the "analogous" concept in Suarez's analogy of intrinsic attribution is really univocal.

[19] See *ibid.*, pp. 238-40.

[20] *Ibid.*, pp. 240-41.

D. RECENT CONTRIBUTIONS

Despite some preliminary work by Gilson[21] and Habbel,[22] the only full-scale study[23] of Thomistic analogy which escapes the limitations of the traditional commentaries has been the doctoral dissertation of Hampus Lyttkens, *The Analogy between God and the World: An Investigation of Its Background and Interpretation of Its Use by Thomas of Aquino.*[24] The first two sections of this work study the sources of St. Thomas' doctrine on analogy and review the traditional interpretations found in the Thomistic and Suarezian commentators. These points have already been discussed. Lyttkens next indicates the basic types of analogy his independent examination of the Thomistic corpus has revealed. Against this textual background he discusses the limitations of the traditional commentaries and their basic categories. Finally he goes on to give a fuller analysis of each of the Thomistic analogies which he has discovered. This analytic

---

[21] Etienne Gilson has published no complete textual discussion of Thomistic analogy. He describes analogy as a similarity between cause and effect, citing texts from the *Summa theologiae* and the *Contra gentiles.* He does not mention proportionality. See his *The Christian Philosophy of St. Thomas Aquinas,* pp. 105-10. His penetrating study of Cardinal Cajetan as a commentator on St. Thomas has made it easier to undertake a fresh examination of the Thomistic doctrine of analogy, apart from Cajetan's categories. See his "Cajétan et l'existence," *Tijdschrift voor philosophie,* XV (1953), 267-86.

[22] See J. Habbel, *Die Analogie zwischen Gott und Welt nach Thomas von Aquin* (Regensburg: Habbel, 1928). Like Gilson, Habbel stresses the causal analogy between God and the world. He thinks that St. Thomas' discussion of proportionality in *Ver.,* q. 2, a. 11, arose out of a desire to show that the essence of God cannot be determined from any creature. See Habbel, *Analogie,* pp. 55 ff. Gilson and Habbel are discussed by Lyttkens, *Analogy,* pp. 241-42.

[23] Incidental discussions of Thomistic analogy are to be found in several recent works, which partly or even entirely break free from Cajetanist categories; see the works of Balthasar, Hayen, Krąpiec, Masiello, and Flanagan listed in the bibliography. But these works either do not deal with analogy as a main topic or study only a limited number of texts. Landry rejected Cajetan's interpretation, but without any full analysis of the texts of St. Thomas.

[24] Lyttkens, as cited in Chap. 1, n. 1. This work is given an extended review by L.-B. Geiger, O.P., in the *Bulletin thomiste,* IX (1955), 416-23.

section of Lyttkens' work is of very high caliber: the textual references are numerous, pertinent, and accurate; the analysis is both cautious and nonreductionist. His conclusions may be summarized as follows.

1. There are three main types of analogy in St. Thomas, all based on the likeness of effect to causes: (*a*) an analogy of attribution in which a concept is drawn from God and used to designate creation extrinsically;[25] (*b*) an analogy in which the image is designated from its archetype, because of an analogous perfection which exists perfectly in God, imperfectly in creatures;[26] and (*c*) an analogy in which the first Cause is designated from its effects, the perfections of which exist in a higher way in their cause.[27]

2. An analogy of proportionality is found in St. Thomas, but it plays only a subordinate role in his metaphysics, where it functions "as a logical aid in stating of God certain properties taken from creation."[28]

Among the criticisms which Lyttkens makes of previous interpretations of Thomistic analogy, the following seem most important from a textual viewpoint.

1. There is no textual foundation for the identification of the *analogia secundum intentionem et secundum esse* (*In I Sententiarum*, d. 19, q. 5, a. 2 ad 1) with the analogy of proportionality discussed in the *De veritate* (q. 2, a. 11).[29] This

---

25 Lyttkens, *Analogy*, pp. 245-66.

26 *Ibid.*, pp. 266-83.

27 *Ibid.*, pp. 283-310.

28 *Ibid.*, pp. 474-75.

29 *Ibid.*, pp. 270-71. An independent study by S. M. Ramirez, O.P., comes to the same conclusion; see his article "En torno a un famoso texto de santo Tomás sobre la analogía," *Sapientia*, VIII (1953), 166-92. Through an examination of the texts themselves and their respective contexts, Ramirez finds that *I Sent.*, d. 19, q. 5, a. 2 ad 1 is *not* parallel to *Ver.*, q. 2, a. 11. He supports his conclusion by comparing the text from the *Sentences* with St. Albert's treatment in the same place. Ramirez finds three types of analogy in this early

criticism deprives the position of Cajetan and his followers of its claim to a textual basis in St. Thomas.

2. Although St. Thomas does discuss an analogy of attribution, he does not do so in the texts usually cited by the commentators. These texts and others like them deal with intrinsic analogies between cause and effect.[30]

3. St. Thomas' use of examples is not a sufficient criterion for classifying texts, since he often cites the same example to illustrate several different types of analogy.[31]

4. There is no textual foundation for the claim of Cajetan's followers that an implied analogy of proportionality is operative in those texts which explicitly describe a direct (and intrinsic) analogy between God and the world.[32]

5. Sylvester of Ferrara's interpretation of the analogy of one-to-another as a general term including proportionality is incompatible with the context of *Summa theologiae*, I, q. 13, a. 6, and *Summa contra gentiles*, Book 1, Chapter 34.[33]

6. The interpretation of the analogy of one-to-another given by Suarez, in which the analogous perfection exists absolutely

text of St. Thomas: analogy of inequality *(secundum esse sed non secundum intentionem)*, of extrinsic attribution *(secundum intentionem sed non secundum esse)*, and of intrinsic attribution *(secundum esse et secundum intentionem)*. He thinks that *Ver.*, q. 2, a. 11 presents a fourth kind of analogy, proportionality. He further identifies *analogia unius vel multorum ad unum* with proportion and *analogia plurium ad plura* with proportionality. The division is neat but somewhat oversimplified.

30 Lyttkens, *Analogy*, pp. 255, 285, 296-98.

31 *Ibid.*, pp. 296-97. The same conclusion is reached by William Meissner, S.J., "Some Notes on a Figure in St. Thomas," *New Scholasticism*, XXXI (1957), 68-84. The article collects and analyzes St. Thomas' uses of the *sanitas* example in analogy contexts.

32 Lyttkens, *Analogy*, pp. 298-307. The doctrine of "mixed" analogies regards one ontological situation as grounding two or more distinct analogies. Valid enough in principle, the doctrine is interpreted by Cajetan's followers so that all intrinsic analogies are automatically proportionalities by their definition, and all *direct* one-to-one analogies are necessarily extrinsic.

33 *Ibid.*, pp. 307-10.

in one analogate and by a relation to this absolute perfection in the other analogates, does not reflect St. Thomas' *analogia unius ad alterum.*[34]

7. Because they have supposed that proportionality is St. Thomas' only intrinsic analogy, Cajetan, Sylvester, and their followers have missed the true role of proportionality within Thomistic analogy and reduced other types of analogy to the analogy of proportionality because St. Thomas presents them as intrinsic analogies.[35]

What about the work of Lyttkens himself? How well has he investigated St. Thomas' doctrine of analogy? His research into the sources of St. Thomas' doctrine, although not complete, and his criticisms of the traditional commentaries are excellent. His positive exposition of Thomistic analogy also has many merits. He handles a large number of texts; he is not an avowed reductionist. The very limited conclusions he draws concerning Thomistic analogy (as summarized above) seem to be supported by the texts he cites. These achievements are considerable; the limitations of Lyttkens' book as a Thomistic textual study in no way minimize them.

What are these limitations? As a study of St. Thomas' doctrine on analogy Lyttkens' work has five major shortcomings.

1. In spite of the large number of textual references, it is still not a thorough textual study. Not all the pertinent texts are treated; of those cited, not all are quoted even in part.

2. The chronological aspects of the textual problem are left more or less unexplored.

3. Lyttkens' treatment of the three causal analogies he finds in St. Thomas is inadequate on several counts. The tripartite division represents an oversimplification of the texts. Little indication is given of the relative importance or unimportance of a

---

[34] *Ibid.*, p. 310.
[35] *Ibid.*, pp. 463-65, 299-302.

particular analogy.[36] The metaphysical significance of the analogy of participation is lost amid the extrinsicist implications of "image-prototype" terminology.[37]

4. A certain literalism is in evidence, especially with regard to the terms *proportio, proportionalitas,* and *analogia;* this results in lengthy discussions of texts which should have been eliminated as irrelevant.[38]

5. Not at home in Thomistic metaphysics, Lyttkens works out in some detail the metaphysical implications of the analogies he finds in St. Thomas. Sometimes this venture goes well, sometimes not so well;[39] but the end result is a textual study whose lines are continuously blurred by distracting speculations on Thomistic natural theology.

THE METHOD OF THE PRESENT BOOK

This study of St. Thomas' doctrine on analogy utilizes Lyttkens' research into the sources of that doctrine and accepts his fundamental criticisms of the traditional interpretations. Yet, while building on Lyttkens' investigations, it attempts to supply

---

[36] For example, the "analogy of extrinsic attribution" found in *Ver.*, q. 21, a. 4, is given much more extensive treatment than the texts on predication *per prius et posterius* which are so prominent in St. Thomas' works.

[37] See Lyttkens, *Analogy*, pp. 342-47. He seems to feel that, because the analogy of participation can be used only *after* the existence of God has been proved, it is nothing more than a logical reformulation of previously attained knowledge. As a result his treatment of the *participatio* texts in St. Thomas is brief and misleading.

[38] See Chap. 4, below. This literalism is also noticeable in his examination of the sources of St. Thomas' doctrine of analogy.

[39] See, for instance, Lyttkens' remarks on the role of the act of existing within Thomistic metaphysics (*Analogy*, pp. 168-70, 257-61, 306-07, 357-59, and 413-14). Lyttkens' conceptualism (or perhaps the conceptualism of the Thomistic commentators he has studied so thoroughly) is evident throughout sect. 5 of Chap. 5, "Logical Aspects of the Three Types of Analogous Statements Based on the Causal Analogy" (pp. 360-414). For his views on the Thomistic proofs for the existence of God see *ibid.*, pp. 405-06. Lyttkens also finds an emanation doctrine latent in Thomistic metaphysics (*ibid.*, pp. 413-14).

for some of the shortcomings of his textual research. To this end a thorough study of the works of St. Thomas has been made, not by means of references gathered by other authors and the helps of indices, but by a page-by-page scanning of all the works. All the texts in which St. Thomas discusses analogy, as well as a number of texts which illustrate various types of analogy, have been collected and are printed in chronological order in Appendix I. A distinct chapter studies these texts for any significant chronological developments. Succeeding chapters analyze them for doctrinal constants. Irrelevant uses of *proportio, proportionalitas,* and *analogia* are identified and eliminated. Proper proportionality, *analogia secundum esse et non secundum intentionem,* and the special problems connected with these analogies are treated separately. Chapter 5 gives the methodological conclusions of this textual analysis. Chapter 6 attempts a synthetic presentation of these various results in the form of a systematic development. Throughout the book an attempt is made to indicate the relative prominence of the various types of Thomistic analogy as found in the texts, as well as to point out their interrelationships.

How are the hundreds of texts to be analyzed and synthesized? Most previous commentators have used the method of "key texts"—selecting and analyzing in detail one or more texts as keys to the rest, and reducing all other texts to the status of variants or completions. But this method has resulted in essentially different syntheses, all of which are open to serious criticism. For practical reasons, therefore, this method is to be avoided. *All* the texts must be dealt with.

Yet if this book is to aid a student of St. Thomas in reading the texts, it must bring some order into a presentation of them. However, a "systematic" approach (working out a theory of analogy and "illustrating" with apt texts) is also open to criticism, for here everything depends on the interpretation, and different interpretations have claimed textual support. The only ordering and classification of texts that does not presuppose an interpretation is a philological one. The basis for an objective analysis of St. Thomas' doctrine can only be what he *literally says*. Hence our first clues must be the explicit language of St. Thomas: the very words and phrases themselves.

The texts, then, will first be studied by comparing and contrasting the terms and expressions which occur in them. In each case one or more texts will be presented in translation. These translations are the author's own.[40]

Each quoted text is immediately identified by the Latin title of the work from which it is taken, together with its code number by means of which the Latin original can easily be found in the Appendix. In this code the first number locates the work in chronological sequence, the second the place of the quoted text in the series of texts taken from the same work. Thus, a text identified as (*S.T.*, I [17.48]) is from the *Summa theologiae*, first part. This is the seventeenth "work" in the chronological series, and the particular text is the forty-eighth one quoted from that work.

---

[40] Though in some cases existing English versions were consulted, the final version given here is our own.

CHAPTER II

Chronological Variations

The many widely divergent interpretations of St. Thomas all have some textual foundation and are derived in one way or another from the text itself. Hence we can legitimately conclude that the diversity of interpretations is to some extent a reflection of the state of the texts. If we turn now to the analytical index to the texts (in Appendix II), we find a wide variety of terms, all used with some frequency. There is then a considerable variation, at least a terminological one.

Recent scholarship has stressed the importance of a chronological study of any author in whose works any variation of expression or doctrine is to be found. In the case of St. Thomas himself the use of the chronological method of investigation has led to brilliant results. Consequently there is no need to argue for the legitimacy or the importance of a chronological study of the texts on analogy.

But a more detailed study of the analytical index shows us that the situation is not simply a matter of chronological variation. Let us begin by considering the thirteen terms which St. Thomas uses most often throughout his works and see how they are distributed. We can take six works whose composition just about spans St. Thomas' career as a writer. In the table on page 21 the number in parentheses after a term indicates the total number of times that the term is found in all the works of St.

Thomas. The numbers in the columns indicate the frequency with which the terms are used in the six works. It will be found that all the terms except one are used in the earliest of the works. The far higher frequency of use in the *Summa theologiae* can be explained by the length and thought content of that work without recourse to the supposition that there was a chronological change in the thinking of St. Thomas. This rather surprising regularity gives no hint of trial and error, of tentative gropings and final synthesis.

Frequency of Use of
Thirteen Terms in Six Works of St. Thomas

Term	*In I Sent.* (1254-1256)	*De veritate* (1256-1259)	*De potentia* (1259-1268)	*Contra gentiles* (1261-1264)	*Summa theologiae Prima pars* (1266-1268)	*In metaphysic.* (1272)
Participation (126)	7	4	6	11	55	4
Likeness (76)	3	14	11	8	18	2
More and less perfect (61)	9	4	3	3	19	1
Per prius et posterius (59)	8	4	3	2	12	5
Proportion (54)	—	6	—	1	9	10
Eminence (37)	6	1	7	2	12	—
Equivocal or analogous cause (30)	1	1	3	2	6	1
Imitation (30)	9	5	5	1	7	—
Proportionality (29)	2	5	—	—	4	4
Deficiency of effect (29)	3	1	4	1	6	1
More or less excellent (27)	2	2	4	1	13	1
Simply vs. *secundum quid* (26)	1	—	1	—	6	4
Attribution, reference, or respect (17)	1	—	—	2	2	—

Not only did St. Thomas employ more or less the same terminology concerning analogy throughout his writings; the main outlines of the doctrine he expressed remained constant as well—at least on superficial observation. But this does not mean that the texts are simple and easily digested. Often a single text will present several different descriptions of the same analogous reality and employ two or more terms to name the diverse relationships within a complex analogy.[1] At other times St. Thomas distinguishes two or more distinct analogies within one complex situation.[2] Even though his discussions of analogy most often center around the relationship of God to the world, this single relationship is viewed from many different aspects. The result is that St. Thomas seems to have many different approaches. If we add to this complexity the independent treatments of other concrete analogies, such as that of substance and accident, we find a rather bewildering variety of texts.

Since this variety is not significantly reduced by a chronological arrangement of the texts, we need to make another hypothesis. The textual studies of St. Thomas by recent scholars have brought out an additional point concerning the philosophy of St. Thomas: he does not expound this philosophy systematically for its own sake, but only partially and for the solution of particular problems, usually theological ones. We can therefore suppose that the diversity of problems and viewpoints rather than doctrinal development[3] is the principal explanation for the variety of terminology—and of solution, should that be found. This hypothesis will be tested in Chapter 3.

---

[1] See, for instance, *I Sent.* (4.2, 15), *Metaphys.* (33.9), *Compend. theol.* (39.5). (This form of reference, with title of the work followed by a number in parentheses, refers to the collection of texts given in Appendix I. The number before the period is the number of the work [or part of the work] in the chronological sequence; the number after the period is the number of the text of that work quoted or to which reference is made. For a list of the abbreviations see p. 158.)

[2] See, for instance, *I Sent.* (4.16) or *Pot.* (14.22).

[3] This is not meant to deny, of course, that St. Thomas' use of such phrases as *per participationem* or *modo eminentiori* became more precise and meaningful as the metaphysical background for these analogies gradually deepened.

To clear the ground for the examination of the constant terminology it will be helpful to remove any confusion created by the presence of chronological variations. This will be the task of the present chapter.

A. DOCTRINAL DEVELOPMENTS

Several instances of development are clear. These are of two types: either a doctrine or a verbal rubric (that is, a word, phrase, or description) employed consistently in earlier works is later abandoned or denied, or a rubric fluctuates through the various works or even within the same work, being either accepted or rejected as its meaning shifts. We shall call the first type "doctrinal development" and the second "terminological shift." We shall examine five instances of doctrinal development. Though these concern relatively minor points, they do seem to be true doctrinal developments; in contrast to the three instances of terminological shift examined in the next section of this chapter, they reveal a change in doctrine (either change or omission), and not merely the floating meaning of some term or rubric of phraseology.

1. *Una ratio vs. diversae rationes.* Three texts in St. Thomas' *Commentary on the Sentences* speak of a single intelligibility *(una ratio)* involved in analogy.

> For that intelligibility [of wisdom] is one according to analogy, existing primarily in God, secondarily in creatures (*I Sent.* [4.22]).
> All such [names] are said of God and creatures not equivocally but analogously, according to a single intelligibility (*I Sent.* [4.24]).
> Since the nature of being has a single intelligibility in all things according to analogy (*II Sent.* [5.1]).

One earlier text and all subsequent discussions of this same point speak of a multiplicity of intelligibilities to be found in every analogy.

Something is said to be predicated analogously which is predicated of several things whose intelligibilities are different but which are attributed to one and the same thing (*Prin. nat.* [3.1]).

For in things which are predicated analogously there is neither a single intelligibility (as in univocation) nor simply different intelligibilities (as in equivocation). Rather, a name which is predicated in several ways signifies different proportions to some one thing (*S.T.*, I [17.31]).

There is a single intelligibility for univocal predicates and simply diverse intelligibilities for equivocal predicates. For analogous predicates, however, a term, taken in one of its meanings, must be put in the definition of the same term, taken in its other meanings (*S.T.*, I [17.41]).

It should be noted that something is predicated of different things in several ways: sometimes according to the very same intelligibility (and it is then said to be predicated univocally, as *animal* is of horse and cow); sometimes according to completely different intelligibilities (and it is then said to be predicated equivocally, as *dog* is the star and the animal); and sometimes according to intelligibilities which are partly different and partly not different (*Metaphys.* [33.9]).

For those things which are predicated [analogously] the same name is predicated of different things according to an intelligibility partly the same and partly different (*Metaphys.* [33.26]).[4]

These texts show St. Thomas changing his answer to the question of the plurality of the analogous intelligibility. In three early texts he speaks of a *single* intelligibility; in all later texts he denies a single intelligibility and speaks instead of different intelligibilities attributed to the same thing or of intelligibilities which are partly the same and partly different.

2. *Reductio ad causam non univocam.* In an early work St. Thomas accepts the dictum "Every equivocal is reduced to a univocal" and yet maintains that in the real order equivocal generation is prior to univocal generation.

---

[4] See similar statements in *Metaphys.* (33.11, 18), and *Ethic.* (34.2).

Although every equivocal is rooted in a univocal, it is not necessary that equivocal generation be reduced to univocal generation.
Rather, it should be reduced to an agent which is univocal in itself.
For we see in nature that equivocal generations are prior to univocal generations. The reason for this is that equivocal causes exercise an influence over the entire species, unlike univocal causes,
which have influence only over a single individual. Univocal causes,
then, are like instruments in relation to equivocal causes (*Boethii
de Trin.* [11.4]).[5]

The next time the question comes up we find that the answer
is slightly different.

An equivocal agent must be prior to a univocal agent because
a univocal agent does not exercise its causality over the entire
species (otherwise it would be its own cause) but only over an
individual within that species. An equivocal agent exercises its
causality over the whole species, and thus the first agent must be
equivocal (*Pot.* [14.25]).

In the *Prima pars* of the *Summa theologiae* a final answer
is given.

And so the universal cause of an entire species is not a univocal
agent. And the universal cause is prior to the particular cause. Nevertheless this universal agent, although not univocal, is not entirely
equivocal either, for otherwise it would not produce its like. Rather,
it can be called an analogous agent; just as in predication every
univocal is rooted in one primary subject which is not univocal but
analogous, being (*S.T.*, I [17.32]).[6]

Thus we see St. Thomas first accepting the dictum that every
equivocal term is rooted in an univocal one, but at the same time
insisting that equivocal generation is prior to univocal genera-

---

[5] A conciliatory gesture is made to the traditional axiom in the phrase "an agent
univocal in itself." But the expression is almost meaningless, and understand-
ably enough is dropped in later works.

[6] *Universale agens non univocum* and *prima causa non univoca* are also mentioned
in *S.T.*, I (17.12, 61) and *De div. nomin.* (18.3).

tion; next speaking of a first agent which is not univocal but equivocal; and finally inverting the original dictum to say that every univocal is rooted in an analogous first subject (in predication) and in an analogous first agent (in causality).

It may not be amiss to point out the parallel between this change and St. Thomas' movement away from a single intelligibility in analogous predication. In both of these instances St. Thomas first bowed to the logical demand for clarity and definability but later rejected this claim in favor of the irreducible diversity of the real order, which cannot be enclosed by man within the limits of a clear concept.

3. *Twofold Exemplarity.* In his earlier works St. Thomas occasionally describes the similarity between God and creatures in terms of a twofold exemplarity, one of the divine idea, the other of the divine nature as model. The following text may be quoted as typical.

> The exemplar cause of things exists in God in two ways. First, it is present as something in his intellect; thus, according to its ideas the divine intellect is the exemplar of all things which come from it, just as the intellect of the artisan, through his art, is the exemplar of all his artifacts. Secondly, it is present as something in his nature; thus, according to the perfection of that goodness by which he himself is good, God is the exemplar of all goodness (*I Sent.* [4.19]).[7]

All of the texts in which St. Thomas discusses the similarity between God and the world in terms of exemplarity will be examined in Chapter 3, section D. These texts describing God as an exemplar both as an intellect and as a nature are cited here because they are significantly confined to St. Thomas' earlier works. Later discussions of exemplarity, as we shall see, either simply refer to the similarity between creatures and their divine exemplar as an unspecified form of imitation or explicitly link

---

[7] See similar texts in *I Sent.* (4.3), *Ver.* (9.7, 18), and *Pot.* (14.2).

exemplarity with efficient causality. Only in these early texts is a twofold exemplarity the basic approach.[8]

4. *Proportionality.* In two passages in his *Disputed Questions on Truth (De veritate)*[9] St. Thomas describes the similarity between God and creatures in terms of proper proportionality. We shall have to discuss these and other proportionality texts in Chapter 4, sections A and B. Here we merely wish to point out an item of chronological interest: these proportionality texts were both written about the year 1256-1257. There are no later texts mentioning proper proportionality in the discussions of the analogy between God and creatures. This fact seems to indicate a definite doctrinal change—we shall have to examine the precise bearing of this point later. We wish only to mention here that as he did with the formal exemplarity of the divine ideas, St. Thomas abandoned explicit proportionality in his later writings as the only description of the analogy between God and creatures.[10]

5. *Participation and the Limitation of Act by Potency.* A recent study has pointed out an interesting development of St. Thomas' handling of participation.[11] The formal, explicit statement that act is limited only by the potency which receives it occurs for the first time in the *Quaestio disputata de potentia Dei.*[12] In that same work the distinction between God and creatures in terms of participation occurs in close proximity to the

---

[8] A somewhat later text, *S.T.,* I (17.114), seems also to be describing this twofold exemplarity, although the text is not clear.

[9] *Ver.* (9.9, 11, 12, 35). One other possible proper-proportionality text occurs in *III Sent.* (6.1). It is noteworthy that one of these major proper-proportionality texts, *Ver.* (9.35), offers proper proportionality merely as one of two valid ways of describing the similarity between God and creatures, the other valid way being proportion.

[10] For a discussion of some apparent exceptions to this statement see below, Chap. 4, pp. 80-86. The pertinent texts are cited in n. 8 of that chapter.

[11] W. Norris Clarke, S.J., "The Limitation of Act by Potency: Aristotelianism or Neoplatonism." *New Scholasticism,* XXVI (1952), 167-94.

[12] *Ibid.,* p. 192. See also *Pot.,* q. 1, a. 2; q. 7, a. 2 ad 9.

limitation principle.[13] In the *Summa contra gentiles* there would seem to be the first occurrence of the explicit blending of the two doctrines in one and the same passage.[14] Later full texts on participation ordinarily use the principle of limitation by potency.

In the *Commentary on the Sentences,* as the table at the beginning of this chapter clearly shows, participation is held by St. Thomas. But most of the texts merely state that the participant is limited, defective, imperfect, and so on.[15] In a very few cases the reason for this imperfection is said to be "the recipient."[16] "The recipient" is a vague term and has no discoverable metaphysical status; it cannot, therefore, be considered to offer anything like a satisfactory explanation.

In the *De veritate* St. Thomas hardly uses the term participation.[17] At the same time there are a number of trenchant, brief criticisms of Platonic participation, and one quite lengthy examination, which concludes by making participation equivalent to *extrinsic* causality (efficient and exemplary).[18]

In the *De potentia* (with less than desirable clarity) and the *Contra gentiles* the imperfection of the participated perfection is said to be the potency which receives that perfection. Now, potency is a clearly and technically defined metaphysical principle, not merely a solution of a special problem. From this

---

[13] *Pot.,* q. 7, a. 2 ad 8 (participation), ad 9 (limitation).

[14] *C.G.* (15.10).

[15] In four passages (*I Sent.* [4.2, 28], *II Sent.* [5.13], *IV Sent.* [7.7]) participation is taken in the sense of the sharing of both analogates in a perfection separated from both, and is rejected.

[16] *I Sent.* (4.4, 10, 20); *II Sent.* (5.20).

[17] *Ver.* (9.12) interprets participation as sharing in a distinct perfection and rejects it as suitable to the analogy between God and creature. *Ver.* (9.8, 34, 36) does use the term, but in no case is the text clear and full; it would seem that all of them could be read as extrinsic.

[18] *Ver.,* q. 3, a. 1 ad 5; a. 5 c.; a. 7 c.; a. 8 c.; q. 4, a. 6 ad 2; q. 5, a. 9 c.; q. 8, a. 9 c.; q. 10, aa. 6, 12; q. 18, a. 7 c.; q. 19, a. 1 c.; q. 21, a. 4 ad 3; q. 23, a. 1 ad 7; q. 26, a. 4 ad 5. The lengthy discussion is q. 21, a. 4; the conclusion of this is given in Appendix I (9.30).

point on, we find that the analogy of participation is no longer merely descriptive, vague, and perhaps extrinsic; it rests on a strictly metaphysical explanation, it is a sharply defined term and idea, and it not only allows for an intrinsic perfection in the participant but actually and formally rests on such an inherent perfection.

We can conclude that the doctrine of participation underwent a development in the works of St. Thomas. In the early works it appears as a vague descriptive term, devoid of any profound metaphysical relations to the basic metaphysical principles of St. Thomas' thought. In its second stage, by being joined with the fully developed doctrine of act and potency, it is a clear, definite, and metaphysical doctrine.[19]

B.   TERMINOLOGICAL SHIFTS

A typical terminological shift takes place within St. Thomas' *Commentary on the First Book of the Sentences,* where the phrase *per prius et posterius* is alternately rejected and accepted as a description of the analogy between God and creatures. The following texts illustrate this pattern.

> [REJECTED.] Such a community [of analogy] may be of two types. Either some things participate in some one perfection according to a relation of priority and posteriority (as do potency and act in the intelligibility of being, and substance and accident in like manner), or one thing receives its being and intelligibility from the other. The analogy of the creature to its Creator is of this latter

---

[19] Father Clarke, "Limitation of Act by Potency" (above, n. 11), considers this development to be a sign of the way in which St. Thomas became progressively more Platonic. Since this present study is not concerned with St. Thomas' sources, an alternative interpretation can be offered only in passing and as a suggestion. Perhaps St. Thomas began his treatment of the relation between God and the world mostly as a theologian, adopting the participation terminology from tradition as a tenable position; as he came to see its philosophical difficulties, he abandoned it; with a new philosophical insight that was compatible with other metaphysical principles, he developed *his own meaning* for the traditional terminology.

type. The creature has existence only insofar as it descends from the First Being and it is called a being only insofar as it imitates the First Being (*I Sent.* [4.2]).

[ACCEPTED.] [God is not an equivocal cause] since effect and cause here are somewhat similar in name and intelligibility according to priority and posteriority. God by His wisdom makes us wise, but in such a way that our wisdom always falls short of the perfection of His wisdom, as an accident falls short of the perfection of being as this is found in substance (*I Sent.* [4.11]).

[REJECTED.] Something is predicated analogously . . . according to intention only and not according to its being; this happens when one intention is referred to several things according to priority and posteriority. [Something may also be predicated analogously] according to intention and according to its being. . . . In such analogies a common nature must be found in each of the things of which it is predicated, although it differs in each according to its greater or lesser perfection. In this manner are truth, goodness, and similar perfections predicated analogously of God and creatures (*I Sent.* [4.17]).

[ACCEPTED.] For that intelligibility [of wisdom] is one according to analogy, existing primarily in God, secondarily in creatures (*I Sent.* [4.22]).

[ACCEPTED.] "Person" is said of God and creatures neither univocally nor equivocally but analogously. . . . It is said antecedently *(per prius)* of God, then of creatures (*I Sent.* [4.26]).

[REJECTED.] There are two types of analogy. One involves a resemblance in some one point which applies to the analogates according to priority and posteriority. This kind of analogy cannot obtain between God and creatures, any more than univocation. The other type is found when one thing imitates another as far as it can, yet does not fully reach that other's perfection. Such is the analogy between creatures and God (*I Sent.* [4.29]).

These texts highlight the shifting meaning of the phrase *per prius et posterius*. Three of them reject and three of them accept the phrase as descriptive of the analogous likeness between God and creatures. In those texts in which it is accepted, the expression seems to mean only that a perfection possessed by God in a more perfect manner and according to (causal) priority is

shared by creatures in a less perfect manner and only consequently upon that possession by God.[20] In those texts in which
it is rejected, it implies that both God and creatures share in
some common perfection which is somehow distinct from both
and prior to both.[21] After the *Commentary on the First Book of
the Sentences* it is used only in the former meaning, and so is
consistently accepted as a description of the analogy between
God and creatures.

Proportion is another Thomistic term which shifts meaning
from text to text, and is accordingly accepted and rejected as a
description of the likeness between God and creatures. The following text is one of several which reject proportion (where
"proportion" is equated with an interdetermining or mutual relationship between God and creatures).

> In those terms predicated according to the first type of analogy
> [that is, proportion], there must be some definite relation between
> things to which something is common by analogy. Consequently it
> is impossible that something be said of God and creature according
> to this kind of proportion (*Ver.* [9.9]).[22]

Numerous texts accept proportion (where it does not imply
either an interdetermining or a quantitative relationship of one
analogate to another). The following text is typical.

---

[20] See *I Sent.* (4.11): "sapientia nostra semper deficit a ratione sapientiae suae,
sicut accidens a ratione entis, secundum quod est in substantia."

[21] See *I Sent.* (4.2): "[Communitas analogiae est] ex eo quod aliqua participant
aliquid unum secundum prius et posterius, sicut potentia et actus rationem
entis, et similiter substantia et accidens." Note the contrast in *I Sent.* (4.29)
between "convenientia in aliquo uno quod eis per prius et posterius convenit,"
which is rejected, and "unum imitatur aliud quantum potest," which is
accepted, because it safeguards God's supremacy.

I Sent. (4.17) describes the relationship not as one *secundum prius et
posterius* (since this phrase is reserved for the analogy *secundum intentionem
tantum*) but as one *secundum rationem maioris perfectionis et minoris*. Thus
this text rejects analogy *secundum prius et posterius* on the ground that it is
purely extrinsic, not because it posits some third thing prior to both God
and creatures.

[22] See also *Ver.* (9.6, 11, 12).

"Proportion" has two meanings. First, it can signify a determined relationship of one quantity to another; thus, double, triple,
and equal are kinds of proportion. Secondly, any relationship of
one thing to another can be called proportion. In this sense, there
can be a proportion between a creature and God, inasmuch as the
creature is related to Him as effect to cause (*S.T.*, I [17.18]).[23]

One text offers both proportion and proportionality as alter-
natively possible analogies.

In the sense in which the term proportion is transferred to signify any relationship of one thing to another . . . , nothing prevents
us from saying that there is a proportion of man to God, since man
stands in some relationship to God, as that he is made by God and
is subject to Him.
Or the answer could be given that, although there cannot be a
proportion strictly so called of the finite to the infinite, yet there
can be a proportionality, which is the likeness of two proportions
(*Ver.* [9.35]).[24]

Proportion, then, is another term which shifts meaning in
St. Thomas' discussions of analogy. Often enough St. Thomas
will give both meanings of proportion[25] and then go on to reject
proportion as an interdetermining relationship and accept it as
a causal (or intentional) relationship between God and creatures. Sometimes he will understand by proportion only an interdetermining relationship and consequently reject it; sometimes
he will accept it without qualification, understanding by it simply a (nonquantitative) relationship of one thing to another.

A third instance of a terminological shift is the phrase "one
in the definition of the other." The following texts, arranged in
chronological order, are representative.

---

[23] See similar texts in *III Sent.* (6.2), *Qq. qdl.*, I (8.2), *Ver.* (9.27), *Boethii de
Trin.* (11.2), and *C.G.* (15.20).
[24] See also *IV Sent.* (7.9).
[25] There are, of course, more than two meanings for *proportio*. See below, Chap. 4,
sect. A.

[REJECTED.] [In a determining proportion, which does *not* obtain between God and creatures] one analogate must be found in the definition of the other, as substance is found in the definition of accident, or else some common note must be put in the definitions of both, inasmuch as both are denominated by their relationship to that one thing, as substance is found in the definitions of both quantity and quality (*Ver.* [9.14]).[26]

[REJECTED.] The first cause, which is God, does not constitute part of the essence of creatures, although existence, which creatures possess, can only be understood as deriving from the divine essence (*Pot.* [14.4]). [This is said in reply to an argument which holds that "the efficient cause does not belong to the nature of a thing," so that the essence of the thing can be completely understood without the cause.]

[ACCEPTED.] Whatever is predicated about things according to priority and posteriority is surely not predicated univocally, since the prior analogate is included in the definition of the posterior analogate, as substance is in the definition of accident inasmuch as it is being. . . . Nothing is predicated of God and other things according to the same order but rather according to priority and posteriority (*C.G.* [15.5]).

[ACCEPTED.] In the case of all names which are predicated analogously of several things, it is necessary that all be predicated with respect to one, and therefore that that one be placed in the definition of all. Because "the intelligibility which a name means is its definition," as is said in the fourth book of the *Metaphysics*, a name must be antecedently predicated of that which is put in the definitions of the others, and consequently of the others, according to the order in which they approach, more or less, that first analogate (*S.T.*, I [17.35]).

[ACCEPTED.] For analogous predicates, however, a term, taken in one of its meanings, must be put in the definition of the same term, taken in its other meanings (*S.T.*, I [17.41]).

[REJECTED.] Although relationship to its cause is not part of the definition of the being which is caused, nevertheless this [relationship] is involved in those notes which are part of its definition (*S.T.*, I [17.74]).

---

[26] See also *III Sent.* (6.5).

[REJECTED.] Being is predicated essentially only of God, since the divine *esse* is subsistent and absolute. Being is predicated of all creatures by participation. . . . But something is participated in two ways. It can be found as part of the substance of the participant, as genus is participated by its species. This is not the way in which *esse* is participated by the creature. For that is part of the substance of a thing which is included in its definition, and being is not included in the definition of a creature, because it is neither a genus nor a difference. Therefore being is participated as something which is not part of the substance of a thing (*Qq. qdl.*, II [28.2]).

[REJECTED AND ACCEPTED.] An accident depends on a subject, although the subject is not part of the essence of the accident, just as a creature depends on its Creator and yet the Creator is not part of the essence of the creature, so that an external essence would have to be put in its definition. Accidents, however, only have existence insofar as they inhere in a subject. . . . Because of this a subject must be included in the definition of an accident, sometimes directly, sometimes indirectly (*Metaphys.* [33.19]).

[ACCEPTED.] This is the nature of every analogon: that about which it is primarily predicated must be part of the intelligibility of all those analogates which are secondary (*Nat. accid.* [42.1]).

The texts just studied are confusing, not to say contradictory, only if a single meaning is postulated for the phrase, "the first in the definition of the others." The "first" may be "first in being" or "first in knowledge"; "to be in the definition of something" may mean either "to be one of the constitutive intelligibilities of an essence" (and since *what* a creature is is not a mere relation, its relationship to God cannot be constitutive); or it may mean "to be part of the complete intelligibility of the creature as creature, or, again, of God as Creator" (and in this sense it is true that its relationship to God is part of the complete intelligibility of a creature as creature; and also true that we human knowers know God naturally inasmuch as He is the cause of creatures, and so the relationship to the creature is part of the intelligibility of God *for us*). In this phrase, then, we find another example of a terminological shift in the Thomistic texts.

CHAPTER III

Doctrinal Constants

This chapter examines the main body of texts of St. Thomas on analogy. The doctrine contained in these texts is investigated according to the various rubrics St. Thomas uses to express his meaning in his description, analysis, and use of analogy. After such a preliminary study the explicit doctrine of St. Thomas can be summarized.

A. GENERAL DESCRIPTIONS OF ANALOGY

We have already mentioned that St. Thomas has written no general treatise on analogy. Here and there, however, throughout his works there are passages which deal with the nature of analogy in general. Let us look at a few of these texts.

[1.] Something is said to be predicated analogously which is predicated of several things whose intelligibilities are different but which are attributed to one and the same thing. For example, *healthy* is predicated of an animal body, urine, and drink, although it does not have entirely the same meaning in each case (*Prin. nat.* [3.1]).

[2.] There are two ways of dividing something common among those things which it includes, just as there are two kinds of community. . . . The second type of division is of that which is common by analogy: namely, that which is predicated of one of the things to which it is common according to its complete intelligibility, and of the other according to an imperfect intelligibility and with some qualification *(secundum quid)*. Thus, being is di-

35

vided into substance and accident and into being in act and being
in potency. This division is, as it were, halfway between equivocity
and univocity (*II Sent.* [5.21]).

[3. Analogous predication] of names occurs in two ways.
Sometimes it is based on the proportion of many things to one. . . .
Sometimes it is based on the proportion of one thing to another.
. . . This type of community is midway between pure equivocation
and simple univocation. For in things which are predicated analogously there is neither a single intelligibility (as in univocation)
nor simply different intelligibilities (as in equivocation). Rather, a
name which is predicated in several ways signifies different proportions to some one thing, as *healthy* predicated of urine means
a sign of an animal's health, while *healthy* predicated of medicine
means a cause of health (*S.T.*, I [17.31]).

[4.] The meaning of univocal terms is entirely the same, that
of equivocal terms entirely different. With analogous terms, however, a word taken in one of its meanings is put in the definition of
the same word taken in other senses (*S.T.*, I [17.41]).

[5.] Whenever something is predicated analogously of several
things, it is realized in its proper intelligibility only in one of them,
from which the others are named (*S.T.*, I [17.51]).

[6.] Something is predicated of different things in several
ways: sometimes according to the very same intelligibility . . . ;
sometimes according to completely different intelligibilities . . . ;
and sometimes according to intelligibilities which are partly different and partly not different. Such intelligibilities are different
insofar as they involve different relationships, the same insofar as
these different relationships are to one and the same thing. Such a
perfection is said to be predicated analogously, that is, proportionately, insofar as each analogate is referred to one thing according
to its own proper relationship (*Metaphys.* [33.9]).[1]

[7.] It is clear that those things which are predicated in this
fashion [that is, analogously] are halfway between univocal and
equivocal predicates. . . . The same name is predicated of different
things according to an intelligibility partly the same and partly
different. The intelligibility is different with respect to different

---

[1] See also *Metaphys.* (33.11).

modes of relationship, the same with respect to the terminus of the relation (*Metaphys.* [33.26]).

[8. In analogy] a name is predicated of many according to intelligibilities which are not totally different but which resemble one another in some respect (*Ethic.* [34.2]).

Two observations seem justified in the light of such texts. First, not every discussion that appears to be a general description applicable to all analogies is such in actual fact. This is true even when the description is couched in categorical language and no qualifications at all are explicitly made. Such categorical language is used in all of the texts just cited, and yet each of them describes a specific type of analogy. Texts 1, 3, 6, and 7 describe analogy as involving different relationships to one and the same thing. Text 3, however, also mentions as a kind of analogy the proportion of one thing to another, which is said to be different from the relationship of many things to one. Texts 2, 4, and 5 all discuss some kind of priority and posteriority. Text 8 speaks of analogates "resembling one another in one respect" and goes on to describe this relationship as reference to a common goal or as a similar relationship to diverse subjects.[2] Text 2 speaks of intelligibilities which are realized in the different analogates perfectly or imperfectly, a point of description lacking in the other texts. Moreover, types of analogy like participation or imitation, so prominent throughout St. Thomas' writings, are nowhere mentioned in these "general" descriptions of analogy. Yet even without adverting to this fact, if we read these texts in context, we see that their categorical language is deceiving. The description they give of analogy *tout court* invariably turns out to be tailored to the exact dimensions

---

[2] *Ethic.* (34.2). The first text cited above, *Prin. nat.* (3.1), after describing analogy in terms of different relationships to a common end, agent, or subject, also goes on to discuss similar relationships among diverse principles. Predication *per prius et posterius* is mentioned in this same text.

of some particular problem.[3] The "general" descriptions are not general.[4]

While no one text can be taken in its entirety and generalized to apply to all analogies, the texts cited above all mention one characteristic. This is the location of analogous likeness midway between univocity and equivocity. Analogous intelligibilities are neither exactly the same nor completely different; they are halfway between these two extremes. Though this is not an especially revealing description, it provides us with a minimum meaning which can be applied to all analogies.

B. REFERENCE; ATTRIBUTION TO ONE

After considering these general texts we can examine one by one the texts which make use of certain verbal formulae. There is no particular reason for considering these various rubrics in a certain order, and our beginning with reference does not imply that it is basic or important, nor that it is the least important. It is merely the case that St. Thomas in a number of texts does describe analogous predication in terms of reference or attribution or denomination. An early text is one of the few which use the term attribution.

> Something is said to be predicated analogously which is predicated of several things whose intelligibilities are different but which are attributed to one and the same thing. For example, *healthy* is predicated of an animal body, urine, and drink, although

---

[3] This is apparent with most of the texts cited above. *S.T.*, I (17.41) and (17.51) present some difficulties, since both insist very strongly on the necessity of a prime analogate in *every* analogy. If true, this would be a genuine characteristic of analogy as such, as well as a description of the particular analogies which St. Thomas wishes to discuss—the predication of the name of God (17.41), or of truth in the mind and in things (17.51). We shall return to this problem after we have discussed causal proportion and participation.

[4] "His texts on . . . analogy are relatively few, and in each case they are so restrained that we cannot but wonder why the notion has taken on such an importance" (Gilson, *The Christian Philosophy of St. Thomas Aquinas*, p. 105).

it does not have entirely the same meaning in each case. It is predicated of urine as the sign of health, of a body as the subject of
health, and of drink as the cause of health. Yet all of these intelligibilities are attributed to one goal, health. Sometimes, then, those
things which are similar according to analogy (that is, proportion
or comparison or agreement) are attributed to one goal, as in the
foregoing example. Sometimes they are attributed to one agent.
Thus, *medical* describes a person who works with technical skill
and a person who works without it (like an old midwife), and even
instruments, but by attribution to a single agent who is the doctor.
Sometimes, too, they are predicated by attribution to a single subject. Thus, *being* is predicated of substance and of quantity, quality, and the other categories. The intelligibility by which substance
is being and that by which quantity and the others are called being
are not entirely the same, for these are all called being because they
are attributed to substance, their subject. Being is predicated first of
substance, consequently, of the others (*Prin. nat.* [3.1]).

Compare the text that has just been quoted with another
early discussion of the problem.

Something is predicated analogously in three ways. First, it
may be predicated according to intention alone and not according
to its being. This happens when one intention is referred to several
things according to a priority and posteriority, and yet this single
intention really exists only in one thing. Thus, the intention of
health is referred to an animal, urine, and diet in different ways,
according to priority and posteriority, but not according to a different being, because health exists only in an animal (*I Sent.*
[4.17]).[5]

The latter text seems to be describing a purely extrinsic denomination. A perfection existing in one being is the terminus of
various relations: the beings so related to this perfection (as
agent, sign, and so on) are denominated from it, though they do
not possess it. The *health* example gives some additional support

---

[5] This is the text that Cajetan uses as the basis for his purely extrinsic analogy
of attribution.

to such an analysis, although St. Thomas' use of examples by itself is never a sure criterion of interpretation.[6] Is the former text from the *De principiis naturae* also describing purely extrinsic denomination? The language of attribution and the *health* example employed would seem to indicate this, but other factors make qualifications necessary. In another context St. Thomas clearly uses a similar language of attribution to describe a likeness which is intrinsic;[7] therefore the terminology does not here necessarily indicate purely extrinsic denomination. Furthermore, the *medical* example, possibly, and the substance-accident application, certainly, involve intrinsic possession of the analogous perfection by both analogates. It does not seem correct, therefore, to limit the analogy described in this text to purely extrinsic denomination, as if by its form alone it necessarily implied that the perfection was not present in any but one analogate. Even though such denomination was probably uppermost in St. Thomas' mind when he wrote this passage, he describes a process of denominating one thing from another which sometimes involves an intrinsic perfection and at other times an extrinsic relation. It should be noted that both this text and the text from his *Commentary on the First Book of the*

---

[6] See the references to Lyttkens and Meissner on this point, cited above, Chap. 1, n. 31. An analogous likeness based on purely extrinsic attribution is not of great philosophical significance, to say the least. The concept of such purely extrinsic attribution seems intelligible, in a Thomistic context, only on the level of *formal* likeness, not on the level of being. Medicine, for example, may be called healthy on a purely extrinsic basis, denominated from the formal perfection of health which is to be found properly only in a living body—but even then medicine possesses a different but equivalent form which enables it to cause health. Being, however, cannot be predicated in this way, for only nonbeing could be completely extrinsic to being. See *S.T.*, I (17.51) cited below, n. 8.

[7] See *Qq. qdl.*, I (8.1), which speaks of *esse* being attributed *proprie et vere* to substance, *ut quo aliquid* (namely, *res*) *est*, to accidents. This text was written about 1256-1259. But see also *S.T.*, I (17.76), where the term *proprie* is used but without the *vere*.

Sentences describe the analogates as related "according to priority and posteriority."

A series of texts written probably fifteen years later shows some striking similarities to these two early texts. Their content is summarized as follows.

1. *S.T.*, I-II, q. 20, a. 3 ad 3 (25.3). A numerically single perfection *(tantum unum numero)* is derived analogously from one analogate to another. The *health* example is used.[8]

2. *Metaphys.*, Book 4, lectio 1 (33.9, 10). Analogates have different intelligibilities insofar as they have different relationships *(habitudines* or *respectus)* by which they are referred to a numerically single *(unum numero)* goal, agent, or subject. The *health* and *medical* examples are used. *Being* predicated of accidents is an instance of reference to a common subject. Priority and posteriority are involved in this analogy.[9]

3. *Metaphys.*, Book 4, lectio 3 (33.11). Analogates with different intelligibilities are referred to one common terminus.

4. *Metaphys.*, Book 5, lectio 8 (33.14). Analogates either have different relationships *(habitudines)* to one common terminus (as urine and medicine to a healthy body) or the *same* proportion to different things (for example, tranquillity : sea :: serenity : air).

---

[8] St. Thomas emphasizes the *single* perfection involved here because he wishes to draw a parallel between such unity and the unity of the interior and exterior components of the human act. An earlier text in the *Prima pars* similarly describes secondary analogates denominated from a perfection existing properly in a primary analogate: "Whenever something is predicated analogously of several things, it is realized in its proper intelligibility only in one of them, from which the others are named. For example, *healthy* is said of an animal, of urine, and of medicine, not because health exists anywhere else but in the animal, but because from the health of the animal medicine is denominated healthy as the cause of that health and urine is denominated healthy as the sign of that same health. Although health is not found in the urine or the medicine, both possess some perfection which makes the one the sign, the other the cause of health" (*S.T.*, I [17.51].

[9] This and the next seven passages occur in commentaries on Aristotelian works.

5. *Metaphys.*, Book 5, lectio 12 (33.15). Two things share a proportional similarity, as quantity and quality share in being.

6. *Metaphys.*, Book 5, lectio 13 (33.16). According to the order of substance to accidents, *being* is predicated primarily of substance, secondarily of accidents. All the meanings of being are reduced to one first subject existing *per se.*

7. *Metaphys.*, Book 7, lectio 4 (33.18). Accidents are denominated being on the basis of their diverse relationships *(respectus)* to one and the same thing, substance. The *medical* example is used. *Being* is here predicated "according to priority and posteriority or according to more and less."

8. *Metaphys.*, Book 11, lectio 3 (33.26). Analogates are proportioned to one common subject. Substance is being *per se;* accidents have different modes of relation to substance and are not beings but *belong to being (non entia sed entis).*

9. *In ethic.*, Book 1, lectio 7 (34.2). Analogates are referred to one source or goal or subject by different proportions or have the same proportion to different subjects. Aristotle says that things are intrinsically good in this latter way. Things are "not as properly" denominated good by reference to a common good as their principle or goal. *Health* and *military* examples are cited.

10. *S.T.*, III, q. 60, a. 1, c and ad 1 (38.1, 2). Things which are variously ordered to one common agent or subject may be denominated from it. *Health* and *medical* examples are cited.

11. *Compend. theologiae*, I, cap. 27 (39.2). Names of creatures, attributed analogously to God according to some order between them, are predicated antecedently *(per prius)* of God. Such analogous perfections are predicated according to a proportion to one common source.

These texts seem to be describing the same type of analogy as the two early texts we analyzed above. One analogate is denominated on the basis of its relationship to some prior analogate; several analogates have different modes of relationship to one common subject, goal, or source to which they are all referred or from which they are all derived. Are such analogies intrinsic or extrinsic? Text 1, which speaks of a numerically single perfection, seems to be dealing with a purely extrinsic attribution, just as the early text from the *Commentary on the First Book of the Sentences* did. Text 2 speaks of reference to a numerically single goal or subject but does not mention a numerically single perfection. Although attribution language is not used, the text is otherwise almost exactly parallel to the early text from the *De principiis naturae*.[10] Like that early text,

---

[10] The parallel is so close in doctrine, phrasing, and examples employed that St. Thomas may well have based this section of his *Commentary on the Metaphysics* on his earlier treatment of the same problem in the *De principiis naturae*, especially if he had originally consulted Aristotle's *Metaphysics* at the time he wrote the *De principiis*. This supposition would explain the close parallels existing between *Metaphysics* (1003a32-b18), the text of St. Thomas in the *Prin. nat.* (3.1), and St. Thomas' own later commentary *Metaphys.*, Book IV, lectio 1.

If this is true, the substitution of *referuntur* and *respectus* in the later passage for the *attributio* language of the earlier treatment appears deliberate and of some significance. Where did St. Thomas find the *attributio* terminology in the first place? It does not appear in the early Latin version of Aristotle as far as we can tell; but it is found in Averroes' *Commentary* on the fourth and seventh books of the *Metaphysics*. See *Aristotelis opera omnia cum Averrois Cordubensis commentariis* (Venice: Juntas, 1573-1575), Vol. 8, Book 4, text 2 (fol. 65r), text 4 (fol. 69r), text 6 (fol. 71v), and Book 7, text 15 (fol. 165rb) (and perhaps as a result of this word in the *Commentary* the Renaissance version of Aristotle's text printed in italics in the same volume inserts the word *attribuitur*, fol. 64vb). This commentary was almost certainly available to St. Thomas in 1255 or when he wrote the *De principiis naturae*; Mandonnet thinks that a Latin translation of this commentary was probably present in Paris before 1215. See P. Mandonnet, O.P., *Siger de Brabant et l'Averroïsme latin au treizième siècle*, second edition, première partie, pp. 13, 14, 16 (Louvain: Institut Supérieur de Philosophie, 1911).

These facts are enough to suggest the conclusion that St. Thomas used not only Aristotle's *Metaphysics* (1003a32-b18) in writing the early passage of the *De principiis naturae* but Averroes' *Commentary* as well. Why was the *attributio* terminology abandoned in the writing of the later passage? It is possible that there is no significance; it is also possible that St. Thomas by then realized the extrinsicist connotations of the attribution terminology, and that these connotations were not desirable in expressing Aristotelian *pros hen* equivocity in the context of a Christian philosophy.

the examples of reference to a common goal or agent give the impression that a purely extrinsic denomination is meant, but the discussion of substance and accident as being indicates that intrinsic denomination is not excluded by this analogy. Texts 3, 4, 5, 6, 7, and 8 all allow for this same interpretation. Text 9 brings in a different type of analogy (also mentioned in text 4) when it offers a like proportion to different subjects as a possible alternative to different proportions to the same subject. Following Aristotle very closely, St. Thomas here says that this alternative expresses the intrinsic goodness of analogously good things better than the standard type of reference to a common source or goal.[11] Text 10 uses the *health* example in a discussion of denomination "by order to one" but does not positively limit such analogy to purely extrinsic denomination. Text 11 reverts to the early attribution terminology, but is obviously discussing intrinsic analogous perfections possessed, according to priority and posteriority, by both God and creatures.

From this analysis we can also conclude that, though several of these later texts seem to be discussing purely extrinsic denomination, most of them treat of an analogy of reference which may be either intrinsic or extrinsic. The basic evidence for this is St. Thomas' consistent application of this analogy doctrine to substance and accidents as being. Accidents, though denominated being by reference to their common subject, certainly intrinsically possess that perfection and, indeed, unite with their common subject to form a complete being. Most of these later texts appear in St. Thomas' Aristotelian commentaries and do

---

[11] Not only this text, the ninth in the present listing, but three earlier texts, summarized above under nos. 2, 7, and 8, follow Aristotle's discussion very closely. The "like relationship of diverse perfections to different subjects" mentioned in text 4 is illustrated there by a simile in which no intrinsic likeness at all is involved. For indirect evidence that St. Thomas is here merely following Aristotle's description of beings as proportionately good, contrast the present text, text 9, with the texts cited below in n. 12, where St. Thomas is definitely developing his own thought.

little more than explain Aristotelian *pros hen* equivocity. Text 9 follows Aristotle's description of beings as proportionately good, but does not positively reject the analogy of reference on the ground that it is a purely extrinsic denomination.

A third series of texts treating the analogy of reference makes clear the openness of this analogy to both extrinsic and intrinsic denomination. The following text is representative of the others in its class.

> In this fashion, then, each being is called good because of the divine goodness, the first exemplar principle as well as the efficient and telic cause of all goodness. Yet it is nonetheless the case that each being is called good because of a likeness of the divine goodness inhering in it, which is formally the goodness by which it is denominated. Thus there is a single goodness common to all and also many goodnesses (*S.T.*, I [17.15]).[12]

Texts such as this reveal a certain polarity in the analogy of reference. If only the relationship to a common source of goal is stressed, the analogy becomes almost purely extrinsic denomination. On the other hand, if the intrinsic perfection which each analogate possesses as a result of its relationship to the common source or goal receives the major emphasis, the analogy becomes an expression of the intrinsic likeness between secondary and primary analogates. In reply to the objection that "a creature is not denominated good by any formal goodness existing in the creature itself, but only by the divine goodness," St. Thomas gives a summary explanation of this difference.

> There are two ways of denominating something with respect to something else. One way makes the very relationship the meaning of the denomination. Thus, urine is called healthy in relationship to the health of the animal. The very meaning of healthy as it is predicated of urine is to-be-a-sign-of-health in the animal. In such

---

[12] See similar discussions found in *Ver.* (9.4, 5, 30, 32, 33); *S.T.*, I (17.51); and *S.T.*, II-II (32.1).

predication that which is denominated with respect to something else is not so denominated because of any form inhering in it but because of something outside it to which it is referred.

The other way of denominating something in relationship to something else does not make the relationship the very meaning of the denomination but rather its cause. Thus, when the atmosphere is called bright because of the sun, this does not mean that the very relationship of the atmosphere to the sun is its brightness, but rather that the location of the atmosphere directly opposite to the sun is the cause of its brightness (*Ver.* [9.31]).

C. CAUSAL PROPORTION

St. Thomas describes the similarity between God and creatures most frequently in terms of a causal relationship. Sometimes he simply states that we are able to rise from a knowledge of creatures to a knowledge of God because of the causal relationship that exists between them.

> In this life God cannot be seen by us in His essence, but He is known by us from His creatures according to His relationship to them as their source (*S.T.*, I [17.25]).[13]

Usually, however, he employs some rubric which emphasizes the ontological similarity between God and creatures which results from this relationship.[14]

The simplest of these rubrics for describing causal similarity is the language of *proportion*. As we have already seen in our examination of terminological shifts in Chapter 2, St. Thomas twice rejects any direct proportion between God and creatures, understanding by the term an interdetermining rela-

---

[13] See similar statements in *S.T.*, I (17.24, 106). St. Thomas' conviction that "Deus non potest habere aliquam relationem ad nos, nisi per modum principii" (*I Sent.* [4.14])—a conviction expressed with equal clarity in the texts of his mature period, just referred to—leads him to highlight the causal relationship which grounds all the major Thomistic analogies.

[14] Often a single passage will employ several rubrics to describe various aspects of the analogous situation under examination.

tionship (such as is found in proportioned quantities).[15] Most frequently, however, he distinguishes two meanings of proportion, rejecting the one which implies an interdetermining relationship and accepting the one which entails only an indeterminate (causal) relationship of one being to another.[16]

The following texts illustrate this process of distinction-rejection-acceptance.

> Proportion has two meanings. In one sense it means the same as a determinate measure of two quantities. This type of proportion can only obtain between two finite things, one of which exceeds the other according to some definite, determinate measure. In its other sense proportion means a relationship of order. It is in this sense that we speak of a proportion between matter and form. . . . In like manner the mover and that which is moved ought to be proportioned. So should an agent and patient: just as the agent can produce some effect, so can the patient receive that same effect. It is not necessary that the passive potency of the patient be commensurate with the active potency of the agent. . . . Thus there is nothing unsuitable about maintaining this type of proportion between God and His creatures, although they are infinitely different (*III Sent.* [6.2]).

> Proportion is nothing else but the relationship of two things to each other when these two things are alike in some respect. . . . In one sense [proportion refers to things] which agree in the same genus of quantity or quality, such as the relationship of surface to surface or number to number. . . . Agreement can also mean that things agree in some sort of order. Such is the proportion existing between matter and form, the maker and his product, and similar things. . . . Thus there is a proportion between the creature and God as an effect to its cause and as a knower to the object known. However, because the Creator infinitely exceeds the creatures, the creature is not so proportioned to its Creator that it receives His causal influence in its perfection, nor that it knows Him perfectly (*Boethii de Trin.* [11.2]).

---

15 *Ver.* (9.9, 11, 12, 35).

16 See below, Chap. 4, sect. B, for a further discussion of proportionality as opposed to proportion.

The proportion of the created intellect to the knowing of God is not a commensurate proportion, but a proportion in the sense in which proportion means any sort of relationship of one thing to another (such as the relationship between matter and form or cause and effect). In this sense nothing prevents a proportion from hold-ing between the creature and God, according to the relationship of one who is understanding to that which is understood, just as it also obtains according to the relationship of effect to cause (*C.G.* [15.20]).[17]

Most of the texts which describe a causal proportion between the creature and its Creator also discuss an intentional propor-tion between the finite intellect and the infinite God whom it knows (in a very imperfect fashion). Of the eight major texts which affirm a proportion between creatures and God, five ex-plicitly describe a causal proportion, five explicitly describe an intentional proportion, three describe both, and one does not specify any particular type of proportion.[18]

These texts reveal one of St. Thomas' basic approaches to the analogy between God and creatures. Creatures resemble God *because they are proportioned to Him as effects to their cause.* Proportion, once it has been purified of unacceptable quantitative connotations, offers one simple way of describing the similarity which obtains between God and creatures as a result of the creatures' relationship to their First Cause.

D. EXEMPLARITY AND LIKENESS

St. Thomas often uses the language of likeness *(similitudo)* to describe the analogy between God and creatures. We can be-gin our examination of the pertinent texts with the most simple and least technical, and advance to more elaborate expositions.

---

[17] See also *S.T.*, I (17.18), quoted above, p. 32.

[18] Causal proportion: *III Sent.* (6.2) ; *Ver.* (9.35) ; *Boethii de Trin.* (11.2) ; *C.G.* (15.20) ; *S.T.*, I (17.18). Intentional proportion: *Qq. qdl.*, I (8.2) ; *Ver.* (9.27) ; *Boethii de Trin.* (11.2) ; *C.G.* (15.20) ; and *S.T.*, I (17.18). Unspecified pro-portion: *IV Sent.* (7.9).

1. *Similarity*. Although occasionally St. Thomas simply refers to God as a "surpassing likeness" of all creation,[19] he is
usually careful to point out that God is not properly said to be
like creatures, but rather creatures are (imperfect) likenesses
of God. The following text is typical:

> As Dionysius says in the eleventh chapter of his book *On the*
> *Divine Names*, God must by no means be called similar to creatures,
> but creatures may be described as in some sense similar to God. . . .
> A man is not said to be similar to his picture, but conversely (*Ver.*
> [9.10]).[20]

Several texts explicitly point out that the likeness which an
effect bears to its cause is not necessarily a reciprocal one. (The
following statement obviously refers to *real* relations.)

> In those things which are related as cause and that which is
> caused, there does not obtain, properly speaking, a reciprocal like-
> ness. We call the statue of Hercules similar to Hercules but not con-
> versely (*Ver.* [9.22]).[21]

As we have already noted in Chapter 2, the term likeness
is one of the commonest analogy terms. Very often creatures
are said to be imperfect or deficient likenesses of God. But when
St. Thomas goes on to explain this likeness (or its deficiency),
he uses additional and more technical terms.

2. *Representation*. Representation is another term used by
St. Thomas to describe the likeness between God and creatures.
Although it sometimes refers to an intentional similitude as contrasted with an ontological likeness,[22] it regularly means an imperfect but real likeness of creatures to God.

> The diverse perfections of creatures . . . imperfectly represent
> the divine perfection. For from the fact that some creature is wise,

---

[19] For example, *Pot.* (14.23, 24).
[20] See also *Pot.* (14.19) ; *C.G.* (15.2) ; *S.T.*, I (17.10).
[21] The same description is given in *Ver.* (9.37) and *Pot.* (14.28).
[22] See *Ver.* (9.26).

it to some extent approaches likeness to God (*Resp. Joan. Ver.* [16.1]).[23]

At times St. Thomas employs the Augustinian distinction between *repraesentatio vestigii* and *repraesentatio imaginis.*

> Every effect to some extent represents its cause; but this happens in various ways. For a certain effect may represent merely the causality of its cause, not its form, as smoke represents fire. Such a representation is called *repraesentatio vestigii,* since a footstep proves the passage of someone but does not tell what sort of person he is. A certain effect may represent its cause through a formal likeness, as fire resembles the fire which produced it or Mercury's statue represents Mercury. Such a representation is *repraesentatio imaginis* (*S.T.,* I [17.78]).[24]

This distinction shows that *repraesentatio* refers, not to any chance likeness but primarily to a likeness between an effect and its cause. The texts examined below on image and on imitation make this quite clear.

3. *Assimilation.* In several places St. Thomas discusses the likeness between God and creatures in terms of assimilation.

> [Creatures resemble God] according to a certain analogy, inasmuch as the very act of existing is common to all. And in this way those things which come from God are assimilated to Him, as to the first and universal source of all existence, inasmuch as they are beings (*S.T.,* I [17.8]).[25]

Sometimes such assimilation is further described as imitation,[26] but usually an analogy is not elaborately described under this rubric. Like representation, assimilation involves more than a chance likeness, and seems to imply either efficient or telic causality, or both.

---

23 See similar statements in *C.G.* (15.22) and *S.T.,* I (17.26, 54, 64, 80, 90, 94).
24 See also *De div. nomin.* (18.6).
25 See also *III Sent.* (6.3) and *C.G.* (15.11).
26 See, for example, *S. Pauli epist.,* lectura (12.1).

4. *Imitation and Images.* St. Thomas frequently describes the relationship between creatures and their Creator as one of imitation: creatures imitate or are images of God. He is careful to distinguish imitation as a special kind of likeness.

> From this consideration it is evident that likeness is a part of the intelligibility of an image, but that an image implies something more than is contained in the notion of a mere similitude: namely, that the similitude be drawn from another. For image is applied to something which is made in imitation of another (*S.T.*, I [17.112]).[27]

As he also did in the *similitudo, assimilatio,* and *repraesentatio* texts cited above, St. Thomas emphasizes that the relationship between God and creature must always be one of analogy. Although there is formal or generic similarity, representation, assimilation, or imitation between creatures, there is only analogous likeness between creatures and their Creator. *A creature is only an imperfect image of God.*[28] While insisting on the imperfect nature of such imitation, St. Thomas is constant in affirming that analogous imitation does obtain between creatures and their Creator. Although he does not always explicitly describe this imitation as causal imitation, many texts clearly point out the causal basis for this analogous likeness.

> [Two things are analogously similar because] one thing receives its being and intelligibility from the other. The analogy of the creature to its Creator is of this latter type. The creature has existence only insofar as it descends from the First Being and it is called a being only insofar as it imitates the First Being. The same

---

[27] See also *S.T.*, I, q. 35, a. 1 ad 1, and *II Sent.* (5.12), where the same definition of an image is given.

[28] See *II Sent.* (5.12) for a typical discussion of this point. *I Sent.* (4.27) and *Ver.* (9.23) both stress the imperfect nature of this imitation. *I Sent.* (4.25, 29) speaks of the creature as imitating God "quantum potest," *I Sent.* (4.7) uses the phrase "secundum possibilitatem naturae suae," *S.T.*, I (17.3), "non perfecte, sed secundum quod possunt," *S. Pauli epist.*, lectura (12.1), "secundum suum posse."

thing holds for wisdom and all the other perfections which are predicated of the creature (*I Sent.* [4.2]).[29]

5. *Exemplarity.* St. Thomas often discusses the relation between God and creatures in terms of exemplarity. These texts are among the most difficult of all Thomistic analogy texts. We shall not attempt to handle all aspects of the problem of Thomistic exemplarity, but shall merely point out some of the more significant elements in that complicated metaphysical position which are prominent in St. Thomas' discussions of analogy.[30]

---

[29] Other texts which bring out the causal nature of this imitation include *II Sent.* (5.12) ; *Ver.* (9.23) ; *C.G.* (15.4, 15) ; *S.T.,* I (17.16, 112) ; *De div. nomin.* (18.2) ; *Compend. theol.* (39.3). Texts in which this causal basis is not explicitly mentioned include *I Sent.* (4.15, 25, 27, 29, 33, 34) ; *Ver.* (9.16) ; *Pot.* (14.6) ; *S.T.,* I (17.115) ; *S. Pauli epist.,* ordinatio (29.1). The larger number of these *imitatio* texts occur in St. Thomas' earlier works. Of the texts cited in nn. 27, 28, and 29, only three were written after the *Prima pars.*

[30] An introductory textual study of Thomistic exemplarity has already been made by Robert J. Henle, S.J. in *Saint Thomas and Platonism,* already cited in Chap. 1, n. 5. The methodological conclusions which guide his doctrinal analysis constitute Chap. 1 of his book and are summarized again in Chap. 11, pp. 420-21. The same material is discussed by Father Henle in "Saint Thomas' Methodology in the Treatment of 'Positiones' with Particular Reference to 'Positiones Platonicae,'" also cited in Chap. 1, n. 5. His general approach entails an examination of all the texts of St. Thomas in which reference is made to Plato or the Platonici in order to determine what doctrinal transformations, if any, take place when originally Platonic doctrines are assimilated into Thomistic thought. Though the major problem examined is that of participation, the closely connected problem of exemplarity is also studied in some detail. See *Saint Thomas and Platonism,* Chap. 5, pp. 358-61, nn. 51-80, pp. 449-52; Chap. 6, pp. 364-69, nn. 18-22, pp. 452-53, and Chap. 7, pp. 379-86, nn. 19-43, pp. 454-58. Although Father Henle's doctrinal and methodological conclusions are explicitly valid only for Plato and Platonici texts, it seems reasonable to extend them to texts which discuss Platonic doctrines like exemplarity and participation without explicitly referring to either Plato or the Platonici. Thus, if we find St. Thomas constantly transforming (as he does) Plato's purely formal, noncausal, often extrinsic participation into an integrated causal explanation of a creature's intrinsic perfection, it seems more reasonable to interpret St. Thomas' own use of participation in the light of this knowledge. Conversely, it seems unreasonable to suppose that St. Thomas in these cases uses a doctrine of participation that is noncausal and tends to extrinsicism, a doctrine which he rejects so forcefully in the explicit Plato and

What is meant by an exemplar? St. Thomas distinguishes it
from the image.

> Properly speaking, an image is made to the likeness of some-
> thing else. That to whose likeness it is made is properly called its
> exemplar, although improperly it may be called an image.[31]

> A third meaning of form signifies that to which something is
> formed. This is an exemplar form, to whose likeness something is
> made. Idea is ordinarily used in this sense, so that idea and the
> form which is imitated are the same (*Ver.* [9.17]).

> The perfection of an image consists in representing its exem-
> plar through its likeness to it (*C.G.* [15.18]).

Thus, whereas an image is that which imitates an exemplar, an
exemplar is that which is imitated. An idea is an exemplar form
existing in the intellect of the efficient cause which produces
the image.[32]

In a dozen or more texts St. Thomas discusses exemplarity
without an explicit reference to the efficient or telic causality involved. These discussions are usually quite brief, with no extensive development of the analogy. The following text is typical:

> "Idea" is a name for an exemplar form. There is one thing
> which is the exemplar of all things, namely, the divine essence,

---

Platonici texts, and which he explicitly modifies in these same texts in a way
that could naturally fit into his own metaphysical thought. The fact that he
does use the same words (or does accept a *positio*) that a Platonist would use
is no argument at all in the light of St. Thomas' methodology. With regard to
exemplarity, Father Henle finds that St. Thomas (1) rejects purely formal,
noncausal Platonic exemplarism, especially if it is also merely extrinsicist;
(2) rejects Aristotle's assertion that the *natural* goal-directedness of finite
agents sufficiently handles the problems which Platonic exemplarity was intended to solve; (3) accepts an exemplarity doctrine which describes a similarity between created effects and (ultimately) a creative intelligence which
is operating *through efficient and telic causality;* (4) transforms the Platonic
forms (and the Augustinian divine ideas) into a *single entity*, the divine
essence, which knows itself as imitable in various ways.

[31] *S.T.*, I, q. 35, a. 1 ad 1.

[32] *S.T.*, I, q. 15, a. 1 c. See *I Sent.*, d. 35 and 36, and *Ver.*, q. 3, for further discussions of the divine ideas.

which all things imitate inasmuch as they exist and are good . . .
(*Qq. qdl.*, II [28.4]).[33]

Most often, however, St. Thomas explicitly links exemplar
causality with efficient or telic causality, using exemplarity as
part of an integrated explanation of the likeness which an effect
bears to the (intellectual) agent who produced it and to the telic
cause to which it is ordered. In more than twenty texts St.
Thomas develops this pattern of integrated causal lines grounding the ontological likeness of creatures to their Creator. Some
of these texts simply describe God as the efficient and exemplar
cause of creatures.

> The divine being is called the being of all things, because from it
> all created being efficiently and exemplarly flows (*I Sent.* [4.11]).[34]

Other texts link God's exemplar causality with His efficient
and His telic causality.

> God can be related to us only as a source. Since there are four
> causes and since He is not our material cause, He is related to us
> as our efficient cause, our telic cause, and our exemplar form,
> though not as an intrinsic formal cause (*I Sent.* [4.14]).[35]

---

[33] Other texts of this sort include *I Sent.* (4.19) ; *III Sent.* (6.4) ; *Ver.* (9.33) ;
Pot. (14.5), and many texts from *S.T.*, such as I, q. 18, a. 4 ad 2; q. 47, a. 1
ad 2; q. 93, a. 1 c.; I-II, q. 61, a. 5 c.; II-II, q. 27, a. 3 c.; III, q. 3, a. 8 c.;
q. 24, a. 3 c. and ad 3. Mention has already been made (Chap. 2, pp. 26-27)
of those half-dozen texts which describe God as the exemplar of creatures
"both as nature and as intellect." These texts are all found in St. Thomas' earlier works; see Chap. 2, nn. 7 and 8. Although it is true that God is the exemplar which creatures imitate both as a being *(ipsum esse subsistens)* and as a
knower *(ipsum intelligere)*, there is no real plurality involved in the distinction between the divine Knower (and His nature) and the objects of the
divine knowledge (including the divine ideas). Consequently, it seems more
meaningful to describe the similarity which creatures bear to their Creator in
terms of a causal relationship whereby they imitate the creative intellect who
is their efficient cause. Except for the six early texts mentioned, this is what
St. Thomas does.

[34] See *I Sent.* (4.7, 18, 35) ; *C.G.* (15.23) ; and *S.T.*, I (17.6, 16, 112). See also
S.T., I, q. 15, a. 2 c.; q. 93, a. 5 ad 4; III, q. 56, a. 1 ad 3.

[35] See *Ver.* (9.3) and *De div. nomin.* (18.5).

Several texts call attention to the fact that exemplar causality, when joined with efficient causality, produces intrinsic likeness in its effects.

> Each being is called good because of the divine goodness, the first exemplar principle as well as the efficient and telic cause of all goodness. Yet it is nonetheless the case that each being is called good because of a likeness of the divine goodness inhering in it, which is formally the goodness by which it is denominated (*S.T.*, I [17.15]).[36]

Finally, several texts offer a summary picture of the whole pattern of integrated lines of causality, with exemplarity a keynote in the explanation of the similarity between creatures and the creative intellect which is their first efficient cause and ultimate goal.

> Every agent is found to produce effects which resemble it. Hence if the first goodness is the efficient cause of all good things, it must imprint its likeness upon the things which it produces. Thus, each thing is called good because of an intrinsic perfection, through a likeness of the divine goodness impressed upon it, and yet is further denominated good because of the first goodness which is the exemplar and efficient cause of all created goodness (*Ver.* [9.30]).[37]

E. PARTICIPATION

The language of participation is found everywhere in the writings of St. Thomas. Some works, like the *Commentary on*

---

[36] See *I Sent.* (4.14, 16); *Ver.* (9.32).

[37] See also *S.T.*, I (17.78) and *Metaphys.* (33.3). Question 44 of the *Prima pars* examines God's causal relationship to the world; here the discussion of God as exemplar cause can be read in context with the discussions of Him as efficient and telic cause of creation. *Metaphys.* (33.3) is the key text in which St. Thomas goes beyond Aristotle's merely negative criticism of Platonic exemplarism to transform Plato's doctrine into a causal exemplarity which respects both the intrinsic perfection of the creature and the complexity of the causal lines which lead from the creature back to God, the creative intelligence. See Henle, *Saint Thomas and Platonism*, p. 379.

Boethius' 'De hebdomadibus' and the *Commentary on the 'Liber de causis,'* in great part consist of discussions of participation in its various meanings. St. Thomas engages in lengthy and quite detailed expositions and criticisms of Platonic participation; after a brief reference to such texts, we shall not further refer to them. On occasion also he speaks of what might be called logical participation, such as the participation of the species in the genus; these texts, though significant for a complete analysis of Thomistic participation, are of no value for a study of analogy. However, many texts dealing with participation explicitly or implicitly discuss analogous likenesses. Of these texts, a large majority explicitly treat of the relationship between God and creatures; a number speak of participation as a distinct kind of analogy. Thomistic participation, then, is of great importance in a study of Thomistic analogy.

"Est autem participare quasi partem capere—To participate is as it were, to have a share of something," says St. Thomas in his *Commentary on Boethius' 'De hebdomadibus.'* This same text goes on to illustrate many different kinds of participation. A species participates in its genus; an individual participates in its species (logical participation); substance participates in its accidents; matter participates in its form (limitation of act by potency); effects participate in the perfections of their causes (analogous participation). Since Thomistic discussions of the analogy of participation between God and creatures always involve causal participation, we are directly interested only in the last of these types of participation, that of an effect in the perfections of its cause.

A good preliminary examination of Thomistic participation has already been made by Robert J. Henle, S.J., in Chapter 7 of his *Saint Thomas and Platonism.*[38] His conclusions contrast

---

[38] See n. 30 above, where the scope and general procedure of this book are described and some of its conclusions summarized.

the Platonic participation which was one of the sources of St. Thomas' doctrine with Thomistic participation itself and carefully distinguish them.

The upshot of this discussion is, therefore, that the Platonic separation and participation, when understood in the light of their proper philosophical principles, result in certain insoluble tensions which turn very largely on the doubtful ontological status of the intrinsic form. It will be remembered that the presuppositions of Platonism—the theory of flux—precisely called in question the ontological reality of the formal determinations of material beings. The Platonic theory requires that we maintain that the Idea (1) is truly separated in being, (2) is truly one, (3) is the real formal cause of the particulars, (4) is truly related to them as a cause, a principle, a justification of knowledge, of predication and of being. If the separation is stressed, the theory tends towards pure extrinsicism; if the invasion of the particulars is stressed, the unity of the form drives towards entitative union and pantheism. These ambiguities and tensions are thus inherent in the pure Theory of Ideas. As we have seen, Saint Thomas himself recognizes these different pressures and their logical conclusions. . . .

As was indicated in the last chapter, when we turn to the Thomistic analogue to participation, namely, the relationship between creatures and God, so often designated in Saint Thomas by the same term, we find the explanation of the relationship to rest in the complex pattern of the four causes. The situation here is far more complex. Therefore: we must think of God, indeed, as the ultimate exemplar cause of all things. But the relationship is mediated by intelligence which is identical with His essence. Further, the exemplarity implies efficient causality, for the resemblance of creatures to God depends upon the efficient action of the Creator, Who, as agent, produces effects resembling, though deficiently, Himself, and, as intelligent and free agent, acts through knowledge and the exemplarity of knowledge (itself reducible as resemblance and as being to the Divine Essence) as well as with the full import of finality. For God acts with determination of ends, and finality runs through the whole of His activity, ordering means to ends and all things to Himself. Moreover, this complexity of ultimate causality is compatible with and does not exclude secondary causes. On the contrary, the reality of the finite world involves the reality of finite agents as such and of intrinsic formal causes determining creatures to being as well as to action.[39]

Several early Thomistic texts, of which the following are typical, reject an unsuitable type of participation between God and creatures.

> The Creator and His creature are reducible to a community not of univocation but of analogy. Such a community may be of two types. Either some things participate in some one perfection according to a relation of priority and posteriority (as do potency and act in the intelligibility of being, and substance and accident in like manner), or one thing receives its being and intelligibility from the other. The analogy of the creature to its Creator is of this latter type (*I Sent.* [4.2]).[40]

> Agreement can be of two kinds. Two things may participate in some one perfection; this type of agreement cannot obtain between the Creator and His creature. . . . Or one thing may exist simply and another participate in that thing's likeness as far as it can. . . . Such is the agreement of the creature with God (*II Sent.* [5.13]).[41]

> A likeness that is found because two things share one thing, or because one has a determinate suitability to the other so that from one the other can be comprehended by the intellect—such a likeness diminishes distance (*Ver.* [9.12].[42]

> The creature is not said to be similar to God as though God participated in the same form which the creature shared. Rather, the reason is that God is the very form substantially, while the creature participates in this form through a kind of imitation (*Ver.* [9.36]).[43]

---

[39] Henle, *Saint Thomas and Platonism*, pp. 378-79.

[40] Note that the participation rejected here is nonetheless an analogous participation. For a text which rejects a logical or univocal participation between God and creatures, see *Qq. qdl.*, II (28.2).

[41] See also *C.G.* (15.5).

[42] This is one of those texts which goes on to reject both participation in a common perfection and determinate proportion as descriptions of the analogy between God and creatures. Proportionality is the only analogy admitted in this text.

[43] For other texts which describe the participation of substance and accidents in the common perfection of being, see *Periher.* (20.4), *Sub. separ.* (31.1), *Metaphys.* (33.18).

These texts, and others like them, reject any analogy of participation which would have both God and creatures sharing, even analogously, in some common perfection prior to both of them. This type of analogy is an analogy of "many-to-one." It may obtain between substance and accidents as principles of being that share in the perfection of being "according to priority and posteriority"; it is not applicable to the relationship between the creature and the Creator.

A second group of texts simply speak of the relationship between God and creatures as one of participation without elaborating on the type of participation involved or even on the basic meaning of the term. Texts like the following late ones are typical (and typically unhelpful in determining the nature of Thomistic participation).

> Since God is existence itself, each thing participates in a likeness of God inasmuch as it exists (*S.T.*, I [17.46]).
> The goodness by which we are formally good is a certain participation of the divine goodness, and the wisdom by which we are formally wise is a certain participation of the divine wisdom (*S.T.*, II-II [32.1]).[44]

A third series of texts from the middle and late periods present St. Thomas' basic description of the analogy of participation (already mentioned in the last text quoted of our first series) between God and creatures as centering around an analogous perfection which God possesses by His essence (or, substance) and which creatures possess by participation.

---

[44] Other texts which mention but do not further explain participation include *I Sent.* (4.16, 20) ; *II Sent.* (5.5) ; *III Sent.* (6.4) ; *Ver.* (9.8) ; *C.G.* (15.10) ; *S.T.*, I (17.4, 21, 58, 62, 70, 72, 80, 82, 83, 86, 93, 97, 123, 124, 125, 127, 128) ; *De div. nomin.* (18.5) ; *S. Pauli epist.*, ordinatio (29.2) ; *Metaphys.* (33.5) ; *Compend. theol.* (39.6). Some of these texts (for example, *I Sent.* [4.16] or *De div. nomin.* [18.5]) explicitly link participation with efficient and telic or exemplary causality. For two texts which discuss participation between cause and effect (but not explicitly between God and creatures) see *S.T.*, I (17.8) and *Lib. de caus.* (35.2).

God alone is being by His very essence; all other things participate in being (*C.G.* [15.16]).[45]

That which is essentially some perfection is the proper cause of that which has that perfection through participation. . . . God alone is being by His very essence; all other things are beings by participation (*C.G.* [15.21]).[46]

Since all things which are participate in existence and are being by participation, there must necessarily be a being at the summit of all things who is existence by his very essence, whose essence is identical with his existence. This being is God, the sufficient, most honorable, and perfect cause of all existence, from whom all things which are participate in being (*In Joann.* [26.1]).

Being is predicated essentially only of God, since the divine *esse* is subsistent and absolute. Being is predicated of all creatures by participation: no creature is its own existence, but rather is a being which has existence. In the same way, God is essentially good, because He *is* goodness itself; creatures are called good by participation, because they *have* goodness (*Qq. qdl.*, II [28.2]).[47]

These texts are representative of the many which contrast a perfection possessed by essence with an analogous perfection possessed by participation. Some simply state the contrast; others explicitly designate one of the beings as the cause of the other; others argue from a given perfection as participated to a being which possesses that perfection essentially; most of the texts deal with being but a number mention other analogous perfections (like goodness) which may be possessed either essentially or by participation. Several texts do not employ the verbal rubric *per essentiam—per participationem*, but use equivalent phrases to describe the same relationship. *Per substantiam* is used occasionally for *per essentiam; esse absolutum* is contrasted with *esse receptum, esse per se* with *esse per par-*

---

[45] See similar texts: *C.G.* (15.1, 8) ; *S.T.*, I (17.4, 91, 109, 110, 118, 129).

[46] See similar statements in *Pot.* (14.10) ; *C.G.* (15.14) ; *S.T.*, I (17.99) ; *Compend. theol.* (39.4).

[47] See also *C.G.* (15.5, 9) and *S.T.*, I (17.102).

ticipationem, esse subsistens with *habens esse*.[48] These expressions all seem to describe the same ontological relationship: one analogate is by His very nature, the other analogates are by participation in the analogous perfection of existence.

Several texts combine this relationship with that of "the one and the many," contrasting *simpliciter* with *multipliciter*, as well as *essentialiter* with *participative (particulariter)*.

> For the goodness which is in God simply and uniformly is found in creatures in many partial forms. Thus, the entire universe more perfectly participates in and represents the divine goodness than does any other creature (*S.T.*, I [17.80]).[49]

A series of texts discusses participation between cause and effect and between God and creatures in terms of *perfect* and *imperfect possession* of an analogous perfection. The following texts are representative.

> When a perfection is found to be shared in different ways by several things, it is necessary that from that analogate in which it is found most perfectly it be attributed to all those analogates in which it is found less perfectly (*Pot.* [14.3]).

> Because that which exists in God is perfect but is found in other things through a certain deficient participation, the perfection which grounds the similitude belongs to God simply, not to the creature (*C.G.* [15.2]).

> It is necessary that all things which are diversified according to diverse participation in being, so that they are more or less perfect, be caused by one First Being, who is most perfectly (*S.T.*, I [17.73]).

> A perfection common to both cause and effect exists in a higher way in the cause than in the effect, for it flows from the cause to the effect. Whatever exists in the lower causes, therefore, and is at-

---

[48] See *I Sent.* (4.12) ; *Ver.* (9.34) ; *Pot.* (14.7) ; *C.G.* (15.18, 19) ; *S.T.*, I (17.14) ; *Qq. qdl.*, II (28.2).

[49] See similar texts: *C.G.* (15.5) ; *S.T.*, I (17.30, 59, 60, 89, 118, 119) ; *Lib. de caus.* (35.3), where *per essentiam* is linked with *universaliter* and *per participationem* with *partialiter* and *particulariter*. See also *Pot.*, q. 3, a. 1.

tributed to the first cause of all, belongs to it in a most excellent way (*Sub. separ.* [31.3]).[50]

These texts, then, describe the creature or the effect of an analogous cause as participating less perfectly or deficiently in the analogous perfection which God or the analogous cause possesses most perfectly or in a higher or most excellent fashion.

Some of the shorter texts on participation may seem to be open to an extrinsicist interpretation. Some of the texts we have already seen should clearly indicate that the participated perfection is intrinsic to the participants. The following text, stressing the numerical plurality of the participated acts, rounds out St. Thomas' teaching, explicitly grounding the plurality and imperfection in receptive potency.

> The first act is the universal principle of all acts, because it is infinite, virtually "precontaining in itself all things," as Dionysius says. Consequently it is participated by things, not as a part but according to the diffusion of its going forth. But potency, since it is receptive of act, necessarily is proportioned to act. But the received acts, which proceed from the first infinite act and are certain participations of it, are diverse (*S.T.*, I [17.98]).

A number of texts combine a description of an analogous perfection which one analogate possesses by its essence and another possesses by participation with a description in terms of more or less perfect possession of such a perfection, without explicit reference to the causal ground of this relation. Two texts in the *De potentia* illustrate this combination.

> A perfection which is predicated of both God and creatures is predicated of God essentially and of the creature by participation. . . . The participated form in the creature falls short of the intelligibility of that which is God (*Pot.* [14.21]).
>
> "More or less" can have three meanings. . . . First, it may refer to the quantity of the thing participated. . . . Such diversity accord-

---

[50] Similar texts include *II Sent.* (5.2, 21); *S.T.*, I (17.7, 15, 44, 65, 102, 104); *Sub. separ.* (31.2); and *Compend. theol.* (39.5).

ing to "more or less" does not make for a different species. Secondly, it may describe one perfection which is participated while another is predicated essentially (as if we were to say, "Goodness itself is better than a good thing"). Thirdly, it may refer to one perfection which belongs to one thing in a higher way than it does to another thing (as heat belongs more properly to the sun than to fire). These last two meanings exclude unity of species and univocal predication. It is in this fashion that something is predicated of God and His creatures according to "more or less" (*Pot.* [14.22]).[51]

The texts in this third group come closest to summarizing the Thomistic analogy of participation between God and creatures;[52] God, the first efficient and exemplar cause of all creatures and their ultimate goal, possesses being, goodness, and similar perfections by His very essence, in a most perfect manner, as identical with that essence and with each other; creatures, the effects of God's causality, participate or share in an imperfect manner in such analogous perfections, and so that these perfections are distinct from each other, because they are received in the creatures' potencies.

A number of texts link causal participation not only with "more or less" perfect possession of the analogous perfection[53] but also with the various kinds of likeness examined in the pre-

---

[51] Similar texts include *I Sent.* (4.10) ; *II Sent.* (5.20) ; *S.T.*, I (17.5, 85) ; *De div. nomin.* (18.7) ; *Lib. de caus.* (35.3). *II Sent.* (5.20), *C.G.* (15.5), and *S.T.*, I (17.5) discuss imperfect participation in terms of priority and posteriority.

[52] Omitted here are a number of texts which describe other varieties of participation which are still analogous. These texts speak of the human reason participating in understanding (noncausal), of the sense appetites perfected by virtue participating in reason (moving cause), and so on. Representative texts are *II Sent.* (5.7, 16) ; *S. Pauli epist.*, lectura (12.4) ; *S.T.*, I (17.17, 22, 23, 101, 104, 126) ; *Virtut. in comm.* (23.1) ; *S.T.*, II-II (32.2) ; *Ethic.* (34.3, 7).

[53] Linkage has also been established with the description according to priority and posteriority; see n. 51 above. Several texts (for example, *Pot.* [14.3]) also use the language of attribution, although the participated perfection is clearly intrinsic, as the context shows.

vious section of this chapter. Thus, there are texts which combine the language of participation with descriptions of the
creature as a likeness, a representation, or an image of God, and
of the Creator as the exemplar and telic cause to which creatures
are assimilated.[54] Furthermore, just as imitation viewed from
the side of God is described as exemplarity, so participation
viewed from the side of God is described as a kind of communication of the divine perfections to creatures, who participate
in this perfection in a limited, diverse, and imperfect manner.
The following text is representative of St. Thomas' doctrine of
communication between God and creatures.

> Because every created substance must necessarily fall short of
> the perfection of the divine goodness, in order that the likeness of
> this divine goodness be communicated more perfectly to things
> there has to be a diversity in things, so that that which cannot be
> perfectly represented by one thing may be represented in a more
> perfect fashion in different ways by different things (*C.G.*
> [15.22]).[55]

The *De potentia* uses this language of communication to express
the themes of the divine goodness, creative causality, the likeness of creatures to God, and the being, goodness, and causal
activity of these creatures. It is thus linked in thought content to
the themes of causal participation and to the doctrine of causal
eminence which we shall see in a later section of this chapter.

F. PRIORITY AND POSTERIORITY

The phrase *per prius et posterius* is one of the most common
of all St. Thomas' descriptions of analogous likeness. It occurs

---

[54] For an example of each of these combinations see *II Sent.* (5.5), *C.G.* (15.9, 10),
S.T., I (17.9, 46, 105, 108), *Sub. separ.* (31.3) —*similitudo*; *S.T.*, I (17.80)—
repraesentatio; *Ver.* (9.36) —*imitatio*; *S.T.*, I (17.15, 16), *Sub. separ.* (31.2),
Compend. theol. (39.5) —*assimilatio*; and *I Sent.* (4.16, 20), *III Sent.* (6.4),
S.T., I (17.15), *De div. nomin.* (18.1) —*exemplaritas*.

[55] See also *S.T.*, I (17.9, 38, 39, 40, 54).

most frequently in descriptions of the relationship of substance and accidents to being. An early text discusses this relationship in terms of analogous predication through reference to a common subject.

> Being is predicated both of substance and of quantity, quality, and the other categories. However, it is not entirely the same intelligibility by which substance is being and quantity is being and the others are being. For all of these are called being because they are attributed to substance, their subject. Thus, being is predicated antecedently *(per prius)* of substance and consequently *(per posterius)* of the other categories. Hence being is not a common genus for substance and quantity, since no genus is predicated of its species antecedently and consequently. Rather, being is predicated analogously *(Prin. nat.* [3.1]).[56]

Other texts describe this same relationship, but employ additional terms to signify priority and posteriority. Substance is designated *ens proprie,*[57] *ens per se,*[58] *ens simpliciter,*[59] and *ens principaliter*[60] as well as *ens per prius*. Accidents are described as *ens secundum quid,*[61] *quo aliquid est,*[62] *non ens sed entis,*[63] as well as *ens per posterius*. One text speaks of substance and accidents as being "according to more and less, or according to pri-

---

[56] Similar texts include *De ente et ess.* (2.2) ; *III Sent.* (6.5, 6) ; *Periher.* (20.1, 3) ; *S.T.,* I-II (25.6, 7) ; *S.T.,* II-II (32.3) ; *Metaphys.* (33.9, 10, 12, 16) and *Nat. accid.* (42.1). Some of these texts also illustrate predication *secundum prius et posterius* of perfections other than being, especially of the other transcendentals, like unity and goodness. For some texts which do not mention being and discuss only these other perfections see *S.T.,* I (17.11, 51) ; *Periher.* (20.5) ; *De instant.* (41.1).

[57] *Qq. qdl.,* I (8.1) ; *Boethii de hebd.* (10.1) ; *De div. nomin.* (18.4) ; *S.T.,* I (17.76).

[58] *Qq. qdl.,* I (8.1) ; *Boethii de hebd.* (10.1) ; *S.T.,* I-II (25.4) ; *Metaphys.* (33.26) ; *Ethic.* (34.1).

[59] *Phys.* (22.3) ; *S.T.,* I (17.81) ; *S.T.,* I-II (25.2, 4) ; *Metaphys.* (33.17, 26).

[60] *Phys.* (22.3) ; *Ethic.* (34.1). The terms principally and secondarily are also used for *analoga* other than being: the "word" in *S.T.,* I (17.69), the "being of reason" in *S.T.,* I (17.49), the "true" in *S.T.,* I (17.48).

[61] *S.T.,* I-II (25.2, 4) ; *Metaphys.* (33.17).

[62] *Qq. qdl.,* I (8.1) ; *Boethii de hebd.* (10.1) ; *De div. nomin.* (18.4).

[63] *Metaphys.* (33.26).

ority and posteriority."[64] Despite terminological differences, the common import of all these texts seems to be that being may be truly and intrinsically predicated of both substance and accidents but pertains more properly to one analogate, substance, than to the other, accident.

Several texts speak of substance and accidents in terms of complete and perfect being in contrast to incomplete and imperfect being.[65] This distinction is based on the different ways in which substance and accidents share in (participant) existence.

> Since being is not predicated univocally of all things, the same mode of existence is not required of all things which are said to be. Rather, some participate in being more perfectly, others less perfectly. Accidents are called beings, not because they exist in themselves but because their existence is to inhere in a substance (*Sub. separ.* [31.1]).[66]

Other texts link analogous predication according to priority and posteriority with the analogy of participation between God and creatures and with the various degrees of participated perfection found in creatures. The following texts are representative.

> Nothing is predicated of God and other things according to the same order but rather according to priority and posteriority. This is so because all things are predicated of God essentially; He is called being by His very essence; He is good by being goodness itself. With things other than God, however, predication is made by participation (*C.G.* [15.5]).[67]

> God is subsistent existence itself. . . . All things other than God are not their own existence but participate in being. It is necessary that all things which are diversified according to diverse participation in being, so that they are more or less perfect, be caused by one First Being, who is most perfectly (*S.T.*, I [17.73]).[68]

---

[64] *Metaphys.* (33.18) ; see also *S.T.*, I (17.100).

[65] *Malo* (24.6) ; *Lib. de caus.* (35.4).

[66] See also *Periher.* (20.4).

[67] See also *C.G.* (15.20), *Pot.* (14.3), *S.T.*, I (17.5, 68), and *Lib. de caus.* (35.3).

[68] See also *II Sent.* (5.5).

Still other texts link analogous predication according to priority and posteriority with causal eminence.[69]

> [God is an analogous cause] since effect and cause here are somewhat similar in name and intelligibility according to priority and posteriority. God by His wisdom makes us wise, but in such a way that our wisdom always falls short of the perfection of His wisdom, as an accident falls short of the perfection of being as this is found in substance (*I Sent.* [4.11]).[70]

A final series of texts contrasts two types of priority in the relationships between God and creatures: a priority in knowledge and a priority in being.

> There are two ways in which a name may be said to apply antecedently to one thing rather than to another: first, according to the imposition of the name; second, according to the nature of the thing. Thus, names predicated of both God and creatures are predicated antecedently of creatures according to the imposition of the name but antecedently of God according to the nature of the thing, since all perfection comes to creatures from God (*Malo* [24.4]).[71]

---

[69] This analogy will be discussed in detail in the next section of this chapter.

[70] See also on this point *Pot.* (14.13) and *Compend. theol.* (39.1). For a discussion of the difference between God's priority to creatures and substance's priority to accidents, in which the analysis is mainly concerned with the logic of the predication involved, see the doubtfully Thomistic work, *Nat. gen.* (43.1): "Being is predicated of God and of His creature, but *per prius* of God, *per posterius* of His creature. . . . Nevertheless it does not follow because of this analogy that being is prior to both God and creature, as it is to substance and accident, of which it is predicated analogously. This can be made clear if we remember that, when the total intelligibility of an analogous perfection is realized in one of the analogates (as the total intelligibility of being is found absolutely in God), there will not be in that case a predicate prior to both analogates, since the predicate does not exceed the subject. However, when the total intelligibility of the predicate is found in neither of the subjects, there must be a predicate prior to and common to both subjects. For example, the whole intelligibility of being is not realized in substance, the first genus, since it does not include the divine being. Consequently being is not a genus but is able to be predicated of all things analogously."

[71] See similar texts: *I Sent.* (4.22, 26); *Ver.* (9.20, 21); *S. Pauli epist.*, lectura (12.3); *S.T.*, I (17.26, 28, 67); *Metaphys.* (33.13); and *Compend. theol.* (39.2).

This distinction enables St. Thomas (1) to distinguish the imperfections involved in our knowledge of God through creatures from the proper perfections which exist in God, prior in nature, although posterior in knowledge, and (2) to explain how the prior analogate in predication according to priority and posteriority is found "in the definition of" the secondary analogates as that to which they are essentially related for their analogous intelligibility. Since God is the primary analogate in the order of being although He is posterior in the order of knowledge, creatures are essentially related to Him as secondary analogates in the order of being, although they may be primary analogates in the order of knowledge. An important text in the *Prima pars* of the *Summa theologiae* sums up this discussion.

> In the case of all names which are predicated analogously of several things, it is necessary that all be predicated with respect to one, and therefore that that one be placed in the definition of all. Because "the intelligibility which a name means is its definition," as is said in the fourth book of the *Metaphysics*, a name must be antecedently predicated of that which is put in the definitions of the others, and consequently of the others, according to the order in which they approach, more or less, that first analogate. . . .
>
> Thus, all names which are predicated of God figuratively are predicated antecedently of creatures rather than of God. . . . The case would be the same for other names as well, which are not predicated of God merely figuratively, if they were predicated of Him merely as cause, as some have held. Thus, when God is called good, this would mean only that God is the cause of the creature's goodness; the goodness thus predicated of God would therefore include in its intelligibility the creature's goodness and goodness would be predicated antecedently of the creature rather than of God.
>
> However, as was shown above, names of this sort are predicated of God not only as cause but also properly. For when God is called good or wise, this signifies not only that He is the cause of wisdom and goodness but also that these perfections exist in Him in a higher way. In the light of these considerations, then, it must be maintained that, as far as the reality signified is concerned, these predications are made antecedently of God rather than of creatures,

because perfections of this sort flow from God to creatures. As far as the imposition of the name is concerned, however, creatures are named first, because we know them first (*S.T.*, I [17.35]).

A final question may be raised concerning predication according to priority and posteriority. Is such an order characteristic of all analogous predication? In every type of analogy we have seen so far, some type of priority and posteriority has been involved. The analogy of reference (or attribution), the analogy of proportion, and the various analogies involving imitation, exemplarity, and participation, all involve predication according to priority and posteriority. This is true even where the analogous likeness is not based on a direct causal relationship.[72] Moreover, St. Thomas says explicitly, in the text from the *Prima pars* just quoted, that in all analogous predication there must be one analogate to which the others refer.[73] But the "all" to which St. Thomas refers—we recall the conclusion of the first section of this chapter—may only be "all the analogies relevant to this problem." The primary analogate need not, of course, possess the analogon in all its perfection in every case of priority (although this is the case in the second kind of the analogy of participation), but must possess it more perfectly or more properly than any of the secondary analogates.[74]

---

[72] See *Ver.* (9.2).

[73] *S.T.*, I (17.35): "In omnibus nominibus quae de pluribus analogice dicuntur, necesse est quod omnia dicantur per respectum ad unum." See similar statements in *III Sent.* (6.6): "Ea quae dividunt aliquod commune analogum se habent secundum prius et posterius," *S.T.*, I (17.51): "Quando aliquid dicitur analogice de multis, illud invenitur secundum propriam rationem in uno eorum tantum, a quo alia denominantur," *Nat. accid.* (42.1): "Haec enim est natura omnis analogi, quod illud de quo primo dicitur, erit in ratione omnium quae sunt post."

[74] When God is one of the analogates involved the primary analogate will always possess the analogous perfection perfectly. See *Nat. gen.* (43.1), quoted above in n. 70. Texts like *Malo* (24.6) and *Lib. de caus.* (35.4) refer to subsistent beings as "perfect and complete beings," but it should be obvious that the word is there used in a relative sense. Several other texts should be mentioned here in connection with this discussion of predication *per prius et posterius.*

G. CAUSAL EMINENCE

In addition to describing the analogy between cause and effect in terms of priority and posteriority, St. Thomas often uses the language of causal eminence, especially in discussing the analogy between God and His creatures. These descriptions in terms of eminence (or its correlate, deficiency) are linked with the analogy of proportion, the analogy of imitation, and the analogy of participation, as well as with predication according to priority and posteriority.[75]

Since the analogy of eminence is always (at least in fact) based on a causal relationship, it is necessary to examine St. Thomas' doctrine on the similarity between cause and effect. Since an agent acts only insofar as it is itself in act, all causes are in act with regard to what they produce in their effects. Conversely, all effects somehow or other resemble their causes with regard to what they receive. This resemblance, however, may be of various kinds. On the basis of the different types of similarity

---

(1) *Ver.* (9.37) discusses *conformatio* between creatures and God in terms of priority: "Unde posteriora prioribus conformantur, sed non e converso." (2) *S.T.,* I (17.71) discusses *quantitas virtualis* in terms of predication *secundum magis et minus* of a perfection which is realized *perfectius vel minus perfecte.* (3) *I Sent.* (4.17) reserves the phrase *per prius et posterius* to describe analogy *secundum intentionem tantum et non secundum esse.* It is an interesting fact for the history of Thomism that this text, which has served as a key text for the interpretation of all other texts in most of the reductionist schemes proposed by the commentators, is the *only* one in the entire Thomistic corpus which employs *per prius et posterius* in this restricted sense. See n. 71 above for texts which contrast priority in knowledge with priority in being. (4) Though the phrase *per prius et posterius* is not employed, texts which describe nonbeing as analogously being or which contrast *ens in anima* with *ens in re* are describing analogous predication *per prius et posterius.* See *Qq. qdl.,* I (8.1) and *Ver.* (9.13); *S.T.,* I (17.49) uses the term "principally."

75 See, for example, *Boethii de Trin.* (11.2)—eminence plus the analogy of proportion; *I Sent.* (4.7)—eminence plus the analogy of imitation; and *C.G.* (15.2) —eminence plus the analogy of participation. Texts linking eminence and predication *per prius et posterius* are discussed in the previous section of this chapter and are cited in n. 70.

between effects and their causes, St. Thomas divides causes into two, sometimes three, categories.

A basic division is into causes whose effects are of the same species as themselves (univocal causes) and causes whose effects are of a different species than themselves (nonunivocal or equivocal causes).

> There are two kinds of agents. One kind is proportioned to the patient receiving its effect, and thus produces a form of the same species and intelligibility as itself in the effect. This is the case with all univocal agents. . . . The other kind of agent is not proportioned to the patient receiving its effect, and thus the effect is not of the same species as the agent but bears a resemblance to the agent as far as it is able to do so. This is the case with equivocal agents (*II Sent.* [5.3]).[76]

Equivocal causes possess the perfection of the effect in a higher way; their effects possess the perfection of their cause only imperfectly.

> In nonunivocal causes the likeness of the effect is in the cause in a more eminent manner, whereas the perfection of the cause is in the effect in an inferior way (*C.G.* [15.17]).

Several texts make this same division in terms of the equality, or lack of equality, of cause and effect—the effect is, or is not, equal to the power of the cause.

> Since every agent acts inasmuch as it is in act and consequently produces effects which resemble it, the form of the effect must in some way be in the agent. This happens in several ways. When the effect is equal to the power of the agent, the form must exist according to the same intelligibility in both the agent and the patient. . . . The agent and patient are in that case of the same species. This is true for all univocal agents. . . . When the effect is not equal to the power of the agent, the form does not exist according to the same

---

[76] See similar texts: *I Sent.* (4.8, 30) ; *III Sent.* (6.2, 3, 6) ; *Pot.* (14.14) ; *C.G.* (15.2, 4) ; *Resp. Joan. Ver.* (16.1) ; *S.T.,* I (17.7, 12, 122) ; *Phys.* (22.12) ; *Malo* (24.2) ; *S.T.,* I-II (25.5) ; *S.T.,* III (38.3) ; *Compend. theol.* (39.3, 5).

intelligibility in both the agent and the patient but exists in the agent in a more eminent manner (*Pot.* [14.11]).[77]

This equality of the effect to the power of the agent is simply another way of expressing the proportion which exists between a univocal cause and its effect.

Several texts speak of three kinds of causes: univocal, equivocal, and analogous causes.

> We find three kinds of efficient causes. The first of these is an equivocal cause, whose effect agrees with it neither in name nor in intelligibility. The sun, for instance, produces heat although it itself is not hot. The second kind is a univocal cause, whose effect agrees with it in name and intelligibility. A man, for instance, generates a man and heat produces heat. God's activity is neither equivocal nor univocal. Not univocal, because nothing univocally agrees with Him. Not equivocal, because effect and cause somehow agree here in name and intelligibility, according to priority and posteriority. God, for instance, by His wisdom makes us wise, but only in such a way that our wisdom always falls short of the perfection of His wisdom, just as an accident falls short of the perfection of being, as this is found in substance. Thus, the third kind of cause is an analogous agent. It is clear, then, that the Divine Being produces the being of the creature as an imperfect likeness of itself (*I Sent.* [4.11]).[78]

A similar text speaks of univocal causes whose effects are of the same species as themselves, of equivocal causes whose effects are of a different species but of the same genus as themselves (the remote or general causes), and finally of an analogous cause whose effects resemble it only analogously (insofar as creatures participate in being from God).[79] Although analogous causes and effects may share common transcendental perfections such as being, goodness, and truth, strictly equivocal causes

---

[77] See similar texts: *Boethii de Trin.* (11.1, 8) ; *Pot.* (14.8).
[78] See also *I Sent.* (4.3, 7), *IV Sent.* (7.3).
[79] *S.T.*, I (17.8, 121).

and effects will differ in specific formal perfections and share generic formal perfections. Thus, an analogous cause like God will possess the perfections of its effects in a higher, more perfect way; an equivocal cause (in the narrow sense) will lack the specific formal perfection of its effect but will possess a different but equivalent specific formal perfection which enables it to cause the perfection of the effect, as well as the common generic perfection. Such fine distinctions are not made in those texts which classify causes into two groups, univocal and equivocal.

The difference in the two texts in the analysis of equivocal causality strictly taken may be due to the sort of causality envisaged. The principle, frequently enunciated by St. Thomas, that cause and effect must somehow resemble each other, obviously applies to causes acting *per se*. A cause, entirely unlike its effect both in name and intelligibility, cannot be producing an effect according to its nature; it must then either be a very remote cause (as the celestial spheres were imagined to be) or a cause acting *per accidens*, in a chance manner.

How does St. Thomas describe the eminence of nonunivocal causes and the deficiency of their effects? He employs a variety of terms. A large number of texts simply speak of the perfection existing more eminently or in a more eminent way in the cause.

> Whatever perfection or nobility belongs to the creature belongs also to God, the equivocal efficient cause of creatures. But these various perfections belong to God in a more eminent way, according to His simple essence (*Resp. Joan. Ver.* [16.1]).[80]

Other texts emphasize the imperfection of the effect and speak of the fact that the creature's perfection falls short of the divine perfection.

---

[80] See similar statements in *I Sent.* (4.6, 9, 27); *Ver.* (9.23); *S. Pauli epist.*, lectura (12.2); *Pot.* (14.12, 13, 14, 22, 23); *C.G.* (15.3, 17); *S.T.*, I (17.7, 27, 28, 35, 53, 55, 57, 63, 65, 85, 88, 92, 103, 116); *De div. nomin.* (18.1); *Q.D. de anima* (27.1); *Sub. separ.* (31.2, 3); *Lib. de caus.* (35.1).

The participated form in the creature falls short of the intelligibility of that which is God, just as the heat of fire falls short of the perfection of the sun's power by which heat is produced (*Pot.* [14.21]).[81]

One group of texts discusses God's eminence within the context of the "triple way."

[Dionysius] says that we go from creatures to God by three ways: through causality, through negation, and through eminence. The reason for this is that the being of the creature is from another. Hence we are led to the cause from which it comes. This can happen in two ways. With respect to the perfection which it receives, we are led by the way of causality. With respect to the manner in which it is received (namely, that it is imperfectly received), we are led by two paths: by negation or removal of the imperfection from God and by the way of eminence, inasmuch as that which is received in the creature exists in the Creator in a more perfect and noble manner (*I Sent.* [4.4]).[82]

Other texts describing the analogy of eminence between God and creatures, or, more generally, between nonunivocal causes and their effects, follow the same pattern but substitute equivalent terms for *eminenter* and *deficienter*. Thus, perfections exist in their nonunivocal causes *excellentius*,[83] *nobilius*,[84] *altius*,[85] *modo excedente*,[86] *modo sublimiori*,[87] whereas these same analogous perfections are found in the effects of nonunivocal causes

[81] See similar statements in *Ver.* (9.23); *Pot.* (14.29); *C.G.* (15.2, 22); *S.T.*, I (17.26, 121, 126); *De div. nomin.* (18.6); *Malo* (24.2); and *Compend. theol.* (39.7).

[82] See also *I Sent.* (4.7); *Boethii de Trin.* (11.1, 3); *Pot.* (14.30, 31); *S.T.*, I (17.24, 37).

[83] See *I Sent.* (4.3); *Pot.* (14.24); *S.T.*, I (17.12, 25, 26, 31, 44, 65, 88, 103); *S. Pauli epist.,* ordinatio (29.2); *Sub. separ.* (31.3); *Metaphys.* (33.4); *De gener. et corrupt.* (37.2).

[84] See *I Sent.* (4.3) and *Ver.* (9.25).

[85] See *Pot.* (14.11); *S.T.*, I (17.26, 47); *Phys.* (22.12).

[86] See *I Sent.* (4.31); *S.T.*, I (17.13, 24); *De div. nomin.* (18.2, 7); *Compend. theol.* (39.7).

[87] See *Ver.* (9.23); *Pot.* (14.8, 12).

modo inferiori.[88] Very frequently the imperfect mode of the effect is not given any special name.

What might be meant by "a perfection existing in a more eminent way" is not often explained by St. Thomas. One way that is mentioned follows the Augustinian-Dionysian suggestion that the "eminence" of a perfection in God lies in the divine simplicity: perfections in God are all identical with each other; there are no distinctions of limited perfections in God.[89] Another way consists in the reduction of all perfections to the act of existing *(omnium perfectiones pertinent ad perfectionem essendi)*, and then pointing out that God is subsistent existence.[90] A third way lies in the doctrine of participation; a perfection which is present, but not by participation, is by that very fact not received, and so must be unlimited.[91] The second and third of these ways are closely connected, and may be considered aspects of St. Thomas' doctrine of the act of being: the first, *as St. Thomas uses it,* is also clearly connected with the doctrine of participation.

This examination of causal eminence brings to a close our investigation of the doctrinal constants in St. Thomas' teaching on analogy. In this chapter we have tried to present, with rather full textual references, the main types of analogy discussed by

---

[88] See *C.G.* (15.17) and *S.T.*, I (17.87).

[89] See the texts cited above, n. 80 and *Pot.* (14.11). Compare: ". . . in Deo praeeminenter . . . quantum ad tria: scilicet quantum ad universalitatem, quia in Deo sunt omnes perfectiones adunatae quae non congregantur in aliqua una creatura. Item quantum ad plenitudinem, quia est ibi sapientia sine omni defectu, et similiter de aliis attributis, quod non est in creaturis. Item quantum ad unitatem; quae enim in creaturis diversa sunt, in Deo sunt unum. Et quia in illo uno habet omnia, ideo secundum illud unum causat omnia, cognoscit omnia, et omnia sibi per analogiam similantur" (*I Sent.* [4.5]). I.-T. Eschmann, O.P. (in Gilson, *The Christian Philosophy of St. Thomas Aquinas*, p. 385) accepts the conclusion that this article is a *Quaestio disputata*, dating probably from 1265-1267.

[90] See, for example, *S.T.*, I (17.7). In *ibid.*, q. 82, a. 3, St. Thomas explains the meaning of eminence in regard to the perfections of intellect and will.

[91] *S.T.*, I (17.44) ; *C.G.* (15.10) ; *Qq. qdl.*, II (28.3) ; *Pot.* (14.20).

St. Thomas. Although his teaching on analogy has been presented according to the various rubrics under which he presents
this doctrine, we have tried to indicate at the same time the extensive linkage which obtains between these various expressions.
In particular, the last two rubrics examined, predication according to priority and posteriority and the analogy of eminence,
occur in conjunction with all the earlier rubrics examined. This
chapter is successful only if it conveys some notion, not only of
the diversity and complexity of St. Thomas' doctrine but also
of the harmony and the interrelationships which pervade it.

CHAPTER IV

Problem Areas

Now that we have examined the main lines of thought found in the majority of Thomistic texts on analogy, we must pay attention to the remaining ones. These are of two kinds: texts which use the terms *analogia, proportio,* and *proportionalitas* in senses which are irrelevant to a doctrine of analogy as we have seen it defined in the preceding chapter; and those which deal with the controversial and much-commented analogy of proportionality and the analogy of genus. In the case of this second group it will be necessary to give a complete textual basis for the discussion, because of divergent interpretations of these passages. Too often, commentators have not treated these passages as a whole and in context.

A. IRRELEVANT USES OF ANALOGY TERMS

There are several contexts in which St. Thomas regularly uses the technical terms of his analogy doctrine in the presentation of quite other positions. This should not surprise us, since the terms which St. Thomas uses to designate those ontological similarities which we call analogy also had and still have other legitimate meanings. To avoid confusion we will simply cite representative texts illustrating these irrelevant meanings (that is, irrelevant to the Thomistic doctrine of analogy) and point out why they are not genuine analogy texts.

1. *Scriptural Analogy.* St. Thomas speaks of an analogy when two scriptural texts are consistent with each other.

> It is an instance of analogy when the truth of one Scripture text is shown not to contradict the truth of another Scripture text (*S.T.*, I [17.1]).[1]

This is obviously a technical usage of the term which is independent of and irrelevant for the Thomistic doctrine of analogy. It is independently derived from the original etymological sense of the compound word, already used in classical times to mean agreement in form (as in grammar) or in sense.

2. *Equality of Proportion.* A number of texts contrast quantitative equality with proportional equality.

> A congruence can be found here according to an equality of proportion. For it seems fitting that God should reward in accordance with His own surpassing power a man who works in proportion to his ability (*S.T.*, I-II [25.8]).

> This, too, is an equality of a sort, according to a proportionality. For just as the debt is related to God, so, too, is the capacity of the debtor related to God. . . . Hence a man cannot make satisfaction [for sins] if this implies a quantitative equality. It is possible, however, if this implies a proportional equality (*IV Sent.* [7.4]).

> The notion of an image does not demand exact equality *(aequalitas aequiparantiae)*, since the image of a large man can be expressed in a small picture, but it does demand an equality of proportions. This means that the mutual relationship of parts be the same in the image and in the exemplar (*II Sent.* [5.14]).[2]

Though these texts employ the terms *proportio* and *proportionalitas*, they are not discussions of analogy at all, but are

---

[1] The use of the term has survived in English in such writers as Butler and Newman. See J. Seynaeve, W.F., *Cardinal Newman's Doctrine on Holy Scripture*, pp. 230-35 (Louvain: Publications Universitaires, 1953). In technical theological writings the expression "analogy of the faith" is perhaps more common.

[2] See other representative texts: *II Sent.* (5.17, 18); *S.T.*, I (17.117); *Meteorol.* (30.1); *Ethic.* (34.4). St. Thomas also speaks of the proportion between mover and moved in *S.T.*, I, q. 105, a. 2 ad 3, and between space and time, *ibid.*, a. 3.

quite clearly describing a relationship which our English word proportion expresses also. The basic instance of a univocal relationship of proportion is that of geometrical proportion (for example, between similar but incongruent triangles). St. Thomas, following Aristotle, extends this description to parallel situations which occur in the image-imaged relationship, in distributive justice, and in a finite creature's acts of merit (or the measure of divine retribution). There is question here of similarity, of proportion; but no analogous community is involved at all, neither in meaning nor in ontological relationship. If there is community (as in the kind of image relationship described), it is a univocal community; if there is no community but a proportion, it is between correlates (for example, sin and satisfaction, functions, burdens, and benefits in a society). There is no analogously common perfection.

3. *Matter's Proportion to Form.* We have seen that matter and form are members of an analogical relationship as instances of potency and act in relation to being. But there are other things to say about the relationship of matter and form. In a series of texts St. Thomas states that primary matter, pure potency, is known only through its relationship to form. The terms *analogia* and *proportio* are both used in this context.

> Primary matter . . . is known by analogy; that is, by proportion (*Phys.* [22.5]).
> The knowledge which is had of matter according to its analogy to form is not sufficient for the knowledge of a singular (*Ver.* [9.28]).[3]

The terms analogy and proportion here mean simply the relationship of pure potency to its act. Form *is proportioned to* mat-

---

[3] See also *Boethii de Trin.* (11.5); *S.T.,* I (17.95); *Phys.* (22.6); *Prin. indiv.* (44.1). The text from *Boethii De Trinitate* also discusses matter as one of four terms in a proportionality: "We call that matter which is related to natural beings the way wood is related to a bed."

ter, just as "act is proportioned to that whose act it is" (*S.T.*, I [17.20]). Matter is not analogously form. (Matter is analogously substance and being, as we have seen.) The relationship in question is that of correlates to each other, not of analogates in an analogous community.

B. PROPORTIONALITY

The texts in which St. Thomas discusses different kinds of proportionality can be grouped in five classes. We shall examine each of them separately.

1. *Proportionality as Transfer.* One series of texts describes a transfer of corporeal attributes to an incorporeal God under the rubric of proportionality.

> There is also a similitude of proportionality. This consists in an identical relationship found in several proportions, as when one says, "Eight is related to four as six is related to three," or "The governor is related to the state as the captain is related to the ship." According to this type of similitude there is a transfer from corporeal beings to the realm of the divine. For instance, God is called a fire because, just as a fire is related to the material liquified by its heat, so, too, God in His goodness diffuses His perfections to all creatures, or something of the sort (*I Sent.* [4.28]).
>
> Some things are predicated properly of God, some figuratively. Those which are properly predicated of Him truly exist in Him. Those which are figuratively predicated of Him are predicated on the basis of a similitude of proportionality with regard to some effect. For instance, in Deuteronomy, Chapter 4, God is called a fire because, just as a fire is related to the consumption of its opposite, so, too, God is related to the destruction of wickedness (*I Sent.* [4.36]).
>
> Another [type of similitude] is that of proportionality. This is found in Scripture when figurative predicates are transferred from the corporeal to the spiritual realm. God, for instance, is called a sun because He is the source of spiritual life as the sun is the source of physical life . . . (*IV Sent.* [7.7]).[4]

---

[4] See similar texts: *II Sent.* (5.9, 15) ; *S.T.*, I (17.35).

The pattern of these texts is consistent. Perfections of physical, or material, beings are predicated figuratively of God. Most often, St. Thomas reduces such predication to a simile, and then explains it as a four-term proportionality; sometimes the intermediate reduction to simile is omitted. The similitude, however, is purely extrinsic. God is certainly not, properly speaking, a fire or the sun. He can be called a fire or the sun only improperly, because He is related to His effects in a way similar to the way in which a fire or the sun is to its effects or properties. Such predication either presupposes proper knowledge previously obtained of how God is related to His effects and properties or lacks such knowledge and so remains in ignorance of what the divine reality hidden behind the figure really is. It is significant that most of the texts discuss passages in Sacred Scripture which make such statements about God. Here the authority of Scripture assures us that such predication is true even if we had no independently valid proper knowledge of God. If we had no previous proper knowledge nor revelation nor any other source of knowledge, such similes about God could not be justified—nor would we know whether to affirm or deny them. As it is, we know full well that not all corporeal traits can correctly be transferred or applied to God. God cannot be designated, even metaphorically, as stupid or ugly or noisome. Even the most figurative language presupposes some previous knowledge of the object so described, at least on the part of the person first employing such language.[5]

---

[5] His audience need not possess this independent knowledge, of course. This explains the constant use of metaphors and similes in teaching. The teacher, knowing both cows and water buffaloes, leads the child to a knowledge of the latter, which he has not experienced, by telling him that they are like cows, which he has experienced. Even here, of course, knowledge by simile is no substitute for direct experience of a water buffalo. It is also to be noted that such a use of simile requires that the learner believe the teacher. Metaphor and simile are grounded in the same kind of ontological similarities which are directly expressed in analogous predication. Neither of them, how-

There is, then, no intrinsic analogy directly and immediately involved in the Thomistic transfer of corporeal predicates to the spiritual order. It designates no analogously common perfection which both God and creatures intrinsically possess (albeit in varying degrees of perfection). The only similitude involved is the similitude of relationships between God and His effects and properties on the one hand, and the creature and its effects and properties on the other. And there is nothing in the very structure of these predications that forces us to say that this similitude is *analogous*. It is, indeed, nonproper predication to say "God is a consuming fire"; but is the very intelligibility of fire different in this case than when we speak of a fire in a furnace? If we interpret this proposition as we have done above, that is, *according to the theory of proportionality*, it would seem not. Indeed, in some of the texts cited in this section, St. Thomas distinguishes analogical predication from such transfer. However, in some of the discussions in the *Summa theologiae*, St. Thomas interprets these predicates as extrinsic causal analogies, predicated antecedently of creatures and containing the creature's perfection in their definition when they are predicated consequently of God. We have seen these interpretations in the preceding chapter under the rubrics of causal proportion, causal eminence, and priority and posteriority.

Hence, we know, independently of figurative predication, that God and creatures share in no univocal perfection and

ever, seems directly reducible to analogy, much less to any one category of analogy; and their purposes are different. For a discussion of the relation of metaphor to analogy see Robert R. Boyle, S.J., "The Nature of Metaphor," *Modern Schoolman*, XXXI (1954), 257-80. The author shows that metaphors do not actually take the form of a proportionality as they are found in literature and in common use, although they have been traditionally described as extrinsic four-term predications. He does not explicitly discuss the relation of simile to analogy, but stresses the difference between simile and metaphor. St. Thomas does not seem to make this distinction; he regularly treats as similes scriptural figures which Father Boyle (and many others also) would insist are genuine metaphors.

that all perfections and operations are found in God as identical with His essence, which is a subsistent act of existing. Thus, we know that any likenesses really obtaining between God and creatures are analogous, not univocal. However, this inference could not be made merely on the basis of the proportional structure of our predication, since the common relationship expressed in a proportionality may just as well be a univocal as an analogous one.

Proportionality in the sense of transfer, as a type of predication about God, thus neither necessarily involves intrinsic analogy nor explicitly expresses (though it ultimately implies) analogous relationships between simply disparate agents and their properties or effects. Furthermore, since figurative predication presupposes some independent knowledge of the reality being extrinsically described, either from experience or some other source such as revelation, such figurative predication about God must necessarily be of a secondary and derivative nature.

2. *Proportionality as Parallel Predication.* As parallel predication proportionality is a comparison of identical or similar proportions.

> Proportion is the relationship of one quantity to another. Thus, six is twice three. Proportionality is a comparison of two proportions, and, if it is disjunctive, has four terms (*Post. analyt.* [21.1]).[6]

Originally a purely mathematical term designating univocal relationships within diverse quantities or figures, proportionality was subsequently applied to any comparison of identical or similar relationships, even those which are not strictly quantitative. Most Thomistic texts on proportionality as parallel predication are simply direct comments on Aristotle's text. The common relationship, even when not quantitative, is often univ-

---

[6] See similar discussions in *Post. analyt.* (21.2) ; *Qq. qdl.*, II (28.1) ; *Metaphys.* (33.14) ; *Ethic.* (34.5). The distinction between *proportio* and *proportionalitas* is not always respected; the terms are sometimes interchanged in the texts.

ocal,[7] only occasionally analogous. As we pointed out in our discussion of proportionality as transfer, the proportional form yields no new knowledge of the related terms and presupposes previous knowledge of the identical or similar relationships. The parallel proportionality, however, though it does not necessarily involve any analogously common perfection, explicitly expresses the univocally or analogously common relationship. The text which describes the univocal relationship of the sea to its calmness and the air to its serenity as proportionally tranquil is a typical case of univocally parallel predication.[8]

3. *Proportionality as a Description of Similar Functions.* Proportionality is also used to describe functional similarities between operative powers and their proper acts and objects. The following text, a direct comment on Aristotle, is typical.

> Another type of proportion obtains when we say that this thing is related to that just as this is to that other. For example, just as the power of sight is related to the act of seeing, so is the power of hearing related to the act of hearing. By this kind of proportion a comparison can be made between motion and the potency which moves, or of any operation and its operative potency (*Metaphys.* [33.23]).[9]

These proportionalities, likewise, do not seem to express any ontological analogy, at least directly. A comparison of two operative powers to their corresponding acts or objects describes no common perfection (at least no specifically common one); it states a relationship which is usually univocal, only rarely analogous; and seems to imply a univocally common perfection. It

---

[7] For example, *Metaphys.* (33.14) and *Ethic.* (34.2).

[8] *Metaphys.* (33.14); see also *S.T.,* I (17.95); *Phys.* (22.10); and *Post. analyt.* (21.2).

[9] See similar texts: *III Sent.* (6.2); *Ver.* (9.9); *Pot.* (14.32); *S.T.,* I (17.43, 111); *S.T.,* I-II (25.1). See also *Metaphys.* (33.22), another direct comment on Aristotle, which describes the identical relationships of the powers of sight and hearing to their respective organs.

results in no new knowledge of the related terms and presupposes previous knowledge of the two proportions that are identical or similar.[10]

4. *Proportionality as a Description of Parallel Relationships.* Another series of Thomistic texts comments on Aristotle's description in the twelfth book of the *Metaphysics* of principles of being as proportionately common. The principles of individual beings are numerically distinct, but exhibit parallel act-potency relationships, as the following texts explain.

> The principles of all things are in some sense the same. They may be the same by proportion. We might say, for instance, that in any genus there are principles which function as matter and form and privation and efficient cause (*Metaphys.* [33.29]).
>
> [Aristotle shows] that the intrinsic principles of things, matter, form, and privation, are not numerically but analogously or proportionately the same for all beings (*Metaphys.* [33.8]).
>
> [Aristotle says] that the principles of all beings are proportionately the same inasmuch as we say that act and potency are the principles of all being (*Metaphys.* [33.27]).[11]

These texts describe how the principles of individuals are proportionately common because of their parallel act-potency relationships. The various sets of correlated principles of act and

---

[10] These limitations apply also to the proportional goodness discussed in *Ethic.* (34.2). The text is a literal comment on Aristotle, explaining Aristotle's statement that goodness predicated proportionately of things ("Sight is a good of the body, understanding a good of the soul") respects the intrinsic goodness of the beings involved better than predication by reference (here understood as extrinsic) to a common source or a common goal. Even though such proportional predication, unlike extrinsic reference, emphasizes that each of the subjects possessing these (univocal) relationships has an intrinsic perfection, it says nothing about an analogously common perfection in which each shares. The text, then, describes an intrinsic perfection, but not an intrinsic similarity (direct analogy).

[11] See also *Boethii de Trin.* (11.6) and *Metaphys.* (33.28). *Phys.* (22.4) discusses the principles of various *opinions* as analogously or proportionately one. *Metaphys.* (33.20) discusses the various potencies within being as (extrinsically) proportioned to each other.

potency within a single being may also be arranged in the form of a proportionality (just as the various acts of the various potencies within a single being may be arranged in the form of a proportion). When we predicate matter and form, for example, of principles which are not literally matter and form (essence and the act of existing, for instance), such predications are extrinsic comparisons—*secundum intentionem tantum*, as St. Thomas remarks in an early text.[12] These predications do not express any analogously common perfection but merely a similar relationship between different act-potency correlations. They give no new knowledge of the principles thus related and presuppose an independent knowledge of the similar relationships. However, as in the case of the third of the quoted texts, the implied act-potency correlation may be explicitly brought out. In this case there is no longer a proportionality but a direct analogy along the lines of an analogy of intrinsic reference.

5. *Proper Proportionality between God and Creatures.* A final series of proportionality texts tries to explain the ontological similarity between God and creatures[13] in terms of propor-

---

[12] St. Thomas himself once at least explicitly noted this point: "nisi secundum intentionem tantum, prout in omnibus invenitur potentia et actus analogice tamen, ut in XII *Metaphys.* dicitur" (*II Sent.* [5.4]).

[13] Not every discussion of proportionality is a discussion of analogy, as we have already seen. *Ver.* (9.6) contains an often-quoted description of proportionality which does not touch analogy at all. Because this text has often been cited in presentations of Thomistic analogy, it is well to quote it in full here and comment briefly on it. It is found in *Ver.*, q. 2, a. 3, arg. 4 and ad 4.

"The medium by which a thing is known is said to be proportioned to that which is known by it. But the divine essence is not proportioned to a creature, since it infinitely surpasses it, and there is no proportion of the infinite to the finite. Therefore by knowing his own essence God cannot know a creature.

"Something is said to be proportionate to another in two ways. In one way, a proportion is found between them. For example, we say that four is proportioned to two, since its proportion to two is double. In the second way they are proportioned according to a proportionality. For example, we say that six and eight are proportioned because, just as six is the double of three, so eight is the double of four; for proportionality is a likeness of proportions.

tionality. These are the texts cited by the numerous Thomistic commentators who have maintained that the analogy of proper proportionality is the only genuine metaphysical or intrinsic analogy. The many texts cited in Chapter 3 of this book which illustrate St. Thomas' multiple approach to a doctrine of analogy ought to be a sufficient comment on such an exclusive claim.

Now, since in every proportion there is a relation to each other of those things that are said to be proportioned according to some definite excess of one over the other, it is impossible that any infinite be proportioned to a finite by way of proportion. When, however, things are said to be proportionate by way of proportionality, they are not related to each other; but there is a similar relationship of two things to two other things. In this way nothing prevents an infinite from being proportioned to an infinite; for, just as some finite is equal to some other finite, so an infinite is equal to another infinite. In this way the medium must be proportioned to what is known by the medium. Thus, just as the medium is related to demonstrating something, so must it be related to that which is known through it in order that the latter be demonstrated. Thus, nothing prevents the divine essence from being the medium by which a creature is known" (The Latin text of the response given in Appendix I [9.6]).

This text employs proportionality to explain, not how an ontological similarity can be found between God and His creatures but rather how the divine essence, an infinite medium, can serve as a means by which God knows creatures, which are finite objects. Presented with the objection that there can be no proportion between such an infinite medium and finite objects, St. Thomas chooses to reply that in divine knowledge medium and object are not directly proportioned to each other, but are proportionate; that is, are each related to their respective acts by a similar relation. Medium and object are not directly related. Rather, the medium is related to the act of demonstrating, as object known is related to the act of being demonstrated. Whether this is a good solution does not concern us here. Nor are we going to decide whether such a proportionality offers more than a verbal solution to the original problem, any more than a study such as ours should question the validity of the original difficulty. We wish only to point out that the whole discussion concerns the relationship between objects of the divine knowledge and the medium by which they are known. In spite of extrinsic resemblances to other Thomistic texts which do discuss analogy, this text is not concerned with that problem. The language of proportionality and the discussion of infinite versus finite excess will not mislead us if we remember the question which is being answered.

Another proportionality text which might be mistaken for an analogy text occurs in *IV Sent.* (7.9). Since this text parallels the text just discussed (*Ver.* [9.6]) quite closely, we shall not quote it in full here, but rather give a brief précis. To the problem of how our finite intellect can know God, an infinite object, St. Thomas replies that, although there cannot be a direct pro-

Moreover, the exclusive claim of one of the classical texts[14] should be considered in the light of other apparently exclusive texts, whose universal applicability we have considered in Chapter 3, section A. We have seen there that an analysis, which out of context seems to be an analysis of all analogies, turns out not to be applicable outside the limits of the problem in answer to which it is given.

But what about proper proportionality itself? Is it a consistently Thomistic analogy? If so, what are its characteristics? How does St. Thomas himself describe it? Before quoting and analyzing the pertinent texts which alone can answer these ques-

---

portion between the finite and the infinite (in the sense of a mutually determining proportion), there may be a proportionality (that is, knower : act of knowing :: object known : act of being known) or a proportion in an extended sense of that term, signifying any relationship of one thing to another. The proportionality explained here allows the finite to know (imperfectly) the infinite and allows the infinite to know the finite. Like the text from the *De veritate,* this text is describing a true proportionality, but it is not at all concerned to describe analogous similarities between God and creatures. The question of the relationship between knower and object known is a valid question, but it is a distinct question from the problem of analogy.

In *S.T.,* I-II, q. 3, a. 5, arg. 1, an effort is made to show that beatitude consists in the operation of the practical intellect, since by that power man becomes like to God who is a creator. St. Thomas answers that the alleged similarity is a proportionality, "for as [the human intellect] is related to its known object, so God is to his" (*S.T.,* I-II [25.1]). But the similarity of the speculative intellect is greater, since it consists in union or "information." This text, similar in manner of solution though not in context to the preceding, obviously presents us with an extrinsic proportionality.

14 We have already seen a number of texts, each of which seems to make exclusive claims, such as "This is the nature of every analogon . . ." (*Nat. accid.* [42.1]) ; see above, Chap. 3, sect. A, and n. 73.

Most medieval writers, indeed, are concerned with solving particular problems, not with the construction of a rational system. Some writers seem never to have thought their solutions through back to their principles, others (like St. Thomas) seem to have a well-developed implicit philosophy. But even these latter ones have not written out this philosophy in systematic form. Hence any piece of philosophical thinking has to be taken in its concrete meaning determined by its function in the context of its special problem. And if this is done, the apparently conflicting exclusive claims vanish, but the reader must himself draw out the implicit lines of connection.

tions, we must first look at the types of arguments which these texts try to meet. The two major proper proportionality texts (both from the *De veritate*) are concerned almost exclusively with meeting two basic arguments. First, there cannot be *any* similarity, even one of analogy, between a finite creature and an infinite Creator.[15] Secondly, any alleged similarity would involve a proportion (*analogia*, to use the Greek term) that would necessarily be mutually determinate and determining, allowing God to be defined in terms of His creatures.[16] These are radical positions. Their uncompromising tone is undoubtedly a partial explanation of St. Thomas' response; certainly he accepts the conditions of the problem in terms of the grave difficulties involved in an ordinary proportion.

Turning now to the proportionality texts themselves, we shall begin by quoting them. St. Thomas first rejects univocation then dismisses pure equivocation. Next he turns to analogy.

> [1.] Consequently it must be said that knowledge is predicated neither entirely univocally nor yet purely equivocally of God's knowledge and ours. Instead, it is predicated analogously, or in other words according to a proportion. Now, an agreement according to proportion can be of two kinds. According to this, two kinds of community can be noted in analogy. There is a certain agreement between things having a proportion to each other because they have a determinate distance between them or some other relation to each other, as two is related to one because it is its double. Sometimes an agreement is also noted between two things between which there is no proportion but rather a likeness of two proportions to each other, as six agrees with four because six is two times three, just as four is two times two. The first kind of agreement is one of proportion; the second of proportionality.
>
> According to the first type of agreement we find something predicated analogously of two things, of which one has a relation to the other, as being is predicated of substance and accident from

---

[15] See *Ver.*, q. 2, a. 11, arg. 1, 2, 3, 4, 5, 7, and 8; q. 23, a. 7, arg. 9.
[16] See *Ver.*, q. 2, a. 11, arg. 6.

the relationship which substance and accident have, or as healthy is predicated of urine and animal because urine has some similarity to the health of an animal. Sometimes, however, a thing is predicated analogously according to the second type of agreement, as sight is predicated of corporeal vision and of the intellect because understanding is in the mind as sight is in the eye.

Because in those terms predicated according to the first kind of analogy there must be some determinate relation between the things to which something is common by analogy, nothing can be predicated analogously of God and creature according to this type of analogy; for no creature has such a relation to God by which the divine perfection could be determined. But in the second kind of analogy no determinate relation is noted between the things to which something is common by analogy; so according to this kind, nothing prevents us from predicating some name analogously of God and creatures (*Ver.* [9.9]).

The Philosopher . . . asserts two kinds of likeness. One is found in different genera and is established according to proportion or proportionality; as when one thing is related to another as a third thing is related to a fourth, as Aristotle himself says in the same place. The second kind of likeness is found between things in the same genus, as when the same thing is present in different subjects. Likeness does not demand a comparison according to the definite relationship which is said in the first way but only according to that which is said in the second way. Consequently it is not necessary that the first kind of likeness be removed from God with regard to creatures (*Ver.* [9.11]).

A likeness that is found because two things share one thing, or because one has a determinate suitability to the other so that from one the other can be comprehended by the intellect—such a likeness diminishes distance. But a likeness according to an agreement of proportion does not; for the latter likeness is also found in things far distant or near. Indeed, there is no greater likeness of proportionality between two and one and six and three than there is between two and one and one hundred and fifty. Consequently the infinite distance of a creature from God does not destroy the likeness mentioned above (*Ver.* [9.12]).

In the second text in the *De veritate* St. Thomas is answering the argument that man's will cannot be conformed to God's because there can be no proportion between God and man, since the creature is infinitely distant from God.

[2.] Man is conformed to God since he is made to the image and likeness of God. Although, because man is infinitely distant from God, there cannot be a proportion between him and God in the sense in which proportion is properly found among quantities, consisting of a definite measure of two quantities compared to each other, nevertheless in the sense in which the term proportion is transferred to signify any relationship of one thing to another (as for example when we say that this is a likeness of proportions: as the prince is to his state, so the captain is to his ship), nothing prevents us from saying that there is a proportion of man to God, since man stands in some relationship to Him, as that he is made by God and is subject to Him.

Or the answer could be given that, although there cannot be a proportion strictly so called of the finite to the infinite, yet there can be a proportionality, which is the likeness of two proportions. We say that four is proportioned to two because it is its double; but six is proportionable to four because four is related to two as six is related to three. In the same way, although the finite and the infinite cannot be proportioned, they can be proportionable, because as the infinite is to the infinite, so the finite is equal to the finite. In this way there is a likeness between the creature and God, because as He is related to the things which belong to him, so the creature is related to what is proper to it (*Ver.* [9.35]).

The simplest approach to these texts may be first to list a number of disconnected observations about the language of the texts and then to discuss their deeper implications. The following points seem significant.

1. The proportionality doctrine in these texts is obviously an extension of mathematical proportionality. The examples of proportionality cited in both texts, with one exception, are drawn from mathematics and illustrate univocal relationships between diverse quantities. The distance metaphor and the language of determinate and indeterminate excess are also mathematical in origin.

2. The one nonmathematical example of a proportionality is the purely extrinsic comparison of the relationship of understanding to the mind and the relationship of seeing to the organ or power of vision. The only similarity involved here is the univocal proportion.[17]

3. The example of proportion in its transferred sense offered in the second text is that of a pilot's relationship to his ship and a ruler's relationship to the commonwealth. It is noteworthy that in its Aristotelian source and in at least one other Thomistic usage (see above, page 80) this example appears under the rubric of proportionality and seems much more reasonably to be a proportionality.

4. The second text offers proportionality merely as an alternative explanation of the ontological similarity between God and creatures. It indicates that a nonquantitative, indeterminate proportion would also be a working solution to the problem of similarity without mutual limitation. (The example illustrating such a proportion, as we have just mentioned, makes a very odd contrast to the proportionality which follows.) However, even in this second text (and certainly in the first text, which does not offer an indeterminate proportion as an acceptable alternative), proportionality appears as an exclusive solution, not as a complementary explanation or a mere variant formulation of some other analogy. Proportionality is intended to be the analogy between God and creatures. Other types of (two-termed) analogies are rejected as unsatisfactory for this situation.

5. A mutually determining proportion seems to be the only kind of proportion considered in these texts when they reject this form of analogy as an explanation of the similarity between God and creatures.

---

[17] The example of the pilot's and the ruler's respective relationships in *Ver.* (9.35) is offered, not specifically to illustrate proportionality but as one possible instance of proportion when proportion signifies "any relationship of one thing to another."

6. Most significant of all, proportionality is presented in these texts as a description of the ontological similarity between God and creatures. Unlike the earlier metaphorical proportionalities and the later comments on extrinsic Aristotelian proportionalities (both of which we have already examined in this section), the proportionality between God and creatures is presented as an intrinsic analogy. Not only is there a common relationship (presumably not univocal but analogous); there is also an analogously common perfection involved, "although in a proportionality no definite relation is involved between things which have something in common analogously." This is not mere metaphorical proportionality, where an attribute or activity of one being is known independently or known only extrinsically. Neither is it the Aristotelian proportionality which compares parallel relationships within independently known beings without predicating any intrinsically common perfection of the beings concerned. Rather, it claims to describe intrinsic (albeit indirect) similarities. Just as "six has something in common with four because six is two times three, and four is two times two," so, too, does the creature's knowledge resemble God's knowledge, *proportionately*.

Let us now turn to the doctrinal implications of these texts. We can note first the structure of the argument. Proportionality is here intended to express intrinsic similarities between God and creatures. Other forms of more direct similarity are rejected. The only alternatives explicitly considered are mutually determining proportion (in which "one thing has such a determinate relation to another that from one the other can be grasped by the intellect") and common participation of two things in a common but prior third perfection. Both of these forms are easily shown to be unacceptable descriptions of the similarity between God and creatures. But they are clearly not the only alternatives to proportionality. A look at the various approaches analyzed in Chapter 3 will confirm this statement.

In these two proportionality texts, St. Thomas makes no use of such acceptable forms of participation and direct proportion, although he has already worked them out in some detail and will employ them consistently in all subsequent discussions of analogy between God and creatures. For a period of some months around the year 1256, St. Thomas either held or considered holding[18] proper proportionality as *the* intrinsic analogy explaining the ontological similarity between God and creatures. This position he had not held previously and would never develop again in subsequent writings.[19] Proper proportionality is therefore a Thomistic analogy in the sense that it is a doctrine taught by St. Thomas for a brief period early in his career.

From a textual standpoint the absence of any subsequent text which teaches proper proportionality between God and creatures constitutes strong evidence that St. Thomas quietly abandoned this doctrine after 1256. More positively, the numerous texts (prior and subsequent to the two proportionality texts) in which St. Thomas clearly teaches more direct analogies between God and creatures indicate that proportionality is not the exclusive analogy between Creator and creatures as these texts teach.

Nothing can be explicitly found in the existing texts which gives any reason for St. Thomas' temporary adherence to pro-

---

[18] We say "considered holding" in view of the proper proportionality text which offers proportionality merely as one of two alternative solutions to objections. This itself is somewhat disconcerting, since the proportionality doctrine which is offered as a mere alternative is presented as the exclusive description of the analogy between God and creatures.

Perhaps, like some of the "agent-intellect" texts in the *Commentary on the Sentences,* this text reflects either St. Thomas' own uncertainty concerning the speculative principles which govern the solution he is sure of, or the technique of a theologian or a controversialist who is saying in effect, "Either of these solutions safeguards what must be safeguarded at this point, and I will not here determine which is the best or correct solution."

[19] St. Thomas had not previously held, and would not subsequently hold, proportionality even as a complementary description of the analogy between God and creatures, much less as the only valid description.

portionality. Two general considerations which could apply to this case might serve as plausible reasons, but they have no probative power. First, the texts occur in a *Disputed Question,* and it is not certain how far St. Thomas, in his "magisterial" reworking of the arguments advanced by the students, was willing to go in reformulating the basic framework of the arguments and solutions. Secondly, in his *Commentary on the Sentences* St. Thomas sometimes proposes alternative solutions, asserting that, whichever is held, the truth of the faith remains intact. This kind of approach is not found often, and hardly ever in the later works, but it does occur in the earlier works. Perhaps St. Thomas in these texts is exercising the theologian's prerogative of showing that a certain truth ("God is truly said to have knowledge") is not in conflict with the arguments of those who would deny it, without considering positively an adequate philosophical defense.

There are two chronological data which we should consider. First, all the texts prior to the two *De veritate* texts deal with analogy in a concrete fashion.[20] They begin with some concrete, qualitatively determinate relationship (such as proportion, priority, participation), or with some concrete example (as health, or substance and accident). This concrete analogy is then analyzed, modified if necessary, applied to the concrete case or rejected, as we have seen St. Thomas do. Of course, St. Thomas is aware of the structure of this analogy,[21] he adverts to the number of terms in the analogy. In the *De veritate* proportionality texts this is still the case. He begins his discussion with the con-

---

[20] These texts are: *II Sent.* (5.13), *III Sent.* (6.2), and *IV Sent.* (7.5). In the case of the distinction of the kinds of analogy as given in *I Sent.* (4.2, 17, 29) we find a different kind of distinction altogether, that of intrinsic and extrinsic, which is not relevant to our present question.

[21] In the texts mentioned the first two speak of a third term; the third speaks of four terms. The point is that the number of terms—though it is known to be present—does not serve as a basis of division.

crete relation of proportionality. In view of the arguments advanced in favor of equivocity, he rejects both the two-term
structure as well as the qualitative determinants associated with
this term by these arguments. He may moreover have been im-
pressed by the fact that the Aristotelian proportions were mutually interdetermining. We can imagine him reflecting that this
limitation would affect all his previous analogies of direct relationship (such as the analogy of imitation). As for the analogy
of reference, this could be viewed either as a related group of
proportions (of the secondary analogates to the primary one)
or as a series of relationships to a perfection prior to all the
analogates. In the first case he would be faced with his original
difficulty with proportion; in the second with the unacceptable
theory of some perfection existing prior to God as well as to
creatures. The latter theory had often been criticized by Christian thinkers with whom St. Thomas was certainly acquainted.
Moreover, he himself had considered and rejected it in his
Commentary on the Sentences. If thoughts such as these entered
his mind, there is no wonder that he turned to proportionality,
which avoided both of these difficulties.

With the *De potentia* there is a different approach.[22] The
formal structure of the analogies is expressed in purely abstract
terms, and a choice is made of the appropriate structure. This
structure is then filled in with qualitative determinants. In the
Contra gentiles[23] and the *Summa theologiae*[24] the same two
stages of analysis appear. From now on it is possible for St.
Thomas to decide the form of his analogy and its concrete description on distinct bases. Hence he can pick and choose among
his illustrations, taking the formal structure from one, combin-
ing it with various qualitative descriptions from others. This
freedom enables him to break out of the dilemma posed in the
De veritate texts.

---

[22] *Pot.* (14.20).   [23] *C.G.* (15.7).   [24] *S.T.*, I (17.31).

Secondly, we have seen in Chapter 2 that the analogy of participation, as St. Thomas first used it, was mostly descriptive and quite vague. What was its difference from Platonic participation? What was its metaphysical status? These questions cannot be clearly answered from the *Commentary on the Sentences*. Already in that *Commentary* St. Thomas submitted Platonic participation to a searching scrutiny. In the *De veritate*, as we have also seen above, St. Thomas again criticizes Platonic participation. He concludes that Platonic participation does not account for—perhaps makes impossible—the existence of creatures with their own intrinsic perfections. In the Platonic explanation it is true that the intrinsic perfection as well as existence of God are safeguarded; "as far as this point is concerned, the opinion of Plato can be sustained" (9.30). But if Platonic participation makes creatures with intrinsic perfections impossible, and if our names of God are derived from the perfections of creatures, then an adequate theology cannot rest on Platonic participation. At this stage of his development it would be readily intelligible for St. Thomas to turn to proper proportionality, since he found Aristotle saying that it more suitably accounts for the intrinsic perfections of the analogates.

However, we have also noted that with the *De potentia* and *Contra gentiles* St. Thomas developed a new, metaphysically grounded participation which also was capable of expressing the intrinsic perfections of creatures. Hence participation was again possible, philosophically as well as theologically, and St. Thomas could turn to it if he wished.

Our textual evidence shows conclusively that St. Thomas did turn to participation, indeed as the most common of all analogy expressions, and entirely abandoned the proportionality structure. Why should he drop this latter completely, rather than keep it as an additional analogy?

If we consider the implications of proper proportionality as an analogy between God and creatures, we can see why St.

Thomas might have been led to accept it only as long as he could see no other defensible analogy. For the intrinsic weakness of the doctrine makes its subsequent abandonment less than surprising. The two proportionality texts attempt to use proportionality as the exclusive expression of the similarity between God and creatures, whereas the proportional form of analogy is presented as unable to perform such a role. We have already seen that proportionality predication involves either agnosticism about one set of the terms of the proportions involved (as in figurative predication not based on an independent knowledge of both the beings referred to), or is merely an extrinsic comparison of beings which are known independently from other sources. St. Thomas does not wish to teach a complete agnosticism about God, as is clear from his criticism of doctrines of equivocation. If he rejects all other analogies between God and creatures, it is difficult to see how he can know even that God and creatures possess analogous perfections, much less what they are or what the relationship is between God and His perfections. It may perhaps be indicative of St. Thomas' realization of this difficulty that the texts in question end very abruptly—there is no attempt to explain what "God truly has knowledge" might mean on the basis of proportionality.

If this is a true limitation of proportionality predication, it seems that St. Thomas ultimately would have to (1) admit complete agnosticism about God (which he definitely does not do); (2) reduce proportionality to a secondary and derivative type of analogy, a reformulation of more direct analogous knowledge, legitimate but clearly dependent upon this previous knowledge;[25] (3) be content with making safe but rather trivial

---

[25] This is certainly a possible way of predicating analogous perfections of God and creatures. However, just as the Aristotelian proportionalities which compared parallel act-potency correlations were derivative and dependent predications, so would such God-creature proportionalities depend upon more primary types of analogous knowledge. It is noteworthy that the analogy of proper propor-

statements to the effect that "the creature stands to the things which are its own as God stands to those which belong to Him" (which is the point he reached in the *De veritate* texts); or finally (4) abandon proportionality as an apt description of the similarity between God and creatures (which is what his subsequent silence on proportionality and positive teaching on other analogies indicate he actually did do).

Another point to be considered is this. Extrinsic proportionality can meaningfully be said to have four terms. In the instance of proportionality as transfer of corporeal attributes, St. Thomas finds the terms of a double relationship between really distinct terms. As he says in one of the texts we have seen above, "God is to the destruction of wickedness as fire is to the destruction of its contrary." But now consider the case of intrinsic proportionality. St. Thomas gives no sign that he ever admitted any real or even formal-real distinction of absolute perfections in God. Hence, in reality, all absolute perfections in God *are* God. St. Thomas holds that "real identity" is a relation of reason. As a result any relation between God and His perfections (being, goodness, and the like) can be only a relation of reason.[26] What are we to make of a similarity of proportions, one of which is

-----

tionality between two or more creatures, so common in Thomistic manuals, is nowhere mentioned in St. Thomas. We shall see later that there is textual ground for holding that any two beings, even of the same species, are analogous in being; but if this analogy is to be expressed as proportionality, it is derivative and depends on previous knowledge of each of the analogates and their respective relationships if this expression is to be at all meaningful. The proportionality set up in *III Sent.* (6.1) between substance and accident and their respective being seems to be valid, and equally derivative: "Things are one by analogy or proportion, as, for instance, substance and quality share in being. For just as substance is related to the being proper to it, so is quality related to the being proper to its genus. . . ."

[26] See ". . . in qualibet proportione oportet esse ad minus duos terminos, nihil enim sibi ipsi proportionatur, sed alteri" (*IV Sent.* [7.5]), ". . . omnis proportionalitas ad minus consistit in quatuor" (*Ethic.* [34.4]). This quaternary is entirely obvious in applications such as those in *Metaphys.* (33.14, 22, 23) and *Ethic.* (34.2). Note also the formal statements of *Post. analyt.* (21.1).

real, the other a being of reason alone, as an explanation of an ontological similarity?

The question of the analogy of proportionality is quite complicated, but the foregoing discussion represents one attempt to report the actual doctrine of the two proper proportionality texts (in distinction from the merely metaphorical or parallel proportionalities), and at the same time locate and critically evaluate that doctrine in the light of St. Thomas' multiple approach to the same analogy situation throughout his other works.

C. ANALOGY ACCORDING TO BEING BUT NOT ACCORDING TO INTENTION

A final series of Thomistic texts on analogy discusses *analogia secundum esse sed non secundum intentionem.*[27] The following three texts are representative of the others in the series.

> Something is predicated analogously in three ways. . . . The second of these is analogy according to being but not according to intention. This occurs when several things are equally matched in the intention of some common note even though that note does not have a being of one and the same sort *(esse unius rationis)* in each of them. An instance of this is that all bodies are made equal in the intention of "body." As a result the logician, who considers only intentions, says that this term body is predicated univocally of all bodies. In reality, however, this nature exists with a being of a different sort in corruptible and incorruptible bodies. Thus, in the eyes of a metaphysician or a philosopher of nature, who consider things according to the being they have, neither body nor any other term is predicated univocally of corruptible and of incorruptible things, as is clear from the words of the Philosopher and of the

---

[27] Most of the texts in the series contain a reference to the tenth book of Aristotle's *Metaphysics*, Chap. 10 (1058b26-1059a16). The Aristotelian text offers some difficulties, but the general meaning is clear: Incorruptibility is an essential property; hence incorruptible things differ in kind from corruptible things; this difference is not merely that which obtains between two species of the same genus. For the textual difficulties, see W. D. Ross's comments *ad locum* in *Aristotle's Metaphysics* (Oxford: Clarendon Press, 1924).

Commentator in the fifth text of the tenth book of the *Metaphysics* ... (*I Sent.* [4.17]).

The Philosopher here is speaking of a natural and not of a logical community. Those things which have a different mode of existing do not share in anything common according to the being which the natural philosopher considers, although they can share in some common intention which the logician considers. Furthermore, according to the natural philosopher, also an elementary body and a celestial body are not in the same genus; but they are for a logician. Nevertheless the Philosopher does not wish to exclude analogous community, but only univocal community. For he wants to show that the corruptible and the incorruptible do not share in the same genus (*Pot.* [14.26]).

For the corruptible and the incorruptible cannot have a common matter. Genus, however, according to the physical philosopher, is taken from the matter. For this reason it was said above that those things which do not have the same kind of matter are in different genera. From the logician's viewpoint, however, they may well have the same generic perfection, inasmuch as they share in a common intelligibility (either of substance or quality or some similar [category]) (*Metaphys.* [33.25]).[28]

These texts all make certain points. (1) The "logician"—in Aristotle's intention a philosopher who deals with real beings only according to the concepts he has of them—is contrasted with the natural philosopher or the metaphysician, "who consider things according to the being they have." The "logician" may legitimately place things in the same logical category (for example, the remote genus of substance) which the natural philosopher, whose knowledge extends to the different modes of the actual existence of things, must describe as generically different. A real, or natural, common genus requires an interchange of matter. (2) Corruptible and incorruptible bodies have a different mode of existence because they have in their very essence

---

[28] See similar texts: *I Sent.* (4.32); *II Sent.* (5.4, 8); *Boethii de Trin.* (11.7); *Pot.* (14.16); *S.T.*, I (17.96, 107); *Phys.* (22.9, 10).

different kinds of matter.[29] This accepted piece of physics forces the natural philosopher to place terrestrial and celestial bodies in different genera, although they may still be analogously similar,[30] and may still be placed together in the logical category of substance.[31]

What is the significance of this type of analogy? For one who believed that the distinction between terrestrial and celestial matter was a valid one (as St. Thomas did), it seems there would indeed be two kinds of material substances, with different kinds of matter, in different genera, but analogously similar.[32] This is the situation which St. Thomas attempts to provide for

---

[29] Four texts extend the contrast between corruptible bodies and incorruptible bodies to one between corruptible bodies and incorruptible *incorporeal beings.* The supposition seems to be that this is where incorporeal substances fit into the categories, if they fit anywhere. See *II Sent.* (5.4) —*angeli; Boethii de Trin.* (11.7) —*immateriales substantiae; Pot.* (14.16) —*aeterna, temporalia; S.T.,* I (17.107) —*immateriales substantiae.*

[30] Some of these texts follow the Aristotelian *littera* and speak of body applied to corruptible and incorruptible substances as an equivocal term describing substances which have only a name in common. Others, like *Pot.* (14.26), make it clear that equivocal in this context means only nonunivocal and does not exclude an analogous community.

[31] Both Aristotle and St. Thomas are trying to make the point that corruptible and incorruptible material substances differ more fundamentally than do species which share a univocally common genus (as rational and irrational share the generic perfection of animal). If there were such a thing as celestial matter distinct in kind from terrestrial matter, the point would be well made. (Perhaps the "antimatter" of contemporary scientific speculation might be considered a potential candidate for the role vacated by the out-dated celestial matter; perhaps also free subatomic particles are body in an analogous sense, though not for the same reason as celestial matter.)

[32] Cajetan and others who reject this analogy while accepting the distinction between terrestrial and celestial matter seem to be misreading the Thomistic texts here. St. Thomas does not say that the logician's indeterminate and univocal predication of body as a remote genus (or as the category substance, the supreme genus) is really a kind of hidden or ignored analogy. He simply says that, besides this univocal logical predication, an analogous ontological one (pertaining to metaphysics or the philosophy of nature) is also possible, on the ground that in the particular cases mentioned there are real differences in the very common perfection itself.

with his *analogia secundum esse sed non secundum intentionem.*
If one does not accept a distinction between terrestrial and celestial matter, then there is not an existence of a different sort for
these bodies, and consequently such an analogy is no longer
necessary,[33] though it might be mentioned for the sake of logical completeness.

---

[33] Some modern interpretations of this analogy maintain that it retains considerable
importance even after the distinction between celestial and terrestrial matter
has been abandoned. See A. Maurer, C.S.B., "St. Thomas and the Analogy of
Genus," *New Scholasticism,* XXIX (1955), 127-44. Father Maurer designates
the *analogia secundum esse sed non secundum intentionem* as the analogy of
genus or the analogy of inequality, and explains it as follows. Generic perfections designate the whole being indeterminately. Fido, a dog, is specifically
different from John, a man; yet both are correctly designated animals. Such
generic designation is not univocal but analogous, since the indeterminate
generic perfection is realized determinately in a different way in Fido and in
John. Father Maurer says that this is St. Thomas' doctrine on *analogia secundum esse et non secundum intentionem.* To support his interpretation he
quotes such texts as *II Sent.* (5.6), and the following passage from *Malo*
(24.5): "All animals are equally animals but yet are not equal animals.
Rather, one animal is greater and more perfect than another. In like manner
all sins do not have to be equal just because they are all sins." Such a text
seems to state the more common interpretation that genera are predicated
univocally of their species: "All animals are equally animals." In this connection, it is worthwhile to recall that indeterminate generic predication remains
indeterminate even when it concerns (as it always does) some specifically
determinate nature (see *S.T.,* I [17.66], and q. 76, a. 3 ad 4).

CHAPTER V

Textual Conclusions

The conclusions of this study can be viewed as being drawn at two levels. There are immediate conclusions which derive from the texts themselves and which have a similar fragmentary and incomplete status. There are also more ultimate conclusions which attempt to provide the entire systematic framework for the more particular conclusions and to fill in the lacunae evident in St. Thomas' various treatments. Such a systematic presentation is of a more speculative nature, more liable to error, less well grounded in the texts. To mark the difference between the two types of conclusions they will be presented in two distinct chapters.

First, then, come the chronological conclusions. The results of the chronological investigation are meager. In addition to several instances of shifting terminology (proportion, priority and posteriority, the first analogate in the definition of the secondary), St. Thomas speaks of a plurality of intelligibilities rather than a single intelligibility in his later discussions of analogy. He gradually develops the doctrine of the primacy of analogous over univocal causality. He comes to reject the primacy of univocal concepts, and places instead the analogous conception, being, as the most basic of all intelligibilities. In his later works he abandons the distinction of God's exemplar causality into *exemplar ut intellectus* and *ut natura*. Also in his later works he makes no further use of proper proportionality as a description of the analogous likeness between God and creatures. St. Thomas' early understanding of the analogy of participation seems to have been quite vague; he seems often to have used it merely descriptively; and he does not show how the analogy itself requires and establishes the intrinsic perfection of the participants. After a period in which he makes almost no use of participation, the analogy recurs in a new form, connected now with the limitation of act by potency. In this second, metaphysical form the analogy of participation establishes the intrinsic perfection of the participants. The participants, as effects, are created in their participated actuality by the being who is such by essence. These same participants, experienced by us according to their inherent participated perfections, cause our knowledge—imperfect but true—of the being by essence.

The first section of Chapter 3, together with the chronological investigations in Chapter 2, established one point of methodology in St. Thomas' treatment of analogy. Though he does consistently describe analogy as the halfway point between univocity and equivocity, many of his other "general" descriptions really are applicable only to specific analogy situations. This is another way of saying emphatically that St. Thomas has no general treatise on analogy. His approach to analogy is both multiple and partial, indicating both the complexity of the doctrine and the diversity occasioned by his shifting interests and deepening metaphysical insights. In the light of this conclusion we can refer back to our originally pragmatic rejection of the method of "key texts"—it is not only a risky business to work out the doctrine of St. Thomas on analogy from selected texts, it is *not possible*.

The analysis carried on in the remaining sections of Chapter 3 reveals another point of methodology. The different rubrics employed by St. Thomas in his discussions of analogy sometimes describe distinct types of analogy and sometimes merely refer to different elements within one complex analogy situation. Thus, the analogy by which health is predicated of both medicine and a patient is simply different from the analogy by which limited beings resemble God by participation. On the other hand, texts which link the analogy of participation with the analogy of eminence are merely isolating two elements within a complex analogy situation. God is by essence what the creature is by participation because God is pure actuality whereas the creature is a limited actuality; God is in an eminent way what the creature is imperfectly because God is the analogous cause of the creature. This linkage of diverse rubrics to describe more adequately the various relationships within a complex analogy situation becomes most extensive in St. Thomas' later discussions of participation through exemplar, efficient, and telic causality. Also apparent here is St. Thomas' propensity to adapt and transform traditional terminology rather than invent new rubrics for his genuinely new thought.[1]

The main doctrinal conclusions of this study are based on the texts discussed in the last six sections of Chapter 3. There we find St. Thomas describing various concrete analogous likenesses in terms of reference, proportion, imitation, priority, participation, and eminence. It is noteworthy that formal discussions of analogy itself appear only within the description and analysis of particular analogates, and often, as we have seen, methodologically go only far enough to handle the concrete problem.

In the analogy of reference one analogate is denominated by reference (or attribution) to another analogate's perfection. If

---

[1] Etienne Gilson has repeatedly pointed out the new meanings which St. Thomas gave to traditional Augustinian and Aristotelian formulae; see, for several examples, *The History of Christian Philosophy in the Middle Ages*, pp. 382-83 (New York: Random House, 1955), and *The Christian Philosophy of St. Thomas Aquinas*, pp. 140, 166-67, 183-85, 467-68, n. 13, 469, n. 32 (first cited in Introduction, n. 1).

only the designation by reference is stressed, the analogy becomes almost purely extrinsic denomination. If the perfection which each analogate possesses as the basis or result of its reference to the other is stressed, the analogy becomes an explanatory description of the intrinsic likeness between secondary and primary analogates.

In applying the language of proportion to the resemblance of creatures and Creator, St. Thomas always eliminates unacceptable quantitative connotations. He maintains that creatures resemble God analogously because they are proportioned to Him as effects to their analogous cause. Proportion thus is taken to mean a general relationship *(habitudo)*, an agreement *(convenientia)*, or a likeness.

The analogy of imitation describes the analogy between God and creatures in terms of similitude, representation, assimilation, image, and exemplar cause. At times St. Thomas points out that the similitude in question is not a mere chance likeness, it is *intended*. The creature is not only like to God, it is *made to* that likeness. Almost always the descriptions either imply or explicitly refer to the efficient (and sometimes telic) causality which is the ontological basis for such similarity.

The analogy of participation, by which one analogate (usually God) possesses essentially or in an unlimited way a perfection which another analogate (some creature) possesses by a limited participation, also is most often linked with the efficient causality by which such participation comes about. At times St. Thomas is at pains to guard against the historical echoes of extrinsicism by pointing out that the participant possesses its own (participated) act, which is limited by the receptive potency.

The Thomistic texts describing resemblance according to priority and posteriority (which is said to be a characteristic of all analogy situations) frequently, though not always, link the possession of an analogous perfection more properly or perfectly by one analogate than by the other(s) with either causal par-

ticipation or the analogy of eminence. In connection with this
rubric we encounter the notion that the prior analogate must
always be placed in the definition of the secondary. What seem
to be difficulties are eliminated by the distinction of two types of
priority: in knowledge and in being.

In the analogy of causal eminence the nonunivocal cause
possesses the analogous perfection of the effect in a more eminent manner than does the effect. Nevertheless the bare causal
relation is compatible with figurative (or extrinsic) denomination. This point becomes clear in St. Thomas' discussion of the
equivocal denomination by causality which he identifies histor-
ically with Maimonides. Further analysis is necessary before
the analogy of causal eminence is shown to be a proper or intrinsic one in the given analogy situation.

All these analogies are employed to describe the relationships of God and creatures. All of them are also employed—the
analogy of participation, however, only in a reduced or in
a noncausal form—to describe the real similarities between
finite creatures, and even those between intrinsic principles of
being, especially substance and accident (except, obviously,
analogies of efficient causality). In addition there is a variety
of participation (which we have referred to as a participation
"of many in one") which is restricted to the relation of accidents
to substance in being, and to similar situations.

The two analogies whose status is most controversial—the
analogy according to being but not according to intention, and
the analogy of proper proportionality—were handled separately. The analogy according to being but not according to intention was seen to be a special case used by St. Thomas to
explain a unique ontological situation: the heavenly bodies were
evidently correctly understood as bodies in a univocal sense, yet
they did not behave as other bodies of our experience. In particular, it was believed that they did not possess the same kind
of matter as terrestrial things, nor interchange matter with

them; hence the two kinds of bodies could not belong to the same *natural* genus of body. And since this is the ultimate genus in the category of substance, there was no further genus in which they could agree and no distinct difference by which they differed. They must, therefore, be bodies analogously, though the intelligibility of "body" did not reveal this diversity. Since it is the nature of this analogy to explain an accepted physical situation, it is at the present time of no doctrinal interest, though it illustrates St. Thomas' technique as an Aristotelian commentator and shows the indirect influence of Aristotelian physics on Thomistic metaphysics.

In dealing with the analogy of proper proportionality some attention was paid to irrelevant usages of the term, and it was distinguished both from univocal proportionalities and from those uses which employ proportional predication but do not describe any analogously common intrinsic perfection nor explicitly express even a common relationship. The two texts in which St. Thomas discusses proper proportionality were quoted, and analyzed in context. Although in these texts St. Thomas presents proper proportionality as the only valid analogy between God and creatures, an analysis of the proportional form of predication reveals that it must either maintain an agnosticism about one of the analogates involved, or must depend upon and reformulate *previous* knowledge of both analogates and of their similarities. This analysis at least partially explains why St. Thomas did not use this analogy in later writings (whereas he continued to use and develop the multiple analogies we have just considered), just as the context of the two texts at least partially explains why he held that doctrine when confronted with the apparent alternatives of the analogy of proper proportionality or no analogy at all. In addition the later texts show a much greater richness of interrelationship and a greater freedom in using the traditional analogies. St. Thomas does not tell us how and why this development took place, any more than he has given us an explicit, complete exposition of analogy itself. A biographer of St. Thomas is baffled by the almost complete lack of self-revelation in the works. Our present interest could easily dispense with the psychological causes of his development, but as historians of his thought we would be very interested in the intelligible reasons for this progress.

It has been noted by historians of ancient and medieval thought that the structure of the monograph is almost unknown to the writers of those periods. An attempt to develop medieval thought in this way, and particularly the attempt to state explicitly the principles we think an author has used, is in some sense a reconstruction, and this will be the task of the next chapter.

CHAPTER VI

Systematic Summary

The thought of St. Thomas as we have followed it through the works is both complex and subtle. We have tried to isolate doctrinal constants in the various texts, and we have seen that certain types or divisions of analogy are given with relative constancy, that certain particular analogies are described with almost complete consistency. But it has also become clear that there is in St. Thomas no general theory of analogy, no explicit presentation of the general structure of analogy. There are at best incidental remarks about elements of such a general structure. Yet the over-all impression is of a remarkably harmonious and consistent use of analogy. Hence we believe that it will not be too difficult to make explicit the structure which is implied in the various particular treatments. But as the preceding chapters should have made sufficiently clear, the implicit structure is not to be discovered by means of an analysis of any *single text*, and perhaps not even by means of a textual analysis at all.

What, basically, is analogy? It has been customary for Thomists to begin with the derivation of the word and its meanings. It is perhaps simpler to say that the meanings presently given in the standard Greek, Latin, and English dictionaries have very little connection with the technical meanings elaborated by St. Thomas. The employment of the term by English logicians and philosophers and by biologists is particularly distracting. It seems more effective to begin unconventionally—though not un-Thomistically[1]—with the very general definition: analogy is a kind of community, that is to say, a kind of unity-of-many.

A. GENERAL CONSIDERATIONS

1. *Analogy and Knowledge.* Even the tyro in the history of philosophy knows that unity is among the very basic, difficult, and therefore controversial philosophical concepts. Many things about unity, and even unity as understood by Thomists, can well be presumed to be known for the purposes of our present exposition. But a few points do have to be made, and they will be controversial points.

Unity has a threefold relation to knowledge. (1) There are unities which are entirely independent of knowledge, such as the so-called numerical unity (that is, of individual things). (2) There are unities that are produced by knowledge in the sense that the mind is responsible for imposing a unity on a multiplicity that is brute and pure, such as the various constellations that people discover in the skies. (3) There are unities which are only intelligible, not existential, and yet are not arbitrarily constructed or imposed by the mind, such as the quidditative concepts which arise by abstraction: blue, chair.[2] Surely most Aristotelians will admit that according to the Aristotelian analysis, the unity of such specific concepts is only in the mind —in themselves all blue things are simply many beings; and also that this admission in no way constitutes a subjectivism nor throws any doubt on the validity of knowledge.

---

[1] On St. Thomas' approach to analogy through the notion of a community (or kinds of community) see *I Sent.* (4.2, 17, 22, 23, 29) ; *II Sent.* (5.1, 21) ; *III Sent.* (6.6) ; *Ver.* (9.9) ; *Pot.* (14.26) ; *S.T.*, I (17.11, 31) ; *Periher.* (20.4) ; *S.T.*, I-II (25.6).

[2] We choose these examples of inanimate objects because natural species of living things are not merely intelligible unities; according to the theory of evolution they are also one by descent, and therefore have a real even if accidental unity.

Concerning this third point there is a statement about the nature of universals which is accepted by at least some Thomists and which is often put this way: "Outside (that is, prior to and independently of) the mind, there is no formally universal or common nature; there is, however, a foundation in singulars for such universal ideas." Now, this thesis is immediately concerned with universal ideas in the strict sense; that is, with quidditative concepts which (in the first instance) arise by abstraction. But there is a sufficient parallel between analogous terms (and concepts) and univocal ones to allow us to understand this thesis in a broader sense. We hold, therefore, that outside the mind there are no *formally common* perfections, whether this community be one of specific unity of identity or of analogical unity.

The community of both univocation and analogy is then a community which formally as such is in the mind. The full implication of this statement can perhaps be set forth more clearly by contrasting it with traditional discussions of the nature and location of analogy. Many authors who write on analogy put their question this way: Does analogy belong to concepts or to things or to both? In our understanding of the relation between human knowledge and the things we know this separation of concept and object of knowledge seems to be misleading, and to involve an unacceptable interpretation of St. Thomas' notion of the nature of human knowledge. We cannot talk properly about the concept in abstraction from the things of which it is the concept except from the point of view of logic. We cannot talk about things as if in talking about them we did not have to know them. Questions about the nature of knowledge are always complex questions, and questions about relationships between beings are equally complex questions.

We can illustrate this problem from the similar area of the case of univocal knowledge. On the one hand we cannot speak correctly and satisfactorily of a univocal concept unless we are referring to the relationships of what is known in this concept to the things outside. On the other hand it is not correct, it is not even possible, to speak of specific identity as existing in things without any relation to knowledge. The attempt to say that there is a species in the real order which is merely discovered by the human mind involves the very serious Platonic difficulties of the one and the many and ultimately should logically involve a Platonic positing of a separated idea or species or to the even more unacceptable consequence of pantheism. It scarcely seems necessary that we here push this interpretation to its full limits. Now, in the same fashion, though with a great deal more emphasis, it must be said that analogy is neither to be predicated of knowledge taken by itself nor of things simply as by themselves. We will consider this question again later when we ask about the real relations and real unities which are to be found among the things of our experience. But it is necessary here to put the question in the way in which we think St. Thomas put it.

St. Thomas is not particularly concerned with the psychology of our conception of being, though he does have some things to say about this. Nor is he concerned with the logic of the analogical concept. The analogical concept—or better, knowledge—is from the point of view of the logician no different from the univocal concept or knowledge and is treated by the logician in exactly the same way. The reason is that the logician does not consider the way in which perfections are in being but only the way in which they are conceived. Now, if we are going to consider analogy as a form of knowledge, then we must consider not only the knowledge as it is in us but also as it is knowledge *of* the things which we know. Therefore it seems to be a more adequate representation of St. Thomas' opinion to say that analogy arises only when the mind and things both enter into the picture. And since both the mind and the things are concerned, it makes relatively little difference whether we speak of the analogy of our knowledge of things or the analogy of things. To make this point more clear, when we speak of the analogy of being we do not mean the analogy of the concept taken as such in the mind. Secondly, we do not mean that there is a Platonic idea of being. Thirdly, we do not mean that there is a formally common nature or formally common perfection in the various things which we denominate being. The expression, the analogy of being, in a Thomistic understanding of that term must be explained this way. *When various, distinct, and independent things are conceived, known, or understood according to their perfection as beings, then they are found neither to be simply the same in this perfection nor to be so diverse that they cannot be conceived according to some kind of common perfection.* The being which is said to be analogous is not the concept, for a concept cannot be predicated of a thing. It is not simply a thing. It is an intelligibility which formally as intelligibility is actually existing only in a mind.

To this extent and in this sense it can be said that the unity or community of analogy is parallel to the unity or community of a univocal concept. But it does not follow that these two communities are necessarily alike in all respects. We find that the Thomistic theory of the univocal concept involves at least these points: the concept of one nature is simply and from all points of view one concept; it arises by abstraction; it can be expanded into a definition which explicates the whole intelligible nature known in the concept and so can have an independent status outside of a judgment; it primarily represents a form or an actuality after the manner of a form; though it is intrinsically related to existence and to singulars, it does not include or require them; as understood, and in abstraction from things, it has no intrinsic relation to any other concept.

On the other hand, in the view of one group of Thomists, and at least as far as the analogy of being is concerned, being is not known simply and immediately in an abstractive concept; being cannot be defined; being is not a form. And it is perhaps also well known that in the Thomistic view the unity of being is not a simple and unqualified one, to say the least. If being is not a concept, then the unity of being cannot be a concept. If, therefore, there is to be any unity of being in knowledge at all, there remains only the judgment. Consequently analogy is primarily an affair of judgment rather than concept.[3]

2. *Types of Analysis of Analogy.* If we are correct in asserting that analogy involves both the judgment of the mind and things, it should follow that analogy can be approached from either of these poles. In fact, it seems that there are even more than two levels of analysis. The following diagram schematically presents the steps of the analysis we will undertake in the remainder of this chapter.

METHODS OF APPROACH TO ANALOGY

1. Predicational Approach: proportion of an analogon to a subject
2. Formal Approach: three possible formal structures:
   a. one to another
   b. many to one
      (1) one is separate from the many
      (2) one is composed of the many
   c. many to many
3. General Material Approach:
   a. qualitative:
      order (prior, posterior)
      proportion
      imitation and exemplarity
      participation
         (1) two-termed
         (2) members in a totality

---

[3] The expression "The concept of being is predicated analogously" is deliberately avoided. It is used by some Thomists who hold that being is completely grasped and understood in itself, and is, as it were, univocal to itself, as any other concept might be thought of as being; and that this single concept is afterward applied differently to various subjects. Such a view seems to be an accurate description of the way in which *secondarily* analogous concepts are used. A secondarily analogous concept has a series of analogous meanings, each of which is predicated univocally of a number of individuals. On the distinction between primarily and secondarily analogous terms see below.

eminence, deficiency (more or less perfect)
simpliciter, secundum quid
reference (attribution)
  b. intrinsic vs. extrinsic (proper vs. improper)
4. Particular Material Approach:
    substance and accidents
    cause and effect
    God and creatures
    created beings
    potency and act
    being and beings of reason
    analoga other than being

These levels of analysis can be described here briefly (detailed application will be made in later sections of this chapter). There is, first of all, a predicational analysis, in which we consider analogical judgments (which, it is true, are about objects) simply as kinds of predication, without explicitly considering the objects known. All other analysis will include the objects of these judgments, but these objects can be looked at from different levels of abstractness and generality. We can first consider the analogous community in the most abstract possible fashion. We can abstract from what the objects are which are analogous, we can abstract from what is analogous about the objects which are analogous and consider the bare, formal notion: "an analogous community of many." In this way we are considering analogy as a form of unity of relation, and when we do so we consider only the sorts of relations that can be found between many things when these many things are not concretely described in any fashion. We shall call this the formal analysis of analogy.

Next, we can consider the analogous community more concretely. On the one hand, relations between many things are not merely relations. They are kinds of relations. In order to consider the relations found between the members of the analogous community as kinds of relations we must consider the individ-

uals in some kind of concreteness. This means that we shall have
to consider the objects which are analogous, at least in some way
with regard to their intrinsic content. Any consideration of analogy which considers the natures, the perfections of the things
which are analogous, can be called a concrete, "material" analysis of analogy. These additional determinants can be considered
in general, as ways of being related. We shall call this level the
"general material analysis" of analogy. Finally, we can consider specifically determined groups of analogates (such as the
substance-accident group), and describe the relations that hold
between these analogates according to their proper concrete
reality. This level of analysis can be considered to be a discussion of the major concrete applications of the structures which
have previously been defined predicationally, formally, and generally. We shall call this the level of "particular (that is, specifically determined) material analysis."

B. PREDICATIONAL ANALYSIS

1. *Types of Predication.* Since analogy is primarily an affair
of judgments, it will be helpful to discover the nature of the
analogous judgment if we contrast it with other types of judgment. Our consideration here is of the way in which various
terms are used in propositions. Traditionally, terms are said to
be of three kinds, but a slightly more complicated approach
commends itself. Terms are either univocal (if they always have
one and the same meaning) or multivocal (if they have several
meanings). Multivocal terms are then subdivided, for the singleness of the term can be merely accidental (dog of animal and
metal claw; bank of financial institution and land bordering a
stream), so that the meanings of this apparently single term are
simply many; or the singleness of term can be "intended," so
that the meanings of this single term are both many and one
("planned ambiguity," as the language analysts like to call it),
and this is the analogous term properly so called. The analogous

term has a meaning which is partly the same and partly different in its various uses.[4]

Univocal terms have a clear and consistent meaning in themselves, and so they should be capable of definition. So we do find that terms which are used univocally in predication are also quidditative in themselves (or at least they are understood as if they were concepts of quiddities).

Analogous terms, however, do not have a single meaning in themselves; that is why they ordinarily are not capable of a definition (that is, one or a single definition) like the definitions of univocal terms.[5] In some vague way an analogous term is one term, and so there can be a vague, somewhat indefinite description of its meaning. As St. Thomas remarks, following Aristotle, the word "is," used by itself, is not entirely meaningless; it has a meaning that can be described in an indeterminate way as asserting the actual existence of a subject in some order or the actual presence in such a subject of some form or perfection.[6] This is indefinite and unsatisfactory; we want to know, "In what order?" or "In what kind of a subject is this perfection?" But we cannot force the analogous term to become determinate *in itself* without immediately destroying its community to the precise extent to which we make it determinate. Is that term, then, condemned to be and to remain vague and indeterminate? No; for it is not a term that is intended to be used by and in itself; it molds itself to its subject; its meaning in any given case is *proportional* to its subject. "Is" denotes the kind of actuality that is suitable, proportioned to the subject which we assert to be. Note that, when we call a term analogous or proportional in the context of predication, we mean "in proportion *to the*

---

[4] On this as a general description of all analogies see above, Chap. 3, sect. A.

[5] Note, however, *Periher.* (20.1), where St. Thomas points out that in an analogy where there is a primary analogate, the analogon, used by itself, is defined (or described) in the same way as that primary analogate.

[6] See *Periher.*, lectio 2 and lectio 5.

subject of which it is predicated," and not "because of any relation of one subject to another, of one analogate to another," nor
"because of the relation of one relation within a subject to another similar relation within another subject."[7]

2. *Cajetan and the Predicational Analysis of Analogy.* The
preceding analysis of univocal and multivocal terms (and no-
tions) is a fairly direct analysis, which St. Thomas often mentions in very brief fashion (for example, to make some division
of terms). But he does not engage in a complete analysis along
these lines, though this analysis is in harmony with his text.

Cajetan, on the other hand, formally begins his treatise with
terms *(nomina).* And it might even be contended that his entire
analysis really remains within predication. Thus, he misses the
point of St. Thomas' *analogia secundum esse et non secundum
intentionem;* he thinks it deals with all generic predication[8] and
concludes that generic terms are called analogous only by an
abuse of that term. Now, had St. Thomas been considering how
generic terms are predicated in propositions, and if in that context he had affirmed that they are "analogous in fact," Cajetan's
solution might have been pertinent. As it was, he misplaced
the problem.

Next, Cajetan takes up the analogy of attribution, which is
an analogy in which the term is properly found only in one subject and is attributed to the others by the mind; he explains it as
a "many-to-one" structure, and uses the example of health. This
is one kind of *analogia secundum intentionem tantum;* but it is
not the only kind, for this Thomistic phrase also describes improper proportionality.

---

[7] These last two meanings are the ones that St. Thomas is using in the *De veritate*
texts analyzed above in Chap. 4, sect. B.

[8] One could, given the same starting point, go in the opposite direction and deny
the existence of generic univocity, as Pedro da Fonseca apparently did. See
Michael P. Slattery, "Two Notes on Fonseca," *Modern Schoolman,* XXXIV
(1957), 197-202.

Finally, Cajetan comes to consider the predication of terms to subjects when the terms are truly and properly but not univocally predicated of each one of these subjects. So far, this is an acceptable, though rather general and vague, description. But at once he goes into the mathematical backgrounds of proportion and the verbal aspects of the problem of a proportion between God and creatures. Moreover, the predicational relation becomes confused with the relation—not within predication—between and within the things about which predication is made, a relation which is either real or of reason. Beginning his consideration of analogy (in the strict sense) within the limited purview of the function of analogous terms in predication, Cajetan correctly concludes that predicates are proportional to their subjects. But since he thinks that this is what St. Thomas said in his analogy of proper proportionality, and since in many cases he finds really or rationally distinct forms or formalities needed to make up a four-termed analogy, he asserts that *all* real analogy is proportionality.[9]

But, a Cajetanist might object, all real analogy *is* proportionality. For St. Thomas clearly teaches—and it is quite evident—that different terms predicated of God are not mere synonyms; in the sentences "God is," "God is wise," and "God is good," "is," "wise," and "good" are quite distinct meanings or intelligibilities *(rationes)*, distinct not only from one another but from their subject, God. Hence there are always four terms in every analogy, and the predicates are essentially proportioned to their subjects, not to each other. Wise as applied to God and wise as applied to Socrates are by no means proportioned to each other, and the meaning of one does not include a reference to the meaning of the other.

---

[9] See Thomas de Vio Cajetanus, *Scripta philosophica.* III. *De nominum analogia,* edited by N. Zammit, O.P., Chap. 3, pp. 23, 25, and esp. p. 27, par. 27. Rome: Angelicum, 1934.

But it is not true to say that God and creatures are not directly related, for in the order of being the creature directly and immediately depends on God; and in the order of knowledge what we naturally know about God can never be completely disengaged from its origin in the experience of creatures. In like manner the predicates themselves which we use of God and creatures are related: in the order of being any perfection of a creature is related to God; in the order of knowledge any perfection predicated of God includes in its definition a reference to the creatures which have been experienced by us as possessing such a perfection. This inclusion of one analogate in the definition of the other is one of the points on which there is a chronological development in St. Thomas, as we have seen.

To say, as the logic of the Cajetanist theory of proper proportionality requires, that neither the analogates nor any of their constituent factors are directly related, leads in the case of the analogy between God and creatures to an awkward dilemma. For example, either we know what wise predicated of God means independently of all reference to creatures, or we use the term neither from a direct knowledge of God nor by any reference to the wisdom of men. The first of these alternatives is ontologism, the second agnosticism.

There does not seem to be any more than a verbal difference between what we have called predicational analysis and Cajetan's analysis of *rationes nominum*. If Cajetan had explicitly stated that he was doing only a predicational analysis and if his followers had so understood him, he would have made a clear contribution. Because his interest in analogy was mainly logical, his exposition is important for studies of the validity of reasoning employing analogous terms. Moreover, certain objections now urged in favor of agnosticism rest on the false assumption that all terms are univocal (or at best only secondarily analogous, to use a distinction to be made in the next section). Against this assumption Cajetan's analysis is entirely valid and

useful even for our contemporaries. When interpreted as remaining on the level of predicational analysis, the work of Cajetan is, then, a real contribution to the theory of analogy, and
entirely faithful to St. Thomas.

But Cajetan does not seem to have realized the relation
between his own and St. Thomas' doctrine. Had he seen the multiple levels of the Thomistic approach, he would not have ab-
sorbed all the other analyses of St. Thomas into the one category
of proportionality. In order to make such a reduction we must
suppose that, when St. Thomas spoke of an analogy between God
and creatures, he meant the same thing as if he had said "an
analogy between our predication about God and our predication
about creatures."

The inadequacies of Cajetan's position are sufficiently clear,
and previous analyses by other authors sufficiently sharp,[10] that
we can dismiss it without further discussion. But one major result of the confusions due to Cajetan is that it is very hard to
write on analogy in St. Thomas without being misunderstood.
We shall, therefore, close this digression by reiterating, "Predicationally speaking, analogy is proportional predication."

3. *Primarily and Secondarily Analogous Terms.* Counting
and identifying meanings is a very difficult task. It is something
like trying to count the meanings of a spoken word, which can
never have the fixity of the written (or other permanent) symbol.
*In the last analysis, counting meanings is analogous to other
countings.* The meaning we use to count with is itself one of the
meanings we are counting, and the process might seem to be
both arbitrary and subjective.

Does this then mean that we cannot distinguish univocal
from multivocal terms? Not entirely; but it does mean that we
cannot attribute fixity and absoluteness to such analyses. Actually, there are very few words which have only one meaning,

---

[10] See Chap. 1, sect. A.

except the highly technical terms of science which have not yet become part of ordinary language. On the other hand, there are not very many that are simply equivocal. Should we then say that most words are analogous? A distinction is in order. We have pointed out that univocal terms properly are the names of concepts of forms (quiddities) or of other perfections treated as if they were forms, and that they have meanings which are capable of complete determination by themselves (that is, apart from any particular subject). For this reason a word like "soft," which has nine meanings according to Webster's Collegiate Dictionary,[11] is basically a univocal term whose various meanings are closely similar, but each of which could in principle be strictly defined, rigorously limited to a specific application, and given nine different verbal forms identifying each meaning. This of course would needlessly multiply words; hence "soft" is primarily a univocal term, but secondarily an analogous one inasmuch as it has a series of similar univocal meanings. These meanings are so related that this term could in time lose one or more of its meanings, or acquire additional ones, particularly in spoken usage.

A primarily analogous term, on the other hand, is one which does not admit of a single determinate meaning in abstraction from a concrete subject.[12] Obviously this kind of term is radically different from a univocal term, and is the one which is

---

[11] Webster's Collegiate Dictionary, fifth edition, p. 945. Springfield: G. and C. Merriam Company, 1946.

[12] Some Thomists have asked this further question: Is it possible that among the meanings of a primarily analogous term there might be one or more which applied equally and without need of further intrinsic determination to many individual subjects? See, for example, Joannes a S. Thoma, Cursus philosophicus thomisticus, Ars logica, edited by Beatus Reiser, O.S.B., pars II, q. 13, a. 3, and q. 14, a. 2; Vol. 1, pp. 485b-486a, 511 (3 vols. Turin: Marietti, 1930). It will be better to discuss this point in connection with the concrete applications of analogy, as a function of the thing about which we make predications, rather than in connection with predication itself; see below, sect. E, "Created Beings as Analogous."

chiefly in question in Thomistic discussions of analogy; this study deals almost exclusively with primarily analogous terms.[13]

C. FORMAL ANALYSIS OF ANALOGY STRUCTURES

Where there is one meaning that refers to a real world, there is one real class of things which is really one by abstraction. But it would appear that, as far as univocal predicates are concerned —at least those simple and primitive predicates that arise by abstraction, there is only one kind of community: the strict logical unity of the species or genus.

Where there are many related meanings, there can only be a community which is in some respects looser than the unity of species or genus. Can we truly speak of the community of beings, of goods, and so on? Without any doubt we do, and even in several different ways.

Now, a community is a unity of many, at the very least of two. Note that we are now concerned with the unity of the objects about which we speak, not of the predication itself. And we must suppose that the objects are objectively many; otherwise the predication is merely erroneous. A manifold which is a real plurality in itself can be combined into a unity; it is not simply a unity by itself. The unity, then, is a relation of the members of the community.

A community, thus unified, can be considered formally as an intelligible structure, without any consideration of the quality .

---

[13] There is one kind of secondarily analogous term which deserves additional attention. Among the positive attributes of God there are some perfections which are named by names that signify these perfections absolutely (S.T., I [17.40]), such as wisdom, knowledge, life. The special status of these names arises from this fact that when they are predicated of God they become involved with the act of existing, and so are predicated not quidditatively but existentially. How this occurs will become clear later; for the time we can content ourselves with saying that these particular secondarily analogous terms behave like primarily analogous ones when they become involved with the act of existing. See Gilson, *The Christian Philosophy of St. Thomas Aquinas*, p. 107 (first cited in Introduction, n. 1).

of the things which enter into this structure. As formally considered, there seem to be three and only three formal structures,[14] one of which has two subtypes.

The first of these consists essentially of two members which are united by a direct relationship between them, and is called by St. Thomas (the analogy of one to another.) There may be other members, but in that case all except one member are each related to that one member by themselves. The second consists of at least two members which are not directly related to each other, but to some thing distinct from them, and they are therefore constituted a community by their relationship to that thing outside them; this is called by St. Thomas the analogy of many to one. In this many-to-one structure we can distinguish two types: the "one" is outside the analogates altogether, or the "one" is made up of all the members. The third of these structures consists of two or more members, each composed of two factors; neither the members nor the factors stand in any relationship to each other, but the relationships of the composing factors are related. This is therefore essentially a four-term analogy, and can be called an "analogy of many to many." Formally speaking, it does not seem possible to find other fundamental types of analogy.

D. GENERAL MATERIAL ANALYSIS

Two quite different kinds of questions can be asked when we come to the material analysis of analogy. For a material analysis considers the things (the "matter") to which a form pertains: in this case, the analogates and their relations. One sort of question concerns the concrete nature of the relations which constitute the various unities, and this kind of question admits

---

[14] Two-term and three-term analogies are mentioned and carefully distinguished in *Pot.* (14.20), *C.G.* (15.7), and *S.T.*, I (17.31) ; two-term and four-term analogies in *Ver.* (9.9).

of a further division into more general and more particular considerations of this concrete nature of the analogates. The general questions will be taken up in this section, the particular ones in the next section. The second sort of question is also general, and asks whether the analogon is or is not intrinsic to the analogates.

1. *Qualitative determinations of analogous relations*

1. *Priority and Posteriority.* We can look at the relations which constitute the unity of an analogous community, and ask whether they are or are not relations of order. A relation of equality between analogates is not possible, since it would con--stitute a univocal community. In the two-term structure, if the analogates are not equal, they must stand in an order to each. other, and thus are necessarily prior and posterior to each other, respectively. In the three-term structure the "one" is necessarily prior to the members, since they formally become members of the analogous community by their relation to it. In the four-term analogies it is clear that the analogates themselves are not in any relationship of priority and posteriority, since they stand in no direct relation at all. As for the relationships themselves, it is difficult to see that they stand in any necessary order.

2. *Proportion.* We can eliminate from consideration the mathematical, quantitative sense of proportion, since it is difficult to see how a relationship like double could be considered as pertaining to analogy at all. In a broader sense the term proportion is equivalent to "relationship of order." And in this broader sense it is found in both the two-term and three-term analogies but not in the four-term ones, just as order itself.

3. *Imitation and Exemplarity.* As we have seen in studying the texts of St. Thomas, imitation implies that one term (the image) is made to the likeness of another (the exemplar). Since this is a direct relationship between the two terms involved, it can qualify only a two-term analogy. But it should be immedi-

ately evident that not every two-term analogy is necessarily an analogy of imitation or exemplarity.

4. *Participation.* If we take participation according to one of St. Thomas' general definitions as meaning to have, as it were, a part or share of something, it can be applied to several different kinds of relationships. First—in a sense irrelevant to our present discussion—it can be used to name the relationship of individuals to the species and species to their genus; this is not analogy at all, but univocation. Secondly, it can be used to describe a three-term analogy, where the one is the whole in which the members share unequally or in a certain order. If we use this sense in the rest of this study, it will always be named fully the analogy of participation in a totality. Thirdly, participation can be used to describe a two-term analogy; in this case one of the analogates is by its essence or by identity what the other is by participation, partially, by reception of a perfection. This kind of participation we will call simply the analogy of participation, without any additional qualifying term.

5. *Eminence vs. Deficiency; (More) Perfect vs. Imperfect (Less Perfect).* This series of terms refers to the way in which the analogon is possessed by two of the analogates when they are compared with each other. It therefore most aptly is applied to those two-term analogies where the order between the analogates consists precisely in the possession of a perfection in different degrees.

6. *Simpliciter, Absolute vs. Secundum Quid.* This set of terms most aptly is used for three-term analogies, and for those two-term analogies where one of the analogates is what the other is only in a qualified sense.

7. *Reference.* This term is most often used for three-term analogies, where one of the analogates has the analogon in itself, simply, without qualification, and the other(s) only by relation to that primary analogate. It can also be used for two-term analogies, as in the "health" instance.

2. *Intrinsic and extrinsic predication*

The scope of this question goes beyond the range of analogy, although it has usually been restricted to it. Univocal predication has usually not been brought into the picture, but there seems to be no valid reason why it should not be included. Our question, then, is: Can predication be divided on the basis of the relation of the predicate to the thing about which it is predicated? That is, is the predicate really in the thing, or is it merely attributed to it (with or without adequate reason)? This is not a predicational question; one cannot tell by looking at a meaning for ever so long whether it does or does not mean an intrinsic perfection of its subject. The question can be answered only by looking at the things themselves; it is therefore a part of a material analysis, or an ontological analysis.

Now, the distinction between predicates which mean intrinsic perfections present in the subjects of which they are predicated and predicates which are denominated of subjects for reasons of various kinds is a traditional and very simple distinction which does not need further elaboration. It can be decided, obviously, only in considering particular predicates and things. We can note, however, that the terms proper and improper often have been used to mean intrinsic and extrinsic respectively.

In general, analogies have always been divided into intrinsic and extrinsic. If, in addition, as we have suggested above (and will refer to the question below), we divide univocal terms in the same way, we will have a fourfold general division (with both a predicational and a material basis): (1) univocal intrinsic terms; (2) univocal extrinsic terms; (3) analogous intrinsic terms; and (4) analogous extrinsic terms.

The division into intrinsic and extrinsic predication does not helpfully pertain to the formal structural analysis of analogy; there is nothing in the formal structure which should or should not involve the presence of the analogon in the analogates. Applied to the general qualitative determinants of the formal structures, some things are clear at once. Priority and posteriority, proportion, eminence, *simpliciter* and reference, all equally admit of division into intrinsic and extrinsic analogies. We can note in passing that the term analogy of attribution has often been an object of controversy, some writers holding that it is always an extrinsic analogy of reference, others that it can also be used to name an intrinsic analogy of reference. On the criterion of ordinary usage the former group would seem to have the better case. The analogies of imitation and participation, on the other hand, seem more naturally to fit cases of intrinsic relationship, and are used awkwardly and with some violence in cases of extrinsic analogy.

E.   PARTICULAR MATERIAL ANALYSIS

To carry on a complete material analysis of all analogies is not only beyond the scope of this book; it seems to be both impossible and undesirable. It seems impossible because it would have to include all extrinsic as well as intrinsic analogies, and it would be difficult to assign limits to possible comparisons. It also seems undesirable because, once the major applications have been made, the rest should be relatively easy. We will therefore content ourselves with a consideration of only a few of the major applications.

1. *Substance and Accidents.* The simplest and most traditional analogical community is that of substances and the accidents. Aristotle already began his consideration of the categories by almost taking for granted that they were all beings, and in various senses. For him the major question rather was: In what way or ways is being said of these various categories?

First of all, we recall that substance is that whose nature is to be in itself, whereas accident is that whose nature is to be in another; that is, in substance. This community is formed by a direct relationship (proportion) between substance and its accidents: substance needs to be completed by its accidents, and accidents are inasmuch as they inhere in and/or perfect their subject. From this point of view substance and accident are related in the analogy of proportion.[15] And since in both cases what is predicated is the direct nature of the analogates, this is an intrinsic analogy of proportion.

Moreover, we can consider substance and accident as principles of that which is (the individual). In this view that which is is the being and its principles are variously related to the whole which they compose. The one is the whole *(id quod est)*; the many are substance in the primary instance, and then in various dependent ways, quantity, quality, and so on. By reason of substance a thing is said to be in itself, and so "substance is"; by reason of accidents a thing is said to be in various qualified ways, and so "accidents are" in substance. This is the analogy of participation in a totality.[16] In this analogy the perfection predicated is none of the analogates;[17] the secondary analogates are related to the analogon by reason of their various relationships to one of the analogates, the primary analogate. From the point of view of the relationships involved, prescinding from the fact that in the example the analogon is extrinsic to the secondary analogates, the health analogy represents this situation well, though it could be misleading if we fail to notice the differences.

Substance and accident can be considered in still another way. We can view substance as entitled to the designation "being" directly and unqualifiedly in itself, whereas accidents can be so called only because of a relation to substance. Accidents are not so much being as "belonging to being." Considered in this way, substance and accident stand in an analogy of refer-

---

[15] See explicitly in *Ver.* (9.9) ; *Metaphys.* (33.9, 18) ; *Ethic.* (34.2).
[16] See *Prin. nat.* (3.1) ; *I Sent.* (4.2) ; *Boethii de hebd.* (10.1).
[17] *I Sent.* (4.2) ; *Nat. gen.* (43.1).

ence.[18] Whether we call this an extrinsic analogy (analogy of attribution) or an intrinsic one depends partly on our view of being (the view of being as essence tends to a view of the analogy as extrinsic, to the extent that being is identified simply with substance), partly on the emphasis, as we have seen earlier.

In all these cases the analogy of substance and accident can be named merely in general as an analogy; as a predication according to priority and posteriority; as a predication differing according as substance is being simply and without qualification, accident is being only qualifiedly, *secundum quid.*[19]

An instance of substance and accident standing in a four-term analogy has not appeared in the texts we have noticed,[20] and it is hard to see how they could be said to be analogous by an analogy of proper proportionality.

On the other hand, the notion of accident is itself an analogous one. Not much can be found in the text of St. Thomas on this point. But it is implicit in the various passages that compare and contrast the accidents one with another. The tradition has insisted strongly that accident is an analogous term, and most often has designated the analogy as an analogy of proper proportionality. The reason brought forward is that the relation of quantity to substance is like the relation of quality, and yet different; and that quantity and quality are intrinsically unlike rather than similar to each other. It seems reasonable enough to say that the various accidents are analogously accidents by an analogy of proper proportionality. But this does not prevent us from considering them at the same time as a series of secondary analogates of substance in the order of being.

2. *Cause and Effect.* There are causes which do not belong to the same species as their effects. Inasmuch as they are differ-

---

18 *Prin. nat.* (3.1) ; *Metaphys.* (33.9, 10, 16, 26).
19 *Prin. nat.* (3.1) ; *Metaphys.* (33.9, 10, 16, 18).
20 Some early texts are indeed ambiguous; see Chap. 4, n. 25.

ent, they cannot form an univocal community; yet a cause cannot really be a cause unless it brings about something in the effect which is at least in some way similar to its cause. Consequently nonunivocal causes come together with their effects in some community of analogy. There is priority and posteriority inasmuch as the cause is at least in nature prior to its effect. The nonunivocal cause is by definition not equal to its effect. It cannot in principle be less perfect; therefore it stands in the relationship of eminence to its effect, it is more perfect than its effect, possesses the produced perfection in a higher way, and so on.[21] Cause and effect are as such always in a two-term analogy, since the relationship of causality is directly between cause and effect. They can also be said to be proportioned one to another.

Nonunivocal cause and effect, as such, are not necessarily intrinsically analogous. The cause must indeed be more perfect, but, in order to be a cause, it need not possess literally the same perfection. Hence if we know only that a cause is a nonunivocal cause of some effect, we can by virtue of the causal relation alone denominate it only extrinsically.[22] Analysis of the nature of the causality, and of the kind of perfection induced in the patient are necessary before we can certainly know that we have to do with an intrinsically analogous cause. (Failure to state this analysis explicitly can make a proof look invalid.)

3. *God and Creature.* Since God is a nonunivocal cause of creatures, we can say that God is prior to creatures (in the order of being); that He possesses in an eminent way, more perfectly, whatever perfections we find in His effects; that the creature is proportioned to its cause, though not adequately. But God is not just "a" cause of the world, He is the first cause, and so the

---

[21] See above, Chap. 3, sects. C and G; esp. *S.T.,* I (17.7, 12), and the detailed analysis in *S.T.,* I, q. 4, a. 2.

[22] St. Thomas explicitly concedes in *S.T.,* I (17.35, 51) that a purely causal knowledge of God—*causaliter tantum*—would be only extrinsic.

cause of the total reality of the effect.[23] Moreover, as first cause
He contains no passive potency, and so is pure act. Inasmuch
as He is the perfection itself, simply, unqualifiedly, whereas the
creature can be considered as related to that perfection, He is
the primary analogate in an analogy of reference.[24] So far we
have analogies truly predicated, but not necessarily intrinsic—
they can be extrinsic to God (as is true of the mixed perfections), or extrinsic to the creature (as, for example, God is the
truth of all truths).

When we begin clearly to distinguish between intrinsic and
extrinsic analogies, we find that the act of existing, the transcendentals, and some acts (such as wisdom, life) which can be considered as nonlimiting modes of being, should be intrinsically
predicated of God.[25] Since whatever is intrinsically in God is
identical with His essence and with Him as well as with His
existence, these perfections are predicated of God by nature,
essentially. On the other hand, in creatures these perfections are
possessed as limited by the subject in which they are received, as
partial, and as multiple. Hence between God and creatures there
is an analogy of participation of all the perfections mentioned
(being, goodness, and so on). If we add to this our previous consideration of God's total causality, we can most adequately name

---

[23] To see how carefully St. Thomas analyzes this special relation one needs to read
in their entirety qq. 44 and 45 of *S.T.*, I.

[24] See, for example, *Compend. theol.* (39.2), and the allowance made for a denomination of truth and goodness in creatures in *S.T.*, I (17.15, 51). Some have
tried to erect this analogy into *the* analogy of being, as Suarez does with his
analogy of intrinsic attribution. But when the analogy of reference is the only
analogy allowed, it becomes impossible to show that it is an intrinsic analogy;
and so, according to the rule of reasoning that requires us to hold as demonstrated only the weaker alternative, we should have no grounds for asserting
that it is an intrinsic analogy. It is therefore admissible as one—and not the
most profound—among several analogies, but not as exclusively valid. As for
the Suarezian terminology, the expression "intrinsic attribution" is permissible
by definition, but is not well calculated to achieve perfect communication.

[25] This point is fully argued by St. Thomas; we can presume knowledge of the
argument here.

the analogy between God and creatures as an analogy of causal participation.[26] Implicit in this description are further qualifications: God is the cause of the world by intellect and will, and so as an intelligent efficient cause He is both the primary exemplar and the ultimate goal of all creatures, and they exist as images, made to the likeness (in imitation) of their Creator.[27]

Attributes predicated of God as denominations known to be extrinsic can also be viewed in different ways. They can certainly be predicated of God by extrinsic causal eminence and by extrinsic reference (attribution). Most commonly, as we have already seen, St. Thomas seems to prefer to consider them as predicated by the analogy of improper proportionality.[28]

4. *Created Beings as Analogous.* Created beings, of course, are analogous, since they are the secondary analogates of all the analogies between themselves and God. But we can legitimately ask whether, outside that situation, they can be said to be analogous to each other. In this connection we have already considered the relation of nonunivocal cause and effect, which, at least to a limited extent, can be found between two creatures.[29]

There are a number of other situations which St. Thomas describes as analogous. For example, St. Thomas often remarks that the act of simple intelligence belongs to the angels by their nature and eminently, whereas the human intellect has such intelligence only by participation and imperfectly.[30] The more general reference to higher and lower creatures often is made

---

[26] See above, Chap. 3, sect. E.

[27] See above, Chap. 3, sect. D.

[28] See above, Chap. 4, sect. B, "Proportionality as Transfer."

[29] See above, Chap. 3, sect. G. Note, however, that the scope of this relation is not so great in our time as it was in St. Thomas'. A great number of effects were then attributed to the heavenly bodies; the reasons for this were on the one hand an ignorance of the presence of adequate causes nearer by, and, on the other, the geocentric structure of the universe.

[30] A large number of texts on this relation have been listed by J. Peghaire, C.S.Sp., *Intellectus et ratio selon s. Thomas d'Aquin*, p. 174 n. (Ottawa: Institut d'Etudes Médiévales, 1936).

by St. Thomas in connection with a very well-known quotation from the Pseudo-Dionysius.[31] This same type of analogy is used extensively in psychological discussions, and, under the rubric of *principaliter-secundario*, is a major key to a much-neglected aspect of the Thomistic theory of the virtues.

In Cajetan and the Cajetanist interpretation creatures of different grades of perfection are said to stand in an analogy of proper proportionality. For example, an angel is said to be to his act of existing somewhat as a man is to the act of existing proper to him. Aside from the difficulty that we know considerably less about the proper nature of the angels than seems to be assumed, this analogy seems to be correctly applied here.

In one area of created being a historical question has been raised: Are two beings of the same species—for example, two men—univocally or analogously beings?[32] It seems perhaps strange that St. Thomas has nothing explicitly on this point; yet it would not be amiss to remark that there was not much of an occasion for him relevantly to discuss it. Moreover, there are asides which indicate his mind. In his *Commentary on the First Book of the Sentences*[33] and in the *Disputed Questions on Truth*[34] he says that univocal terms name a nature, and not the *esse* of a thing, and that, if they named the act of existing, they could

---

[31] ". . . semper fines priorum coniungens principiis secundorum" (*De div. nomin.*, cap. 7, no. 4). For Thomistic uses of this hierarchial view see, for example, *II Sent.*, d. 24, q. 2, a. 1 ad 3; *III Sent.*, d. 26, q. 1, a. 2; d. 35, q. 1, a. 2, qa. 2 ad 1; *Ver.*, q. 24, a. 1 ad 9; *In libros De anima*, lectio 13 (Pirotta, no. 397); *S.T.*, I, q. 78, a. 4 ad 5.

[32] For a reference to John of St. Thomas see above, n. 12.

[33] In *I Sent.* (4.29), St. Thomas says of univocal terms that in them there is a community "secundum rationem naturae et non secundum esse." See *S.T.*, I, q. 30, a. 4, and q. 39, a. 4 ad 4. Put positively, being is concrete, not abstract: "Sed id quod est, sive ens, quamvis sit communissimum, tamen concretive dicitur" (*Boethii de hebd.*, lectio 2).

[34] *Ver.*, q. 2, a. 11: "Si enim in Petro non differret homo et hominem esse, impossibile esset quod homo univoce diceretur de Petro et Paulo, quibus est esse diversum." See *S.T.*, I, q. 3, a. 5 c.

not be univocal. This point is indicated even less explicitly in the *Summa theologiae*.[35] The argument, however, seems clear enough. In Thomistic metaphysics, to consider any thing as a being is to consider it according to the existence which it actually has *(ens dicitur id quod est, habens esse)*.[36] But according to its actual existence, each being is distinct, different, unique. Hence no two beings inasmuch as they are signified as beings can univocally be beings.

The situation is not quite so clear when we try to answer the question, According to what kind of analogy? Most Thomists agree in analyzing this analogy as the analogy of proper proportionality. That a proportionality can readily be found is clear: each individual being is proportioned to its own proper act of existing, just as any other individual is to its. This is also a proper proportionality, for each being intrinsically is something and possesses its own act within it. But if we are speaking about two beings of the same species, it is hard to see why we should not have to say that the proportion of one man's individual nature to his act of existing is the same as another man's to his own *(eadem proportio)*. True, the four terms are different; on the other hand, the difference of terms of itself does not make for an analogous relationship. Consequently the analogy of two beings, at least when these beings belong to the same species, does not seem to be suitably described as an analogy of proper proportionality.[37]

What about a three-term analogy? If there were a direct abstractive concept of being or of the act of existing, or if being were a totality consisting of all finite beings, a three-term struc-

---

[35] *S.T.*, I, q. 13, a. 5.

[36] *Metaphys.*, Book 4, lectio 2 (Cathala, nos. 556-58); Book 12, lectio 1 (Cathala, no. 2419).

[37] In addition the ordinary condition, that none of the four terms be the same (except in the series 2 : 4 :: 4 : 8), seems hardly fulfilled, since both analogates have the "same" act of existing; see below, n. 39.

ture could be thought of. In the former case, however, the logical unity of the concept seems to bring about univocation; in the latter case, being would pertain to the universe primarily, and this would compromise the independence of things.

There is left, then, only the two-term structure. Among two-term structures, analogies of proportion or order and priority-posteriority do not seem to apply;[38] *a fortiori*, analogies which describe kinds of priority (such as nonunivocal causality, imitation, participation) are excluded. This leaves us with the very general designation of similarity as a way to describe the immediate relationship of two beings (at least, two belonging to the same species). Unfortunately, this does not advance our knowledge, since the term *similitudo* can be applied to all analogies, and even to univocal predicates. But we can compare the likeness of two beings as beings—St. Thomas does not do so—to the likeness of two individuals in a species. Usually, likeness is predicated according to an agreement or communication in a form. There are then as many kinds of likeness as there are ways of communicating in a form. If the form is the same and the way it is possessed is the same, the likeness is equality. If it is possessed in a different way, the likeness is one of more or less. If the form is the same but is differently specified, the likeness is only remote and generic. Finally, there is a likeness which is not based on any form in any species or genus, but rests on a nonformal perfection, "as the very act of existing is common to all."[39] Now, since the act of existing is common to all, any two

---

[38] If one wished to assert that in fact all the members of a species differ in degree of perfection, this would not change the case, since in fact we do not know of such a difference. And see *S.T.*, I, q. 50, a. 4 and ad 1; q. 75, a. 7; *S.T.*, I (17.84).

[39] The argument here given is a summary of *S.T.*, I, q. 4, a. 3. For the quoted words see *S.T.*, I (17.8). That the act of existing is common to all (created) things is asserted and implied by St. Thomas in a large number of places. See, among others, *I Sent.* (4.11); *Ver.*, q. 5, a. 9 ad 7; *Pot.*, q. 3, a. 1; *C.G.*, I, cap. 42, (15.11); III, cap. 66; *S.T.*, I, q. 8, a. 1; q. 14, a. 6;

beings are alike inasmuch as they communicate, not in the same form or formality but in the same act. This communication is most significant, for existence is the basic act of a being.

Moreover, on the very reasonable ground that the similarity of any two beings in the same species is quite different from the relation of substance to accident or God to creature, we should expect a different analogy in all three cases. To put it most simply, it is an analogy of being of individuals in a species; the analogous community is precisely that of individuals.[40] To follow St. Thomas' method, we might label this analogy the analogy of individual communication.

This solution raises a question, for it insistently calls for a real, or ontological, grounding of the common act which all finite things have. But this is all to the good, for the fact of many finite beings is one of the evidences for the existence of God. The analogy of individual communication by which the many beings of experience are related to one another, then, can-

q. 45, a. 5 and ad 1; q. 65, aa. 1, 3; q. 104, a. 1; *S.T.*, I-II, q. 66, a. 5 ad 4. There is a long treatment in *Lib. de caus.*, prop. 4 (ed. Saffrey, p. 29). The contemporary interest in the unique character of the I-thou relationship is not irrelevant here. We can abstract from the special philosophical and literary elaborations of this theme to point to the fundamental experiential fact that the relation of one human person to another, because it is concrete and entirely existential, is always one of analogy, not of abstract univocation. This is a basic relationship, since in human experience the relationship of one person to another seems to be the primary instance of all individual-to-individual relations. Moreover, in the first instance the material individual is known through sense, in the analogously shared "here-and-now" of actual sensation. On the knowledge of the material singular in the material conditions of space-time analogously common to object known as active and to knower as passive see George P. Klubertanz, S.J., "St. Thomas and the Knowledge of the Singular," *New Scholasticism*, XXVI (1952), 140, 166.

[40] This means that the totality of the created beings as such is only an intelligible unity. There are real unities from this partial point of view, but not in being: they are to be found at the level of activity. Through knowledge and causality the whole of created reality is accidentally unified. The only real unity in being can be found when we take a more complete point of view; all created beings have a common source and goal. This real unity is expressed explicitly in the analogy of causal participation. See *S.T.*, I, q. 47, a. 3.

not be completely understood until it is seen to be a partial aspect of the analogy of participation.

5. *Being in Act and Being in Potency; Potency and Act.* St. Thomas several times remarks that being in act is being simply, without qualification, whereas being in potency is being only in a certain way; that is, inasmuch as it is able to be. The analogy here is a simple two-term analogy of priority and posteriority, or proportion, where the prior analogate is without qualification, the posterior analogate is only qualifiedly.[41]

On the other hand, the terms potency and act do not always involve an analogy. Used by themselves, as they are used often by St. Thomas and most Thomists—for example, in the high-level generalizations that are known as principles[42]—they are not properly analogous; rather, they are the very analogon, or similar proportion itself, of analogous proportions (such as matter and form, substance and accident). Again, in expressions like the act of seeing and the power of seeing, the term seeing is univocal; the terms act and power are proportioned but correlatively opposite, not members possessing an analogously common perfection.

In a different kind of example, the terms potency and act, precisely because they are not expressed in it, reflexively designate secondary and primary analogates. Thus, when we say of a sleeping man and a working mathematician, "He knows mathematics," the term knowledge is used analogously in the two cases, according to an analogy of intrinsic proportion.

---

[41] These relations are most fully discussed in *Metaphys.*, Book 5, lectio 9 (Cathala, no. 897), Book 9, lectio 9 and 10. See, for briefer remarks, *I Sent.* (4.2), and *S.T.*, I, q. 14, a. 9. Compare *III Sent.* (6.2); *Ver.* (9.27); *C.G.* (15.20); *S.T.*, I (17.18).

[42] These are really not principles in the strict sense, since at times St. Thomas engages in what is at least a rational analysis to show forth their truth. Consider, for example, how St. Thomas explains a proposition like "Act is simply prior to potency" in the passages referred to in n. 41. For this reason these propositions can well be called theorems.

6. *Ens in Anima—Beings of Reason.* Analyzing Aristotle, St. Thomas says that the first division of being is into the being which is in the soul (being of reason) and the being which is in nature.[43] By the being which is in the soul he means the true; and nonbeing is the false. Of the true, St. Thomas says that it is called being because the mind deals with it "as it were with beings" *(quasi de quibusdam entibus).* Thus, the being in the things of nature is being simply, without qualification, whereas the being which is in the soul is a qualified being. There is therefore priority and posteriority, and the analogy can be called an analogy of proportion. But since the being which is in the soul does not show anything of the nature of being,[44] nor share the essence of being,[45] the analogy is one of extrinsic proportion. Or, considering that the mind imitates the structure of reality in some sense, we could call it an analogy of extrinsic imitation.

The being of reason in a narrower sense is that which is not, but is conceived as if it were. In a weaker sense than the true, the being of reason is called being by the same kind of extrinsic analogy.

We can ask further whether, in addition to the two similar types (the being in the mind and the being of reason), any other analogies are to be found in this area. For example, if we say, "Humanity is being," is this predication any different from a proposition like "Whiteness is a being"? The answer would seem to be in the negative: all second-level abstractions seem to be equally, and so univocally, beings of reason.[46]

---

[43] Explicitly in *Metaphys.,* Book 4, lectio 1 (Cathala, no. 540); see also Book 5, lectio 9 (895), and Book 6, lectio 4 (1233).

[44] ". . . natura entis," *Metaphys.,* Book 6, lectio 4 (Cathala, no. 1244), *S.T.,* I, q. 14, a. 6, and *S.T.,* I (17.77), *I Sent.* (4.6), *II. Sent.* (5.1).

[45] ". . . essentia entis," *Metaphys.,* Book 5, lectio 9 (Cathala, no. 889), and *S.T.,* I, q. 19, a. 6; see *Ver.* (9.1).

[46] See Francis A. Cunningham, S.J., "A Theory on Abstraction in St. Thomas," *Modern Schoolman,* XXXV (1958), 254-56, 262-63, and A. M. Krąpiec, O.P., "Analysis formationis conceptus entis existentialiter considerati," *Divus Thomas* (Placentiae), LIX (1956), 348.

7. *Analoga Other Than Being.* In all these considerations the analogon dealt with has been being. But some of the texts have explicitly treated other analoga; chief of these are truth and goodness. Inasmuch as truth and goodness are transcendentals, they are convertible with being, and to this extent we should expect to find similar analogies. If now we turn to the *Summa theologiae*, we find, in a paragraph remarkable for its compression and for the number of concrete analogy expressions, a statement of the analogy of God and creature in goodness that is very like the fullest expression of the analogy of being.

> Therefore everything can be called good and being from the first being, which is good and being by its essence, inasmuch as everything participates it after the manner and measure of a particular likeness [*per modum cujusdam assimilationis*], though remotely and deficiently, as is evident from the preceding articles. In this fashion, then, each being is called good because of the divine goodness, the first exemplar principle as well as the efficient and telic cause of all goodness. Yet it is nonetheless the case that each being is called good because of a likeness of the divine goodness inhering in it, which is formally the goodness by which it is denominated. Thus there is a single goodness common to all and also many goodnesses (*S.T.*, I [17.15]).

In this single text the analogies of (extrinsic) causal reference, of eminence, and of causal participation are woven together. However, the "good" is not only the transcendental good, but also the proper good of some nature which is the good-without-qualification *(bonum simpliciter)*. This sense of good is analogous to the former one, as the very names indicate. Moreover, proper (unqualified) goods are proportioned to different natures. Hence a series of proper goods will be analogous with the analogy of proper proportionality. Proper goods, of course, are based on transcendental goodness. But they formally consist in a suitability to a specific (or generic) nature, and so are not an absolute quality. Hence, also, there is no common intrinsic perfection by which various proper goods are good. And as a

further consequence, proper goods cannot be compared or related unless they are first independently known.

The true is another analogous conception with which St.
Thomas deals at some length. Again, the *Summa theologiae*
gives an almost complete treatment in the articles of Question
Sixteen. Truth, in its proper sense, is a property of the judgment
of the mind; things are denominated true by an analogy of
reference, inasmuch as they are ordered to the mind (as causes
of human knowledge, as effects of the divine knowledge); propositions are denominated true, not as possessing truth but as
signifying the truth in the mind, and so they are true by an analogy of reference which is simply extrinsic. Human truth and divine truth are analogous in that the divine truth is subsistent,
perfect, and simple, whereas human truth is possessed by participation, is finite, limited, and multiple. Finally, things can be
called more or less true (as in the "fourth way"), insofar as
they possess a greater or lesser intelligibility (based on their
greater or lesser actuality), or insofar as they more clearly man-
ifest their distinctive nature or are less distinguishable.

Finally, there are some special analogous terms predicated
of creatures and of God, such as life, knowledge, wisdom,
mercy. We adverted to these terms earlier in discussing secondarily analogous terms. The most complete analysis is given by
St. Thomas in his question about the life of God. First, life is a
term like other terms naming the essences of things. Such terms
are derived from observable accidents, and are used to name the
nature which is the principle of proper accidents. So life principally names a kind of nature, and secondarily the activities
which are characteristic of such a nature. This is a simple analogy of proportion. But to live also means more: not only to have
a nature suited to vital operations, not merely to carry out vital
activities, but to exist in such a nature—as we often say in English, "to be alive." This is another step in the analogy of proportion, where we have moved from operation to nature to the act

of existing. Life can thus, thirdly, mean being alive. Thus life becomes a complex conception, sharing in the primarily analogous nature of being itself. Hence we can find a series of degrees of participation in life (vegetative, sensitive, rational), culminating in the First Cause of life, which is life by essence. Similarly, God has knowledge perfectly and simply; creatures have knowledge by participation; God has will perfectly and simply, creatures by participation; God is wise, as being wisdom itself; creatures have wisdom.

But wisdom can also be considered in relation to creatures, and then it is like mercy, justice, and providence. Inasmuch as these conceptions name God intrinsically, they name Him according to nonlimiting modes of being, and so are reducible to knowledge and goodness.

> . . . to give perfections to things pertains indeed to divine goodness, and also to justice, liberality, and mercy, but according to different intelligibilities. For the communication of perfections, taken absolutely, pertains to goodness, as was shown above. But inasmuch as perfections are given by God to things according to their proportion, communication pertains to justice, as was shown above. Inasmuch, however, as He does not give perfections to things for His own advantage, but only out of His goodness, communication pertains to liberality. Finally, inasmuch as the perfections given by God to things remove imperfections, communication pertains to mercy (S.T., I [17.56]).

This passage shows that the very intelligibility of some perfections involves creatures, which are distinct from God. It can therefore be said that perfections of this sort are also analogous with the analogy of proper proportionality. It is a proportionality, because, as the wisdom of man suitably disposes the works of man, so the wisdom of God suitably disposes His creation. It is a proper, or intrinsic, analogy, for we know through the analogy of causal participation that knowledge is an intrinsic perfection of God, present in Him most perfectly and as identical with Him. These cases show that proportionality is a legitimate way of expressing the analogy of some perfections present in both God and creatures; they also show in what sense it is a secondary and derivative analogy. For unless we know that God intrinsically possesses the perfection of wisdom, an application of the term "wisdom" to His governing of creatures will be purely extrinsic. Other terms that can be analyzed in the same way are "Lord" and "judge."

F. RELATED SUBSIDIARY QUESTIONS

1. *Extrinsic Analogy vs. Metaphor.* Traditionally, Thomism has tended to reduce all extrinsic predication to the analogies of attribution and improper proportionality.[47] One of the reasons for this has been the ambiguity of the term proper. This has sometimes been used to mean univocal and sometimes intrinsic; this confusion has been increased by the vague meaning of the Latin term, *metaphora,* which usually means figure of speech (occasionally the Latins use the literal equivalent, *translatio*). Unfortunately, St. Thomas was interested only in scientific predication, and so did not undertake an accurate analysis of rhetorical and poetic language, nor investigate the content and nature of prephilosophical knowledge.

Moreover, many of those who professionally analyze language are logicians, who import their own sober approach to predication into the highest reaches of poetry. A logical person could not mean to say that John Doe is a pig; he must mean only that John is *like* a pig! True, if the term pig is used often enough to designate people who eat to excess or in some unmannerly fashion, the makers of dictionaries, recognizing a secondarily analogous term, will define it as "a person who resembles a pig." But by this time the term has ceased to have the force of the original metaphor, and in becoming analogous has become a commonplace epithet.

---

[47] See, for example, Cajetanus, *De nominum analogia,* Chap. 7, pars. 75-76.

To claim that the original metaphor is the same kind of predication as the much less effective analogous epithet seems to disregard the facts. Such a reduction has very often been done by Thomists in their attempt to explain metaphor and make it rational. Had they instead inquired into the foundations of metaphor, and found that direct metaphor rests upon underlying analogy, or that one or the other kind of analogy is presupposed, their work would have been relevant.

There is a particular need for this investigation of metaphor because of the modern concern with the transcendence of God on the part of some theologians (such as Tillich or Barth), or with the very knowability of God on the part of some language analysts. Both of these groups, it seems, more or less consistently conceive of all predicates as primarily univocal. We have seen earlier that primarily univocal predicates designate formal perfections whose relation to being is that of formal quidditative limitation. Such predicates, when applied to God, are used by extrinsic denomination. A theology resting on this supposition would be a so-called negative theology. It would insist on the refusal to let God be limited by the imperfections of creatures.

On the positive side theologians of this stamp have exercised great ingenuity in pointing out what is "really" meant by the predicates attached to God. For example, when God is said to be great, this means that man feels his littleness before the Unknown God; when God is said to be good, this means that man feels his sinfulness; when God is said to be Creator, this means that man feels insecure in the face of transcendent reality—and so on down the line. Surely these are all good points, and they show much more sensitivity to the modes of religious language than the rationalist reductions to improper proportionality.

In the face of this situation two things seem to be important. One is to insist again on the nature of our intrinsically analogous knowledge of God, keeping it within its proper limits and explaining it according to the rich and meaningful analogy of causal participation. The other is to recognize the proper nature of metaphor. It would seem much more natural to take metaphor at its face value, as univocal predication. It is, of course, extrinsic predication; the man who sees John Doe as a pig does not intend to put him on a spit and roast him for supper. But he does attribute this nature univocally, and so we can well call metaphor extrinsic univocal predication.[48] In this case metaphor will be interpreted quite differently than if it were an analogy, and some of the modern work done on metaphor could be of great use to a theologian.

In interpreting metaphor as extrinsic univocal predication we have removed it from the scope of a book on analogy. As a consequence only enough needed to be said to make this removal distinct and consistent.

2. *The Unity of an Analogous Conception.* What does it mean to ask about the unity of an analogous conception such as that of being? Obviously there is only one word; is there one or more than one concept or conception? This has been a controverted point for years, and partisans of quite different solutions have distinguished two concepts: an obscure or imperfect concept and a clear or perfect one. Both Cajetan and Sylvester of Ferrara agree that the former (imperfect) concept is numerically one; Sylvester holds that the perfect concept is actually many; Cajetan, that the perfect concept is that of the various analogates and no longer that of the analogon.

This question can be clarified somewhat if we consider what we actually do. If one thinks of being—for example, if he is defining being as that which is, or if he is judging, "Every being is good"—in cases like these he obviously has only one conception. Moreover, there is nothing particularly imperfect or no-

---

[48] See Robert R. Boyle, S.J., "The Nature of Metaphor," *Modern Schoolman,* XXXI (1954), 257-80; "The Nature of Metaphor: Further Considerations," *ibid.,* XXXIV (1957), 283-98.

tably obscure about this conception. But when being is simply conceived (that is, neither affirmed nor denied), or when it is made the subject of propositions, it is neither analogous nor even multiple in any way, for it is not formally common in this usage.

But we can also predicate being. More often, when we talk about predicating being, we rather mean that we predicate the verb *is* than the noun predicate (is a) being. Now, as we have seen, analogous predicates are precisely proportional to their subjects, and this is primarily true of the verb is. Hence we ought reasonably to conclude that, as proportional to their subjects, the analogous conception as verb predicate is multiplied just as its subjects are multiplied. In a similar fashion, even when we make use of the noun predicate being, as in "John is a being," the noun predicate being (which retains some of the traits of its original verbal root) is proportional and multiplied as the *is* is. In this sense it seems that Sylvester has the better of the argument, though the distinction between obscure and clear concepts should be dropped in favor of the distinction between subject and predicate.

Of course, the real question is not about the number of acts (conceptions) which we perform when we think or use an analogous conception, but rather about the unity of that which is predicated. Now, if we are predicating being, the question about the unity of being means: Is there one or more than one being? or—to make Heidegger sound like a Platonist—Is there being *(Sein)* over and above and in addition to beings *(Seiende)?* In the Thomistic analysis there are many beings, and there is no being (neither separate form nor formality nor logical abstractive concept) which is not either one of the things which are or their common cause, Subsistent Being. Are these many beings in any sense one? St. Thomas has always held that there is one universe, inasmuch as all things proceed from one cause and tend toward one over-all goal, act on one another and are acted on in causality, and form an intelligible whole in that each thing shares in one and the same act of existing which is the very essence of its cause. In addition to this, there are various other unities corresponding to the various analogies we have seen: the ordered unity of the grades of being according to the analogy of proper proportionality; the unity of analogous causes and effects, through proportion, eminence, and reference; and the unity of all beings as individual beings according to the analogy of individual communication. Within each being there is a unity of principles which are proportioned to each other as act and potency, and in turn are ordered by the whole to which they are related according to the analogy of reference, and of participation in a totality.

3. *The Abstraction of the Analogous Conception.* This is another traditional problem. The problem is set by the origin of univocal concepts: a species simply abstracts from its individuals, a genus from its species; and the differences themselves are outside the formal intelligibility of the species and genus respectively. But—to take the comparison in inverse order—all the differences of being are themselves being, otherwise they could not determine being; being itself cannot be indeterminately, but must be in some way, so that it also cannot be abstracted from its differences.

In the face of this difficult problem Thomists have had recourse to various subterfuges: they have said that there is an imperfect abstraction, concealing the differences in each analogate, confusing (mingling together) or indeterminately grasping the various modes of difference. Some authors merely restate the problem: in the "third degree of abstraction" differences are not actually explicitly stated, but they are actually implicitly contained. How can something be *actu implicite?*

Most simply, St. Thomas provides a solution to this problem. Univocal concepts, he reminds us, abstract from individuals, or from specific differences, by leaving these differences out of consideration. The univocal concept is perfectly intelligible without these differences, and consequently need not refer to them except potentially or implicitly.

But there are a number of conceptions which could not have arisen in this way; simple nonconsideration of relevant factors would distort the intelligibility. For these conceptions, St. Thomas says, the process of abstraction is not used, but another, which he calls separation, and by which, as he explicitly says, we reach "being and substance and act and potency."[49] First, we experience an individual, determinate being. Upon reflection and analysis we can come to understand that, though this being exists in its own individual way, it is not its particularity, its mode of existing, that makes it a being. By this negative judgment we separate in our mind the mode from the being possessed in such a mode. In principle, this could be done with any of the beings of our experience. We need not speculate on the possibility of doing it after the experience of only one being, since by the time it occurs to us to reflect (either by ourselves or through the influence of a teacher), we have already experienced many beings. No matter what being we begin with, though the mode negated would be different in each case, the concrete conception of concrete being attained would provide an equally good starting point to move to all other beings. St. Thomas points out that "the Pythagoreans and the Platonists . . . , because they did not understand the differences [between the two kinds of abstraction and separation] fell into error";[50] and we would not badly misinterpret history if we added that in ignoring the difference between abstraction and separation some Thomists fell into what are at the very least great difficulties.

Conclusion: Rationalism, Agnosticism, and Analogy. Rationalism holds that we first know clearly what God is, and then

---

[49] *Boethii de Trin.*, q. 5, aa. 3, 4.
[50] *Ibid.*, a. 3.

prove His existence. Agnosticism, its contrary, agreeing that we would have to have a clear concept of what God is before we could prove His existence, maintains that we cannot have such a concept, and hence cannot prove that God exists. St. Thomas did not know these doctrines in their contemporary form, but he was familiar with the negative theology of the Pseudo-Dionysius and the equivocation doctrine of Maimonides on the one hand, as well as with the rationalism of Berengarius, Roscellin, and Avempace on the other. And, of the two, the negative theology received the gentler treatment.

For St. Thomas repeatedly rejected any pretended proper human concept of God. The assertion that we have a concept of God's essence appeared to him to be simply false. Surely whatever man can clearly conceive is by that very token finite. Our natural abstractive concepts are knowledges of formal natures—and to build a knowledge of God out of such concepts, be it by addition or by subtraction, is nothing short of idolatry. On this score St. Thomas makes his own the doctrine of Dionysius: our best knowledge of God is the knowledge that we are ignorant of what He is.[51]

Yet, for all that, St. Thomas is not a Dionysian, not an agnostic. He does not limit man's knowledge of God to the negative attributes like eternity, immensity, infinity, immateriality. He serenely asserts that we can know that God exists, that He is good, wise, holy, loving. But in his explanation of our knowledge of God he avoids even a trace of concession to rationalism. We have seen that he denies the reduction of knowledge to a basis of univocal concepts. In the matter of method he stands—strangely enough, armed with an Aristotelian weapon—diametrically opposed to rationalism. We do not first have a

---

[51] See *Ver.*, q. 2, a. 1 ad 9; *I Sent.*, d. 13, q. 1, a. 1, qa. 4; *Periher.*, lectio 14; *Pot.*, q. 7, a. 2 ad 1; *Qq. qdl.*, I, 9, a. 3; *S.T.*, I, q. 13, a. 12 ad 1; q. 22, a. 3. For the explicit rejection of the *method* of Avempace, see *S.T.*, I, q. 88, a. 2.

concept of what something is; with Aristotle, he avers that we must first know *that* something is before we can legitimately ask *what* it is. But is he not thereby caught in the dilemma proposed by Plato: If we do not already know what we are seeking to know, how shall we recognize it?

To see how St. Thomas escapes this difficulty we need but reflect on some of his distinctive metaphysical principles. What, for St. Thomas, is it to be a *per se* cause of something? It is, first, to exist, and second, to, exist in a way relevant to the particular effect which is caused. Now—assuming for our present purposes an extensive knowledge of Thomistic metaphysics— the things of our experience show themselves, upon a difficult but rigorous analysis, to be effects, not only in their particular and individual characteristics but also, and most importantly, in that they are. Hence their very existence and activity imply the existence of a cause. But this cause cannot belong to the same order of caused being, since the same question would recur indefinitely. The cause of the beings of experience, then, is a cause whose nature is other than theirs. The ground of the being of the world cannot itself have a ground. This ground is called God; and we have, in proving His existence, identified Him relationally as the cause of the world.

In this case, too, the metaphysical implications of cause must be admitted. This means, first, that the cause of existing things exists, and that it exists, being a *per se* cause, relevantly to its effects.[52] Further metaphysical analysis—whose details are again presumed to be known—shows that the cause of good in things is goodness; that the cause of true, beautiful, living, knowing, personal beings is truth, beauty, life, knowledge, personality. Still further metaphysical reflection shows us that the simply uncaused cannot be thought of as potential; it must be judged to be wholly actual, and thus purely and entirely exis-

---

[52] See above, Chap. 3, sect. G.

tential. Thus, the attributes of goodness, truth, beauty, knowledge, life, personality are each identical with the subsistent, unlimited, unfractionated act of existing. In brief, the analogy of causality becomes the analogy of causal eminence and ultimately the analogy of causal participation.

Now, in the light of this, what do our words about God mean? The meaning of negative attributes is clear, and constitutes no epistemological problem. When we say that God is not a stone, we mean by "stone" in that proposition what we always mean. Metaphorical terms used about God have a very rich and complex meaning, a meaning which often reflects historical and cultural contingencies. The metaphysician does not ordinarily use such terms in his own investigations; but, finding them in existence, he is concerned only with showing how they reflect the intrinsically analogous knowledge he has previously obtained in his own way. The meaning of intrinsically analogous terms is the crucial issue. When we say "God is," we mean that "the cause of all that is, Himself is, and in the same positive sense of exercising an act of existing; yet in such a way that His nature as cause constitutes no limitation on His actuality; 'God is,' though expressed in a judgment which asserts actuality of a definite subject, represents the simple reality, 'God-is.' "

Again, take the statement, "God is good." According to the fundamental metaphysical meaning of good, good is that which has nothing lacking to it of the perfection it should have as such and such. Evil is always a defect, good a fullness, an overflow— "bonum est diffusivum sui." A man is good; a cabbage is good; but a man is not good by sprouting cabbages on his shoulders. Similarly, the goodness of God is not the goodness of a man, not even the goodness of all the things He has made. Hence "God is good" means that God, who simply is, by being is the fullness of all that belongs to Him. In saying that God is good we do not and cannot mean that we know in what His goodness consists. Indeed, it is more accurate to say that His goodness does not consist in some mode or character of His activity or being—it is His being, simply. Though this is not conceptual identification, it is also not equivocation.[53] It is proportional predication; and the meaning of this predicate, for us (in St. Thomas' terms, "with regard to the mode of knowledge and the priority of the origin and imposition of the name") is defined in relation to the meaning it has in the beings of experience: The goodness of God is the kind of being that is relevant to causing the goodness of things we experience, and God is not qualified by goodness, but is absolute goodness by His very essence and being.[54]

At the risk of being obvious we would like to make, in similar vein, an analysis of the proposition, "God is love."[55] Love, as we find it in the beings of experience, is the basic act of appetency toward the good: being open to and directed toward the good, tending to and embracing it, holding it precious for its own sake. Now, love is a relational term, and so is predicated by an analogy of proportionality in addition to the basic analogy of causal participation.[56] So in saying "God is love" we mean that God is the kind of being who creates beings capable of love, and who is Himself an act of conscious adherence to the good, and who, moreover, in creating (and in all His other dealings with man[57]) and communicating goods to creatures acts as one who fully and unselfishly loves another.

---

[53] In the beatific vision the blessed shall indeed wonder at the goodness of God and shall agree with St. Paul that man has not experienced in this life, and could not conceive, what God is in Himself (I Cor. 2:9). But we should not therefore imagine that they will exclaim, "This is not in any sense what I mean by goodness." See St. Thomas, *In I Cor.*, cap. 2, lectio 2.

[54] See above, Chap. 3, sects. E and G.

[55] This illustration is chosen because some contemporary philosophers have said the expression is meaningless. See, for example, W. T. Stace, *Time and Eternity*, pp. 57-58 (Princeton: Princeton University Press, 1952).

[56] See above, pp. 142-45.

[57] Naturally, the revelation of God's love for us in the incarnation, suffering, and death of Jesus makes the Christian's comprehension of this statement incomparably richer.

Against such a human knowledge of God the strictures of the existentialist and "crisis" theologians have no effect. St. Thomas did not seek to reduce God to the categories of human thinking, nor model his concept of God on a blown-up anthropocentrism. He admits entirely that what God is in Himself is unknown to us and naturally unknowable.

But the countercharge of "mystification" and "meaninglessness" hurled by analysts against existentialist theologians who use words of professedly unknown meaning likewise misses St. Thomas. St. Thomas not only has a definite meaning for his words about God; he goes so far as to insist that all meanings have their origin in sense (and the process of displaying such an origin he calls the reduction to sense[58]). The only unanswerable objection that an analyst can raise against St. Thomas is that his philosophy is "metaempirical." For it is indubitable that St. Thomas thought that the human mind, though resting on experience, could and did validly judge about things not presented immediately in such experience. The empiricist can be accused of making a nonempirical statement himself, but this will not disturb him. Like the skeptic, he is in an impregnable position, granted his unproved premises. But the sheer logical impregnability of a position is not enough to commend it.

St. Thomas chose to accept himself as a man, to admit his limitations of knowledge but also his power. This is real courage and honesty: to take the responsibility of all one's powers, to push, in a carefully disciplined and critical way, our intellect to its fullest extent, the analogous knowledge of the existence and nature of God.

---

[58] On this see Louis-M. Régis, O.P., "Analyse et synthèse dans l'oeuvre de saint Thomas," in *Studia mediaevalia in honorem admodum reverendi R. J. Martin, O.P.*, pp. 321-22 (Bruges: De Tempel, n. d.), and Umberto Degl'Innocenti, O.P., "Omnis nostra cognitio incipit a sensibus," *Aquinas*, I (1958), 379-91.

Texts

of St. Thomas

on Analogy

Boethii de hebd.: *Expositio in librum Boethii De hebdomadibus* [10]
Boethii de Trin.: *Expositio super librum Boethii De Trinitate* [11]
C.G.: *Summa contra gentiles* [15]
Compend. theol.: *Compendium theologiae* [39]
De div. nomin.: *Expositio in Dionysium De divinis nominibus* [18]
De ente et ess.: *De ente et essentia* [2]
De gener. et corrupt.: *In libros De generatione et corruptione expositio* [37]
De instant.: *De instantibus* [41]
Ethic.: *In decem libros Ethicorum expositio* [34]
In Joann.: *Expositio in evangelium Ioannis* [26]
Lib. de caus.: *Super librum De causis expositio* [35]
Malo: *Quaestiones disputatae de malo* [24]
Metaphys.: *In duodecim libros Metaphysicorum expositio* [33]
Meteorol.: *In libros Meteorologicorum expositio* [30]
Nat. accid.: *De natura accidentis* [42]
Nat. gen.: *De natura generis* [43]
Periher.: *In libros Perihermeneias expositio* [20]
Phys.: *In octo libros Physicorum expositio* [22]
Post. analyt.: *In libros Posteriorum analyticorum expositio* [21]
Pot.: *Quaestiones disputatae de potentia* [14]
Prin. indiv.: *De principio individuationis* [44]
Prin. nat.: *De principiis naturae* [3]
Q.D. de anima: *Quaestio disputata de anima* [27]
Qq. qdl., I; *Qq. qdl.*, II: *Quaestiones quodlibetales*, VII-XI; I-VI, XII [8, 28]
Resp. Joan. Ver.: *Responsio ad Joannem Vercellensem . . . de articulis CVIII* [16]
S. Pauli epist., lectura; *S. Pauli epist.*, ordinatio: *Expositio in S. Pauli epistolas*, lectura; *Expositio in S. Pauli epistolas*, ordinatio [12, 29]
S.T., I; *S.T.*, I-II; *S.T.*, II-II; *S.T.*, III: *Summa theologiae*, prima pars; pars prima secundae partis; secunda pars secundae partis; tertia pars [17, 25, 32, 38]
I Sent.: *Scriptum super primum librum Sententiarum* [4]
II Sent.: *Scriptum super secundum librum Sententiarum* [5]
III Sent.: *Scriptum super tertium librum Sententiarum* [6]
IV Sent.: *Scriptum super quartum librum Sententiarum* [7]
Sub. separ.: *De substantiis separatis, seu de angelorum natura* [31]
Ver.: *Quaestiones disputatae de veritate* [9]
Virtut. in comm.: *Quaestio disputata de virtutibus in communi* [23]

158

This appendix reproduces all the texts formally dealing with analogy which we have found in the Thomistic corpus. Also included are a number of texts which illustrate different types of analogy.[1] The texts are assembled in chronological order. Each work of St. Thomas (and in several cases, each major part) in which we have found texts to be quoted has been assigned a number in this chronological sequence; thus, the *Quaestiones disputatae de veritate* has the identifying number 9. Within each work each text has been assigned a number indicating its order of appearance within the work cited. Thus, *Ver.* (9.23) refers to the twenty-third text cited from the *De veritate*, which is question 4, article 6. All references to the texts collected here will be made by thus naming the work in which the text is found and the code number of work and text.

The chronology followed is that of Ignatius Eschmann, O.P.[2] For purposes of convenience a list of those works of St. Thomas examined in connection with this study is given here, with approximate dates. Those works in which texts on analogy were discovered are the ones that have a preceding code number. Unless otherwise indicated, all

---

[1] A few texts in which irrelevant usages of the terms *proportio, proportionalitas,* and *analogia* occur are included in this collection for purposes of contrast. No attempt has been made to include all the texts in which analogy is actually used. A fairly heavy sampling of texts describing causal participation is given. On the other hand, very few texts are cited which deal with noncausal participation (particularly those which occur in the areas of psychology and ethics) or with the analogy between *ens in re* and *ens in anima;* similarly, very little is quoted in which the difference between act and potency is described. Our intention has been to list the texts which explicitly mention and discuss analogy (even when the name is not mentioned); we hope that the list, if not complete, is at least comprehensive enough so that the texts inadvertently omitted will not appreciably affect our conclusions.

[2] Ignatius Eschmann, O.P., "A Catalogue of St. Thomas' Works," in Gilson's *The Christian Philosophy of St. Thomas Aquinas,* pp. 381-437, cited in Introduction, n. 1.

159

works cited are certainly authentic. Where no special edition is referred to, the reading is that of the Parma edition.

A Chronological Sequence of St. Thomas' Works

1. *De fallaciis ad quosdam nobiles artistas.* Very probable. 1244-1245.
   De propositionibus modalibus. Very probable. Possibly 1244-1245.
2. *De ente et essentia.* Before 1256. Ed. Charles Boyer, S.J. Rome: Gregorian University Press, 1933.
3. *De principiis naturae.* Before 1256. Ed. John J. Pauson. Fribourg: Société Philosophique, 1950.
4. *Scriptum super primum librum Sententiarum.* 1254-1256.
5. *Scriptum super secundum librum Sententiarum.* 1254-1256.
6. *Scriptum super tertium librum Sententiarum.* 1254-1256. Ed. M. F. Moos, O.P. Paris: Lethielleux, 1933.
7. *Scriptum super quartum librum Sententiarum.* 1254-1256.
   Contra impugnantes Dei cultum et religionem. 1256.
   Expositio in evangelium S. Matthaei. 1256-1259.
   Expositio in Isaiam prophetam. 1256-1259.
8. *Quaestiones quodlibetales,* VII-XI. 1256-1259.
9. *Quaestiones disputatae de veritate.* 1256-1259.
10. *Expositio in librum Boethii De hebdomadibus.* 1256-1261.
11. *Expositio super librum Boethii De Trinitate.* 1256-1261. Ed. Bruno Decker. Leiden: E. J. Brill, 1955.
12. *Expositio in S. Pauli epistolas,* lectura (from *In I Cor.,* cap. 10 to end, with the possible exception of *In Heb.*). 1259-1265.
13. *Expositio super primam decretalem "De fide catholica et sancta Trinitate" et super secundam "Damnamus autem."* Possibly 1259-1268.
14. *Quaestiones disputatae de potentia.* 1259-1268.
    Expositio in Job ad litteram. 1260.
    De regno ad regem Cypri. About 1260-1267.
    De articulis fidei et Ecclesiae sacramentis. Possibly 1261-1262.
    De rationibus fidei contra Saracenos, Graecos, et Armenos. 1261-1264.
15. *Summa contra gentiles.* 1261-1264. *Opera omnia jussu impensaque Leonis XIII* (ed. Leonine). Vols. XIII-XV. Rome: Commissio Leonina, 1920-1930.
    De emptione et venditione ad tempus. Probably 1262.
    Contra errores Graecorum, ad Urbanum IV Pontificem. 1263.

Catena aurea (Glossa continua in Matthaeum, Marcum, Lucam, Joannem). About 1264.

16. *Responsio ad Joannem Vercellensem . . . de articulis CVIII.* 1264-1266.

17. *Summa theologiae,* prima pars. 1266-1268. Ed. Leonine, vols. IV-XII, 1896-1906.

18. *Expositio in Dionysium De divinis nominibus.* Before 1268.

Expositio in Threnos Jeremiae prophetae. Very probable. 1267-1268 (possibly 1254).

Expositio in Jeremiam prophetam. Very probable. 1267-1268 (possibly 1254).

19. *In libros De anima expositio.* 1267-1271.

In librum De memoria et reminiscentia. Possibly 1267-1271.

In librum De sensu et sensato expositio. Possibly 1267-1271.

De spiritualibus creaturis quaestio disputata. After 1267.

20. *In libros Perihermeneias expositio.* Authentic through Book II, Lectio 2. 1268-1271.

21. *In libros Posteriorum analyticorum expositio.* Possibly 1268-1271.

22. *In octo libros Physicorum expositio.* 1268-1271.

23. *Quaestio disputata de virtutibus in communi.* 1268-1272.

24. *Quaestiones disputatae de malo,* I-V, VII-XVI. Probably before 1269.

De secreto. 1269.

De mixtione elementorum. 1269-1271.

25. *Summa theologiae,* pars prima secundae partis. 1269-1271. Ed. Leonine.

De forma absolutionis, ad generalem magistrum ordinis. 1269-1272.

De sortibus ad Dominum Iacobum. 1269-1272.

26. *Expositio in evangelium Ioannis.* 1269-1272.

27. *Quaestio disputata de anima.* Possibly 1269-1272.

Quaestio disputata de caritate. 1269-1272.

Quaestio disputata de correctione fraterna. 1269-1272.

Quaestio disputata de spe. 1269-1272.

Quaestio disputata de unione Verbi Incarnati. Possibly 1269-1272.

Quaestio disputata de virtutibus cardinalibus. 1269-1272.

28. *Quaestiones quodlibetales,* I-VI, XII. 1269-1272.

29. *Expositio in S. Pauli epistolas,* ordinatio (from beginning to *In I Cor.,* cap. 7, 9, and possibly *In Heb.*). 1269-1272.

30. *In libros Meteorologicorum expositio* (through 363a20). 1269-1273.

Quaestio disputata de malo, VI. After 1269.

Contra pestiferam doctrinam retrahentium pueros a religionis ingressu. 1270.

De perfectione vitae spiritualis. 1270.

31. *De substantiis separatis, seu de angelorum natura.* Possibly 1270.

De unitate intellectus, contra Averroistas. 1270.

De motu cordis ad Magistrum Philippum. 1270-1271.

De aeternitate mundi, contra murmurantes. 1270-1272.

De regimine Iudaeorum, ad Ducissam Brabantiae. 1270-1272.

32. *Summa theologiae,* secunda pars secundae partis. 1270-1272. Ed. Leonine.

Responsio ad Ioannem Vercellensem . . . de articulis XLII. 1271.

Responsio ad Lectorem Venetum de articulis XXXVI. 1271.

33. *In duodecim libros Metaphysicorum expositio.* Before 1272.

34. *In decem libros Ethicorum expositio.* 1271-1272.

In libros Politicorum expositio. (Authentic to 1280a6.) Possibly 1271-1272.

35. *Super librum De causis expositio.* 1272. Ed. H.-D. Saffrey, O.P. Fribourg: Société philosophique, 1954.

36. *In libros De caelo et mundo expositio.* 1272-1273.

37. *In libros De generatione et corruptione expositio.* (Through 321b-34.) 1272-1273.

In Psalmos Davidis expositio. 1272-1273.

38. *Summa theologiae,* tertia pars. 1272-1273. Ed. Leonine.

39. *Compendium theologiae.* 1273 (or possibly 1261-1269).

Ad Bernardum, abbatem Cassinensem. 1274.

40. *De immortalitate animae.* Very probable. No date. Ed. E. Gomez. Madrid: Feda, 1935.

De demonstratione. Dubious. No date.

41. *De instantibus.* Dubious. No date.

De iudiciis astrorum ad quendam militem ultramontanum. No date.

De modo studendi. Dubious. No date.

42. *De natura accidentis.* Dubious. No date.

43. *De natura generis.* Dubious. No date.

De natura verbi intellectus. Dubious. No date.

44. *De principio individuationis.* Dubious. No date.

De occultis operationibus naturae, ad quendam militem ultramontanum. No date.

De quatuor oppositis. Dubious. No date.

Responsio ad lectorem Bisuntinum de articulis VI. No date.

1.1 De fallaciis (1244-1245)

cap. 4:

Species autem sive modi aequivocationis sunt tres. . . . Secunda species est quando unum nomen principaliter unum significat, et aliud metaphorice sive transumptive; sicut hoc verbum "ridere" principaliter significat actum hominis proprium; metaphorice autem sive transumptive significat prati floritionem. . . . Et ad hanc speciem reducitur multiplicitas nominum analogorum quae dicuntur de pluribus secundum prius et posterius; sicut sanum dicitur aliquando de animali, urina et diaeta.

2.1 De ente et essentia (before 1256) Ed. Boyer

cap. 4:

Et ita invenitur potentia et actus in intelligentiis, non tamen forma et materia, nisi aequivoce. Unde etiam pati, recipere, subiectum esse et omnia huiusmodi quae videntur rebus ratione materiae convenire, aequivoce conveniunt substantiis intellectualibus et corporalibus, ut in tertio *De Anima* Commentator dicit.

2.2

cap. 6:

Et quia accidentia non componuntur ex materia et forma, ideo non potest in eis sumi genus a materia, et differentia a forma, sicut in substantiis compositis; sed oportet ut genus primum sumatur ex ipso modo essendi, secundum quod ens diversimode secundum prius et posterius de decem generibus praedicatur; sicut dicitur quantitas ex eo quod est mensura substantiae, et qualitas secundum quod est dispositio substantiae, et sic de aliis, secundum Philosophum in quarto *Metaphysicae*.

Page 65

3.1 De principiis naturae (before 1256) Ed. Pauson

cap. 6 (102.3-104.19) :

. . . Quaedam autem sunt diversa in genere, sed sunt idem solum secundum analogiam; sicut substantia et quantitas, quae non conveniunt in aliquo genere, sed conveniunt solum secundum analogiam. Conveniunt enim solum in eo quod est ens; ens autem non est genus, quia non praedicatur univoce, sed analogice.

Ad huius autem intelligentiam sciendum est quod tripliciter aliquid praedicatur de pluribus; univoce, aequivoce et analogice.

Univoce praedicatur quod praedicatur secundum idem nomen et secundum eamdem rationem, idest definitionem, sicut animal praedicatur de homine et de asino. Utrumque enim dicitur animal, et utrumque est substantia animata sensibilis, quod est definitio animalis. Aequivoce praedicatur quod praedicatur de aliquibus secundum idem nomen et secundum diversam rationem, sicut canis dicitur de latrabili et de caelesti, quae conveniunt solum in nomine et non in definitione sive significatione; id enim quod significatur per nomen est definitio, sicut dicitur in IV *Metaphysicae*. Analogice dicitur praedicari quod praedicatur de pluribus, quorum rationes diversae sunt, sed attribuuntur alicui uni eidem, sicut sanum dicitur de corpore animalis et de urina et de potione, sed non ex toto idem significat in omnibus. Dicitur enim de urina ut de signo sanitatis, de corpore ut de subiecto, de potione ut de causa; sed tamen omnes istae rationes attribuuntur uni fini, scilicet sanitati. Aliquando enim ea quae conveniunt secundum analogiam, idest in proportione vel comparatione vel convenientia, attribuuntur uni fini, sicut patet in praedicto exemplo; aliquando uni agenti, sicut medicus dicitur et de eo qui operatur per artem et de eo qui operatur sine arte, ut vetula, et etiam de instrumentis, sed per attributionem ad unum agens quod est medicus [*var.*, medicina]. Aliquando autem per attributionem ad unum subiectum, sicut ens dicitur de substantia et de quantitate et qualitate et aliis praedicamentis. Non enim ex toto est eadem ratio qua substantia est ens et quantitas et alia; sed omnia dicunter ens ex eo quod attribuuntur substantiae, quae quidem est subiectum aliorum. Et ideo ens dicitur per prius de substantia et per posterius de aliis; et ideo ens non est genus substantiae et quantitatis, quia nullum genus praedicatur per prius et posterius de suis speciebus, sed praedicatur analogice. Et hoc est quod diximus quod substantia et quantitas differunt genere, sed sunt idem secundum analogiam.

Eorum igitur quae sunt idem numero, et forma et materia sunt idem numero, sicut Tullii et Ciceronis. Eorum autem quae sunt idem specie, sed diversa numero, etiam materia et forma non est eadem numero, sed specie, sicut Socratis et Platonis. Et similiter eorum quae sunt idem genere, et principia sunt idem genere; ut anima et corpus asini et equi differunt specie, sed sunt idem genere. Et similiter eorum quae conveniunt secundum analogiam tantum, principia sunt eadem secundum analogiam tantum, sive proportionem. Materia enim et forma et privatio, sive potentia et actus, sunt principia substantiae et aliorum generum. Tamen materia substantiae et quantitatis, et similiter forma et privatio, differunt genere, sed conveniunt solum secundum proportionem in hoc quod, sicut se habet materia substantiae ad substantiam in ratione materiae, ita se habet materia quantitatis ad quantitatem. Sicut tamen substantia est causa caeterorum, ita principia substantiae sunt principia omnium aliorum.

Pages *24*, *35*, 37, *38-39*, **43-44**, *65*, 131, 132[1]

4.1 In I Sententiarum (1254-1256)

prol., q. 1, *a.* 2, *arg.* 2:

Item, una scientia est unius generis, sicut dicit Philosophus in I *Posteriorum* [text. 43]. Sed Deus et creatura, de quibus in divina doctrina tractatur, non reducuntur in unum genus, neque univoce, neque analogice. Ergo divina scientia non est una. Probatio mediae. Quaecumque conveniunt in uno genere univoce vel analogice, participant aliquid idem, vel secundum prius et posterius, sicut substantia et accidens rationem entis, vel aequaliter, sicut equus et bos rationem animalis. Sed Deus et creatura non participant aliquid idem, quia illud esset simplicius et prius utroque. Ergo nullo modo reducuntur in idem genus.

4.2

prol., q. 1, *a.* 2, *ad* 2:

Ad secundum dicendum quod Creator et creatura reducuntur in unum, non communitate univocationis sed analogiae. Talis autem communitas potest esse duplex. Aut ex eo quod aliqua participant aliquid unum secundum prius et posterius, sicut potentia et actus rationem entis, et similiter substantia et accidens; aut ex eo quod unum esse et rationem ab altero recipit; et talis est analogia creaturae ad Creatorem; creatura enim non habet esse nisi secundum quod a primo ente descendit, nec nominatur ens nisi inquantum ens primum imitatur; et similiter est de sapientia et de omnibus aliis quae de creatura dicuntur.

Pages 22, 28, *29-30*, 31, *51-52*, *58*, 95, 112, 131, 140

---

[1] Regular (roman) numerals indicate a passage that has been cited; italic numerals indicate a passage that has been translated; bold numerals indicate a passage that has been discussed.

4.3

d. 2, q. 1, a. 2, c.:
Quod autem est causa alicuius, habet illud excellentius et nobilius. Unde oportet quod omnes nobilitates omnium creaturarum inveniantur in Deo nobilissimo modo et sine aliqua imperfectione. . . . Inde est quod ipse non est causa rerum omnino aequivoca, cum secundum formam suam producat effectus similes, non univoce, sed analogice. . . . Unde ipse est exemplaris forma rerum, non tantum quantum ad ea quae sunt in sapientia sua, scilicet secundum rationes ideales, sed etiam quantum ad ea quae sunt in natura sua, scilicet attributa. . . . Res creata dicitur sapiens inquantum imitatur divinam sapientiam.
Pages 26, 72, 74

4.4

d. 3, divisio primae partis textus:
[Dionysius] dicit enim quod ex creaturis tribus modis devenimus in Deum: scilicet per causalitatem, per remotionem, per eminentiam. Et ratio huius est, quia esse creaturae est ab altero. Unde secundum hoc ducimur in causam a qua est. Hoc autem potest esse dupliciter. Aut quantum ad id quod receptum est; et sic ducimur per modum causalitatis: aut quantum ad modum recipiendi, quia imperfecte recipitur; et sic habemus duos modos, scilicet secundum remotionem imperfectionis a Deo et secundum hoc quod illud quod receptum est in creatura, perfectius et nobilius est in Creatore; et ita est modus per eminentiam.

Aliae duae rationes sumuntur per viam eminentiae. Sed potest dupliciter attendi eminentia, vel quantum ad esse vel quantum ad cognitionem. Tertia ergo sumitur ratio per viam eminentiae in esse et est talis. Bonum et melius dicuntur per comparationem ad optimum. Sed in substantiis invenimus corpus bonum et spiritum creatum melius, in quo tamen bonitas non est a seipso. Ergo oportet esse aliquod optimum a quo sit bonitas in utroque.
Pages 28, 74

4.5

d. 2, q. 1, a. 3:
Et haec eminentia attenditur quantum ad tria: scilicet quantum ad universalitatem, quia in Deo sunt omnes perfectiones adunatae quae non congregantur in aliqua una creatura. Item quantum ad

plenitudinem, quia est ibi sapientia sine omni defectu, et similiter
de aliis attributis, quod non est in creaturis. Item quantum ad unitatem; quae enim in creaturis diversa sunt, in Deo sunt unum. Et
quia in illo uno habet omnia, ideo secundum illud unum causat
omnia, cognoscit omnia, et omnia sibi per analogiam similantur. Secundum ergo hanc opinionem, conceptiones quas intellectus noster
ex nominibus attributorum concipit sunt vere similitudines rei quae
Deus est, quamvis deficientes et non plenae, sicut est de aliis rebus
quae Deo similantur. . . . Pluralitas nominum venit ex hoc quod ipse
Deus nostrum intellectum excedit. . . . quia bonus est, ideo bona facit, et alia participando eius bonitatem ad modum eius se habent.
    Page 75

4.6

d. 3, q. 1, a. 1, ad 1:
Dicendum quod Deus non est hoc modo existens sicut ista existentia, sed in eo est natura entitatis eminenter; unde sicut non est
omnino expers entitatis, ita etiam non omnino est expers cognitionis, quin cognoscatur.
    Pages 73, 141

4.7

d. 3, q. 1, a. 3, c.:
Dicendum quod, cum creatura exemplariter procedat ab ipso Deo
sicut a causa quodammodo simili per analogiam (eo scilicet quod
quaelibet creatura eum imitatur secundum possibilitatem naturae
suae), ex creaturis potest in Deum deveniri tribus modis quibus
dictum est, scilicet per causalitatem, remotionem, eminentiam.
    Pages 51, 54, 70, 72, 74

4.8

d. 3, q. 1, a. 3, ad 5:
Dicendum quod creatura est effectus non proportionatus Creatori;
et ideo non ducit in perfectam cognitionem ipsius sed in imperfectam.
    Page 71

4.9

d. 4, q. 1, a. 1, c.:
Quidquid perfectionis invenitur in creatura de Deo dici potest
quantum ad id quod est perfectionis in ipsa, omni remota imper-

fectione. . . . Si autem imponitur ab eo quod est perfectionis, dicitur proprie, quamvis secundum modum eminentiorem.
Page 73

4.10

d. 8, q. 1, a. 2, sed contra 2:
Praeterea, nihil habet esse, nisi inquantum participat divinum esse, quia ipsum est primum ens, quare causa est in eo per modum participantis: quia nihil potest recipere ultra mensuram suam. Cum igitur modus cuiuslibet rei creatae sit finitus, quaelibet res creata recipit esse finitum et inferius divino esse quod est perfectissimum. Ergo constat quod esse creaturae, quo est formaliter, non est divinum esse.
Pages 28, 63

4.11

d. 8, q. 1, a. 2, c.:
Invenimus enim tres modos causae agentis. Scilicet causam aequivoce agentem, et hoc est quando effectus non convenit cum causa nec nomine nec ratione: sicut sol facit calorem qui non est calidus. Item causam univoce agentem, quando effectus convenit in nomine et ratione cum causa, sicut homo generat hominem et calor facit calorem. Neutro istorum modorum Deus agit. Non univoce, quia nihil univoce convenit cum ipso. Non aequivoce, cum effectus et causa aliquo modo conveniant in nomine et ratione, secundum prius et posterius; sicut Deus sua sapientia facit nos sapientes, ita tamen quod sapientia nostra semper deficit a ratione sapientiae suae, sicut accidens a ratione entis, secundum quod est in substantia. Unde est tertius modus causae agentis analogice. Unde patet quod divinum esse producit esse creaturae in similitudine sui imperfecta: et ideo esse divinum dicitur esse omnium rerum, a quo omne esse creatum effective et exemplariter manat.
Pages *30*, 31, *54, 67, 72*, 138

4.12

d. 8, q. 2, a. 1, c.:
Illud enim in quo non est esse absolutum, sed terminatum per recipiens, non habet esse perfectum, sed illud solum quod est suum esse: et per hoc dividitur esse aeternum ab esse rerum immobilium

creatarum, quae habent esse participatum, sicut spirituales creaturae.

Page 61

4.13

d. 8, *q.* 4, *a.* 2, *ad* 1:

. . . Propter diversum modum praedicandi non dicitur substantia de Deo et creaturis univoce, sed analogice.

4.14

d. 18, *q.* 1, *a.* 5, *c.*:

Deus non potest habere aliquam relationem ad nos, nisi per modum principii. Cum autem causae sunt quatuor, ipse non est causa materialis nostra; sed se habet ad nos in ratione efficientis et finis et formae exemplaris, non autem in ratione formae inhaerentis. . . . Quaedam horum abstractorum important rationem principii efficientis et exemplaris, ut sapientia et bonitas et huiusmodi . . . , ut cum dicimus, Deus est sapientia nostra causaliter, per modum quod dicitur spes nostra: quia per eius sapientiam efficitur in nobis sapienta exemplata a sua sapientia, per quam sapientes sumus formaliter.

Pages 46, *54*, 55

4.15

d. 19, *q.* 1, *a.* 2, *c.*:

Quandoque autem qualitas aliqua est proprie et pléne in uno, et in alio est tantum quaedam imitatio illius secundum aliquam participationem: et tunc illa qualitas non dicitur utriusque, sed eius tantum quod eam plene possidet.

Pages 22, 52

4.16

d. 19, *q.* 5, *a.* 2, *c.*:

Dicendum quod sicut dictum est ratio veritatis in duobus consistit: in esse rei, et in apprehensione virtutis cognoscitivae proportionata ad esse rei. Utrumque autem horum quamvis, ut dictum est, reducatur in Deum sicut in causam efficientem et exemplarem; nihilominus tamen quaelibet res participat suum esse creatum, quo formaliter est, et unusquisque intellectus participat lumen per quod recte de re iudicat, quod quidem est exemplatum a lumine increato. Habet etiam intellectus suam operationem in se, ex qua completur ratio

veritatis. Unde dico, quod sicut est unum esse divinum quo omnia
sunt, sicut a principio effectivo exemplari, nihilominus tamen in
rebus diversis est diversum esse, quo formaliter res est; ita etiam
est una veritas, scilicet divina, qua omnia vera sunt, sicut principio
effectivo exemplari; nihilominus sunt plures veritates in rebus
creatis, quibus dicuntur verae formaliter.

Pages 22, 55, 59, 64

4.17

d. 19, *q.* 5, *a.* 2, *ad* 1:

Dicendum quod aliquid dicitur secundum analogiam tripliciter: vel
secundum intentionem tantum, et non secundum esse; et hoc est
quando una intentio refertur ad plura per prius et posterius, quae
tamen non habet esse nisi in uno; sicut intentio sanitatis refertur ad
animal, urinam, et dietam diversimode, secundum prius et posterius; non tamen secundum diversum esse, quia esse sanitatis non
est nisi in animali. Vel secundum esse et non secundum intentionem; et hoc contingit quando plura parificantur in intentione
alicuius communis, sed illud commune non habet esse unius rationis
in omnibus, sicut omnia corpora parificantur in intentione corporeitatis. Unde Logicus, qui considerat intentiones tantum, dicit, hoc
nomen corpus de omnibus corporibus univoce praedicari: sed esse
huius naturae non est eiusdem rationis in corporibus corruptibilibus et incorruptibilibus. Unde quantum ad metaphysicum et naturalem, qui considerant res secundum suum esse, nec hoc nomen
corpus nec aliquid aliud dicitur univoce de corruptibilibus et incorruptibilibus, ut patet, X *Meta.* [text. 5], ex Philosopho et Commen-
tatore. Vel secundum intentionem et secundum esse; et hoc est
quando neque parificatur in intentione communi, neque in esse; sicut ens dicitur de substantia et accidente; et de talibus oportet quod
natura communis habeat aliquod esse in unoquoque eorum de quibus dicitur, sed differens secundum rationem maioris vel minoris
perfectionis. Et similiter dico, quod veritas, et bonitas, et omnia
huiusmodi dicuntur analogice de Deo et creaturis. Unde oportet
quod secundum suum esse omnia haec in Deo sint, et in creaturis secundum rationem maioris perfectionis et minoris; ex quo sequitur,
cum non possint esse secundum unum esse utrobique, quod sint
diversae veritates.

Pages 7-8, 14, *30*, 31, 39, **70**, 95, *100-01*, 112, *120-21*

4.18

d. 19, *q.* 5, *a.* 2, *ad* 3:

Dicendum quod similiter dico de bonitate, quod est una bonitas, qua sicut principio effectivo exemplari omnia sunt bona. Sed tamen bonitas qua unumquodque formaliter est bonum diversa est in diversis. Sed quia bonitas universalis non invenitur in aliqua creatura, sed particulata, et secundum aliquid, ideo dicit Augustinus quod si removeamus omnes rationes particulationis ab ipsa bonitate, remanebit in intellectu bonitas integra et plena, quae est bonitas divina, quae videtur in bonitate creata sicut exemplar in exemplato.

Page 54

4.19

d. 19, *q.* 5, *a.* 2, *ad* 4:

Dicendum quod exemplar rerum est in Deo dupliciter. Vel quantum ad id quod est in intellectu suo, et sic secundum ideas est exemplar intellectus divinus omnium quae ab ipso sunt, sicut intellectus artificis per formam artis omnium artificiatorum. Vel quantum ad id quod est in natura sua, sicut ratione suae bonitatis qua est bonus, est exemplar omnis bonitatis; et similiter est de veritate.

Pages *26*, 54

4.20

d. 22, *q.* 1, *a.* 2, *c.*:

Dicendum quod quamvis omnis perfectio quae in creaturis est exemplariter a Deo descendat, sicut a principio praehabente in se unice omnium perfectiones; nulla tamen creatura potest recipere illam perfectionem secundum illum modum quo in Deo est. Unde secundum modum recipiendi deficit a perfecta repraesentatione exemplaris. Et ex hoc etiam in creaturis est quidam gradus, secundum quod quaedam quibusdam plures perfectiones et nobiliores a Deo consequuntur, et plenius participant.

Pages 28, 59, 64

4.21

d. 22. *q.* 1, *a.* 2, *sed contra* 1:

Quidquid dicitur de aliquibus per prius et posterius, magis proprie convenit ei de quo per prius dicitur; sicut ens per prius convenit substantiae quam accidenti.

4.22

d. 22, *q.* 1, *a.* 2, *ad* 3:
Dicendum quod sapientia creata magis differt a sapientia increata
quantum ad esse, quod consistit in modo habendi, quam floritio
prati a risu hominis: sed quantum ad rationem a qua imponitur
nomen, magis conveniunt; quia illa ratio est una secundum analogiam, per prius in Deo, per posterius in creaturis existens; et secundum talem rationem significatam in nomine, magis attenditur
veritas et proprietas locutionis, quam quantum ad modum significandi, qui datur ex consequenti intelligi per nomen.

   Pages *23, 30,* 67, 112

4.23

d. 22, *q.* 1, *a.* 3, *ad* 2:
Dicendum quod aliter dividitur aequivocum, analogum et univocum. Aequivocum enim dividitur secundum res significatas, univocum vero dividitur secundum differentias; sed analogum dividitur secundum diversos modos. Unde cum ens praedicetur analogice
de decem generibus, dividitur in ea secundum diversos modos. Unde
unicuique generi debetur proprius modus praedicandi. Et quia in
divinis non salvantur nisi duo genera quantum ad rationem communem generis, scilicet substantia et ad aliquid; ideo dicuntur in
divinis duo modi praedicandi. Unumquodque autem genus dividitur univoce in species contentas sub genere, et ideo speciebus non
debetur proprius modus praedicandi. Et propter hoc quamvis
quaedam contenta in praedicamento qualitatis dicantur de Deo secundum rationem speciei, non tamen afferunt novum modum praedicandi, etsi afferant novam rationem significandi. Unde, quamvis
in Deo non sint nisi duo modi praedicandi, sunt tamen plures rationes significandi secundum quas divina nomina multiplicari possunt.

   Page 112

4.24

d. 22, *q.* 1, *a.* 3, *ad* 4:
Omnia enim huiusmodi dicuntur de Deo et creaturis non aequivoce,
sed secundum unam rationem analogice.

   Page *23*

4.25

d. 24, *q.* 1, *a.* 1, *ad* 4:

Quamvis Deus et creatura non conveniant in aliquo uno secundum aliquem modum convenientiae, tamen est considerare communitatem analogiae inter Deum et creaturam, secundum quod creaturae imitantur ipsum prout possunt.

Pages 51, 52

4.26

d. 25, *q.* 1, *a.* 2, *c.*:

Dicendum quod persona dicitur de Deo et creaturis non univoce nec aequivoce sed secundum analogiam; et quantum ad rem significatam per prius est in Deo quam in creaturis, sed quantum ad modum significandi est e converso, sicut est etiam de omnibus aliis nominibus quae de Deo et creaturis analogice dicuntur.

Pages *30*, 67

4.27

d. 34, *q.* 3, *a.* 1, *c.*:

. . . Et ideo cum de omnibus quae de Deo dicimus, intelligendum sit quod non eodem modo sibi conveniunt sicut in creaturis inveniuntur, sed per aliquem modum imitationis et similitudinis; expressius ostendebatur huiusmodi eminentia Dei per ea quae sunt magis manifesta ab ipso removeri.

Pages 51, 52, 73

4.28

d. 34, *q.* 3, *a.* 1, *ad* 2:

Dicendum quod similitudo est duplex: quaedam enim est per participationem eiusdem formae; et talis similitudo non est corporalium ad divina, ut obiectio probat. Est etiam quaedam similitudo proportionalitatis, quae consistit in eadem habitudine proportionum, ut cum dicitur: sicut se habet octo ad quatuor, ita sex ad tria; et sicut se habet consul ad civitatem, ita se habet gubernator ad navem; et secundum talem similitudinem fit transumptio ex corporalibus in divina: ut si Deus dicatur ignis ex hoc quod sicut se habet ignis ad hoc quod liquefacta effluere facit per suum calorem, ita Deus per suam bonitatem perfectiones in omnes creaturas diffundit, vel aliquid huiusmodi.

Pages 28, *80*

4.29

d. 35, *q.* 1, *a.* 4, *c.*:
Dicendum quod tribus modis contingit aliquid aliquibus commune esse, vel univoce, vel aequivoce, vel analogice. Univoce quidem non potest aliquid de Deo et creatura dici. Huius ratio est quia cum in re duo sit considerare: scilicet naturam vel quidditatem rei, et esse suum, oportet quod in omnibus univocis sit communitas secundum rationem naturae, et non secundum esse, quia unum esse non est nisi in una re; unde habitus humanitatis non est secundum idem esse in duobus hominibus; et ideo quandocumque forma significata per nomen est ipsum esse, non potest univoce convenire, propter quod etiam ens non univoce praedicatur. Et ideo cum omnium quae dicuntur de Deo natura vel forma sit ipsum esse, quia suum esse est sua natura, propter quod dicitur a quibusdam philosophis, quod est ens non in essentia, et sciens non per scientiam, et sic de aliis, ut intelligatur essentia non esse aliud ab esse, et sic de aliis; ideo nihil de Deo et creaturis univoce dici potest. . . . Et ideo dicendum quod scientia analogice dicitur de Deo et creatura, et similiter omnia huiusmodi. Sed duplex est analogia. Quaedam secundum convenientiam in aliquo uno quod eis per prius et posterius convenit; et haec analogia non potest esse inter Deum et creaturam, sicut nec univocatio. Alia analogia est secundum quod unum imitatur aliud quantum potest, nec perfecte ipsum assequitur; et haec analogia est creaturae ad Deum.
Pages *30*, 31, 51, 52, 95, 112, 136

4.30

d. 35, *q.* 1, *a.* 4, *ad* 1:
Dicendum quod ab agente secundum formam non producitur effectus univocus, nisi quando recipiens est proportionatus ad recipiendum totam virtutem agentis, vel secundum eamdem rationem; et sic nulla creatura est proportionata ad recipiendum scientiam a Deo per modum quo in ipso est; sicut nec corpora inferiora possunt recipere calorem univoce a sole, quamvis per formam suam agat.
Page 71

4.31

d. 35, *q.* 1, *a.* 4, *ad* 2:
Dicendum quod scientia Dei non est mensura coaequata scientiae nostrae, sed excedens; et ideo non sequitur quod sit eiusdem ra-

tionis secundum univocationem cum scientia nostra, sed secundum analogiam.
Page 74

4.32

d. 35, *q.* 1, *a.* 4, *ad* 5:
Dicendum quod dictum illud est intelligendum quantum ad esse, et non quantum ad intentionem rei quae communiter praedicatur; quia corpus, etiam secundum hoc quod dicitur ibi, aequivoce de corruptibilibus et incorruptibilibus praedicatur, cuius tamen ratio eadem est in utroque si secundum intentionem communem consideretur.
Page 101

4.33

d. 35, *q.* 1, *a.* 4, *ad* 6:
Dicendum quod inter Deum et creaturam non est similitudo per convenientiam in aliquo uno communi, sed per imitationem; unde creatura similis Deo dicitur, sed non convertitur, ut dicit Dionysius.
Page 52

4.34

d. 35, *q.* 1, *a.* 4, *ad* 7:
Dicendum quod scientia non praedicatur de Deo, secundum rationem generis sui, qualitatis scilicet accidentalis, sed solum secundum rationem differentiae, quae ad perfectionem pertinet, secundum quam a natura attenditur per imitationem, ut dictum est.
Page 52

4.35

d. 38, *q.* 1, *a.* 1, *c.*:
Haec omnia habent unum modum causalitatis, scilicet per modum communem efficientis exemplaris, ut dicimus, quod a primo bono sunt omnia bona, et a primo vivente omnia viventia. . . . Constat enim quod scientia sua est causa per modum efficientis et exemplaris omnium scientiarum.
Page 54

4.36

d. 45, *q.* 1, *a.* 4, *c.*:
Dicendum quod de Deo quaedam dicuntur proprie, quaedam metaphorice. Ea quae proprie de ipso dicuntur, vere in eo sunt; sed ea

quae metaphorice, dicuntur de eo per similitudinem proportionabilitatis ad effectum aliquem, sicut dicitur ignis *Deuter.* 4, eo quod
sicut ignis se habet ad consumptionem contrarii, ita Deus ad con-
sumendum nequitiam.

Page *80*

5.1 In II Sententiarum (1254-1256)

d. 1, *q.* 1, *a.* 1, *c.*:

. . . cum natura entitatis sit unius rationis in omnibus secundum
analogiam.

Pages *23*, 112, 141

5.2

d. 1, *q.* 1, *a.* 2, *c.*:

Cum autem quaelibet res, et quidquid est in re, aliquo modo esse
participet, et admixtum sit imperfectioni, oportet quod omnis res,
secundum totum id quod in ea est, a primo et perfecto ente oriatur.

Page 62

5.3

d. 1, *q.* 2, *a.* 2, *c.*:

Dicendum quod finis et agens proportionantur ad invicem, sicut
materia et forma. Unde secundum differentiam agentis est differentia finis. Est autem duplex agens. Quoddam quod suscipienti
suum effectum est proportionatum; unde formam eiusdem speciei
vel rationis in effectum inducit, sicut in omnibus agentibus univocis,
ut ignis generat ignem, et domus quae est in anima artificis causat
domum quae est in materia. Quoddam vero agens non est proportionatum recipienti suum effectum. Unde effectus non consequitur
speciem agentis, sed aliquam similitudinem eius quantum potest,
sicut est in omnibus agentibus aequivoce, ut sol calefacere dicitur.

Page *71*

5.4

d. 3, *q.* 1, *a.* 1, *ad* 2:

Dicendum quod aliqua sunt unius generis logice loquendo, quae
naturaliter non sunt unius generis, sicut illa quae communicant in
intentione generis quam logicus inspicit, et habent diversum modum essendi: unde in X *Metaphys.* [text. 26], dicitur quod de corruptibilibus et incorruptibilibus nihil commune dicitur, nisi communitate nominis: et ideo non oportet angelos cum corporalibus

eadem principia communicare, nisi secundum intentionem tantum, prout in omnibus invenitur potentia et actus analogice tamen, ut in XII *Metaphys.* dicitur [text. 26].
Pages **86**, 101, 102

5.5

d. 3, *q.* 1, *a.* 5, *c.*:

. . . quod quidem habet possibilitatem secundum quod de se non habet esse, et complementum prout est quaedam similitudo divini esse, secundum hoc quod appropinquabilis est magis et minus ad participandum divinum esse.
Pages 59, 64, 66

5.6

d. 3, *q.* 1, *a.* 5, *ad* 3:
Dicendum quod genus praedicatur aequaliter de speciebus quantum ad intentionem, sed non semper quantum ad esse, sicut in figura et numero, ut in III *Metaphys.* dicitur. Sed hoc in speciebus non contingit.

5.7

d. 3, *q.* 1, *a.* 6, *ad* 2:
[Intellectus humanus] non habet intellectum ut naturam propriam, sed per quamdam participationem. [See *In IV Sent.*, d. 50, q. 1, a. 1, c.]
Page 63

5.8

d. 12, *q.* 1, *a.* 1, *ad* 1:
Corporeitas secundum intentionem logicam univoce in omnibus corporibus invenitur; sed secundum esse considerata, non potest esse unius rationis in re corruptibili et incorruptibili: quia non similiter se habent in potentia essendi, cum unum sit possibile ad esse et ad non esse, et alterum non; et per modum istum dicit Philosophus in X *Metaphys.* quod de corruptibili et incorruptibili nihil commune dicitur nisi communitate nominis.
Page 101

5.9

d. 13, *q.* 1, *a.* 2, *c.*:

Et hoc quidem videtur magis verum: quia nihil per se sensibile spiritualibus convenit nisi metaphorice, quia quamvis aliquid commune possit inveniri analogice in spiritualibus et corporalibus, non tamen aliquid per se sensibile, ut patet in ente et calore; ens enim non est per se sensibile, quod utrique commune est; calor autem, quod per se sensibile est, in spiritualibus proprie non invenitur. Unde cum lux sit qualitas per se visibilis, et species quaedam determinata in sensibilibus, non potest dici in spiritualibus nisi vel aequivoce vel metaphorice.

Sciendum tamen quod transferuntur corporalia in spiritualia per quamdam similitudinem, quae quidem est similitudo proportionabilitatis; et hanc similitudinem oportet reducere in aliquam communitatem univocationis vel analogiae; et sic est in proposito: dicitur enim lux in spiritualibus illud quod ita se habet ad manifestationem intellectivam sicut se habet lux corporalis ad manifestationem sensitivam.

Page 80

5.10

d. 16, *q.* 1, *a.* 1, *arg.* 3:

Praeterea, in imagine importatur convenientia quaedam cum aliquo uno. . . . Sed quaecumque conveniunt in aliquo uno, habent aliquid prius et simplicius se, sive sit convenientia analogiae, sive univocationis: est enim ens prius substantia et accidente, sicut animal prius homine et equo. Deo autem nihil est prius et simplicius. Ergo non potest esse eius imago in creatura.

5.11

d. 16, *q.* 1, *a.* 1, *arg.* 5:

Item, infinite distantium non potest esse indiscretio et unio. . . . Ergo creatura non potest esse ad imaginem Dei, a quo in infinitum distat.

5.12

d. 16, *q.* 1, *a.* 1, *c.*:

Respondeo dicendum quod imago proprie dicitur quod ad alterius imitationem est: nec tamen quaelibet imitatio rationem imaginis perficit; ut si hoc sit album et illud album, non ex hoc dicitur eius imago: sed ad rationem imaginis exigitur imitatio in aliquo quod speciem exprimat et essentiam. . . . Haec autem imitatio potest esse dupliciter: aut simul quantum ad speciem et signum speciei, et sic imago hominis est in filio suo, qui ipsum in humana specie et figura imitatur, et haec est perfecta imago: aut quantum ad signum tantum, et non quantum ad veritatem speciei, sicut imago hominis est in statua lapidea; et haec est imperfecta imago. Et primo modo filius est imago patris, sicut in natura communicans; secundo autem modo imago Dei est in creaturis; et ideo creatura potest esse imago Dei, licet non perfecta.

Pages 51, 52

5.13

d. 16, *q.* 1, *a.* 1, *ad* 3:

Dicendum quod convenientia potest esse dupliciter: aut duorum participantium aliquod unum, et talis convenientia non potest esse Creatoris et creaturae, ut obiectum est; aut secundum quod unum per se est simpliciter, et alterum participat de similitudine eius quantum potest; ut si poneremus calorem esse sine materia, et ignem convenire cum eo, ex hoc quod aliquid caloris participaret: et talis convenientia esse potest creaturae ad Deum, quia Deus dicitur ens hoc modo quod est ipsum suum esse; creatura vero non est ipsum suum esse, sed dicitur ens, quasi esse participans; et hoc sufficit ad rationem imaginis.

Pages 28, *58*, 95

5.14

d. 16, *q.* 1, *a.* 1, *ad* 4:

Dicendum quod ad rationem imaginis non exigitur aequalitas aequiparantiae, cum magni hominis in parva pictura imago exprimatur; sed exigitur aequalitas proportionis, ut scilicet eadem sit proportio partium ad invicem in imagine quae est in imaginato.

Page *78*

5.15

d. 16, *q.* 1, *a.* 2, *ad* 5:

Proprietates divinae ostenduntur in creaturis dupliciter: vel secundum similitudinem analogiae, sicut vita, sapientia, et huiusmodi, quae analogice Deo et creaturis conveniunt . . . vel secundum similitudinem proportionis,* secundum quod spirituales proprietates corporalibus metaphorice designantur. . . . Sed haec similitudo non facit rationem imaginis, unde Dionysius vocat eam [in 2 cap. *Caelest. Hierar.*] dissimilem similitudinem. [Mandonnet has "proportionalitatis."]

Page 80

5.16

d. 27, *q.* 1, *a.* 2, *ad* 3:

Dicendum quod in definitione accidentis non debet poni nisi subiectum eius. Quamvis autem contingat virtutem in aliqua potentia ut in subiecto esse quae essentialiter mens non est, non tamen habet quod sit subiectum virtutis, nisi inquantum aliquid mentis et rationis participat; unde Philosophus, in I *Ethic.*, cap. ult., dicit quod rationale est subiectum virtutis, vel rationale essentialiter, vel rationale per participationem.

Page 63

5.17

d. 27, *q.* 1, *a.* 3, *c.*:

Est enim duplex aequalitas, scilicet aequalitas quantitatis et aequalitas proportionis.

Page 78

5.18

d. 27, *q.* 1, *a.* 5, *ad* 1:

Non intelligitur commensuratio quantitatis praemii ad principium merendi secundum aequalitatem, sed proportionalitas quaedam.

Page 78

5.19

d. 34, *q.* 1, *a.* 2, *ad* 1:

Dicendum quod genus dupliciter potest accipi. Uno modo proprie, prout praedicatur de pluribus in eo quod quid est, et sic neque bonum neque malum sunt genera, quia sunt de transcendentalibus quia bonum et ens convertuntur. Alio modo communiter, ut genus dicatur omne id quod sua communitate multa ambit et continet, et sic bonum et malum dicuntur genera omnium contrariorum.

5.20

d. 37, q. 1, a. 2, c.:

Dicendum quod ens invenitur in pluribus secundum prius et posterius. Illud tamen verissime et primo dicitur ens cuius esse est ipsum quod est, quia esse eius non est receptum, sed per se subsistens. In omnibus autem quae secundum prius et posterius dicuntur, primum eorum quae sunt, potest esse causa, et per se dictum, est causa eius quod per participationem dicitur; et ideo oportet quod illud ens quod non per participationem alicuius esse quod sit aliud quam ipsum, dicitur ens, quod primum inter entia est, sit causa omnium aliorum entium. Alia autem entia dicuntur per posterius, inquantum aliquod esse participant quod non est idem quod ipsa sunt, et haec procedunt usque ad ultima entium; ita quod quamcumque rationem essendi aliquid habeat, non sit sibi nisi a Deo, sed defectus essendi sit ei a seipso.

   Pages 28, 63

5.21

d. 42, q. 1, a. 3, c.:

Dicendum quod duplex modus dividendi commune in ea quae sub ipso sunt, sicut est duplex communitatis modus. Est enim quaedam divisio univoci in species per differentias quibus aequaliter natura generis in speciebus participatur, sicut animal dividitur in hominem et equum, et huiusmodi; alia vero divisio est eius quod est commune per analogiam, quod quidem secundum perfectam rationem praedicatur de uno dividentium, et de altero imperfecte et secundum quid, sicut ens dividitur in substantiam et accidens, et in ens actu et in ens potentia: et haec divisio est quasi media inter aequivocum et univocum.

   Pages *35-36*, 62, 112

5.22

d. 42, expositio primae partis textus:

Hoc dicitur ad ostendendum quod divisio peccati in mortale et veniale non est univoci divisio: quia sic mortale et veniale dicerentur duae species peccatorum; sed est divisio analogi: et propter hoc dicuntur mortale et veniale esse genera peccatorum, quasi non communicantia unum genus.

6.1 In III Sententiarum (1254-1256) Ed. Moos

d. 1, *q.* 1, *a.* 1, *c.*:

. . . Vel unum analogia seu proportione, sicut substantia et qualitas in ente: quia sicut se habet substantia ad esse sibi debitum, ita et qualitas ad esse sui generis conveniens. . . . In uno autem genere vel specie Deum et creaturam convenire impossibile est; sed per analogiam possibile est.

Pages 27, *99*

6.2

d. 1, *q.* 1, *a.* 1, *ad* 3:

Dicendum quod proportio dicitur dupliciter. Uno modo idem est proportio quod certitudo mensurationis duarum quantitatum. Et talis proportio non potest esse nisi duorum finitorum, quorum unum alterum excedit secundum aliquid certum et determinatum. Alio modo dicitur proportio habitudo ordinis. Sicut dicimus esse proportionem inter materiam et formam, quia materia se habet in ordine ut perficiatur per formam, et hoc secundum proportionalitatem quamdam. Quia sicut forma potest dare esse, ita materia potest recipere idem esse. Et hoc modo etiam movens et motum debent esse proportionalia, et agens et patiens, ut scilicet sicut agens potest imprimere aliquem effectum, ita patiens possit recipere eumdem. Nec oportet ut commensuretur potentia passiva recipientis ad potentiam activam agentis; nec secundum numerum, sicut unus artifex per artem suam potest inducere plures formas, ut formam arcae et formam serrae, sed lignum non potest recipere nisi unam illarum; nec etiam secundum intentionem, quia artifex per artem suam potest producere pulchram sculpturam, quam tamen lignum nodosum non potest pulchram recipere. Et ideo non est inconveniens ut hic modus proportionis inter Deum et creaturam salvetur, quamvis in infinitum distent. Et ideo possibilis est unio utriusque.

Pages 32, *47, 48*, 71, 84, 95, *140*

6.3

d. 4, *q.* 1, *a.* 2, *qa.* 2, *ad* 2:

Dicendum quod Christus dicitur "primogenitus in multis fratribus" secundum humanam naturam, non quasi univoce filius cum aliis, sed per analogiam, quia ipse est filius naturalis propter unionem in persona, alii autem filii adoptivi per assimilationem ad Deum quae est per gratiam.

Pages 50, 71

6.4

d. 27, *q*. 2, *a*. 4, *qa*. 3, *ad* 1:

Alio modo dicitur forma exemplaris ad cuius similitudinem aliquid fit et per cuius participationem esse habet; sicut divina bonitas est forma exemplaris omnis bonitatis, et divina sapientia omnis sapientiae.

Pages 54, 59, 64

6.5

d. 33, *q*. 1, *a*. 1, *qa*. 2, *ad* 1:

Dicendum quod quando aliqua condividuntur, aequaliter recipientia communis praedicationem, tunc unum non ponitur in definitione alterius; sed quando commune praedicatur de eis per prius et posterius, tunc primum ponitur in definitione aliorum, sicut substantia in definitione accidentium.

Pages 33, 65

6.6

d. 33, *q*. 2, *a*. 1, *qa*. 1, *ad* 2:

Dicendum quod ea quae dividunt aliquod commune univocum, simul sunt quantum ad intentionem generis, quamvis unum possit esse causa alterius quantum ad esse, sicut motus localis est causa aliorum motuum contra quos dividitur. Sed ea quae dividunt aliquod commune analogum se habent secundum prius et posterius, etiam quantum ad intentionem communis quod dividitur, sicut patet de substantia et accidente. Unde ex hoc quod una virtus condividitur alteri, non oportet quod una non sit altera principalior.

Pages 65, 69, 71, 112

7.1 In IV Sententiarum (1254-1256) Ed. Moos (to d. 23)

d. 1, *q*. 1, *a*. 4, *qa*. 1, *ad* 4:

Dicendum quod causa univoca vel non univoca, proprie loquendo et simpliciter sunt divisiones illius causae cuius est similitudinem habere cum effectu; hoc autem est principalis agentis et non instrumentalis. . . . Et ideo proprie loquendo, neque instrumentum est causa univoca, neque aequivoca. Posset tamen reduci ad utrumlibet, secundum quod principale agens, in cuius virtute instrumentum agit, est causa univoca vel non univoca.

7.2

d. 1, q. 1, a. 4, qa. 2, c.:
[Instrumenta et] huiusmodi entia consueverunt intentiones nominari et habent aliquid simile cum ente quod est in anima quod est ens diminutum, ut dicitur in VI *Metaphys.*

7.3

d. 1, q. 1, a. 4, qa. 4, c.:
Dicendum quod quia omne agens agit sibi simile, ideo effectus agentis oportet quod aliquo modo sit in agente. In quibusdam enim est idem secundum speciem; et ista dicuntur agentia univoca, sicut calor est in igne calefaciente. In quibusdam vero est idem secundum proportionem sive analogiam, sicut cum sol calefacit. Est enim in sole aliquid quod ita facit eum calefacientem sicut calor facit ignem calidum et secundum hoc calor dicitur esse in sole aequivoce, ut dicitur in libro de *Substantia orbis.*

7.4

d. 15, q. 1, a. 2, c.:
. . . Et hoc etiam est aequale aliqualiter, scilicet secundum proportionalitatem; quia sicut se habet hoc quod Deo esset debitum ad ipsum Deum, ita hoc quod iste potest reddere ad eum. . . . . Unde non potest homo satisfacere, si li "satis" aequalitatem quantitatis importet: contingit autem, si importet aequalitatem proportionis, ut dictum est.
Page 78

7.5

d. 16, q. 3, a. 1, qa. 1, c.:
Et quia in qualibet proportione oportet esse ad minus duos terminos, nihil enim sibi ipsi proportionatur, sed alteri.
Page 99

7.6

d. 41, q. 1, a. 1, qa. 5, c.:
Duplex est modus quo aliquid ex alio procedit. Unus secundum quem procedit in similitudinem speciei, sicut ex homine generatur homo; alius secundum quem procedit dissimile in specie; et hic

processus semper est in inferiorem speciem, ut patet in omnibus agentibus aequivoce.

7.7

d. 45, *q.* 1, *a.* 1, *qa.* 1, *ad* 2:
Duplex est convenientia vel similitudo. Una quae est per participationem eiusdem qualitatis, sicut calida ad invicem conveniunt; et talis convenientia incorporalium ad loca corporalia esse non potest. Alia per quamdam proportionalitatem, secundum quam in Scripturis metaphorae corporalium ad spiritualia transferuntur ut quod dicitur Deus esse sol, quia est principium vitae spiritualis sicut sol vitae corporalis, et secundum hanc convenientiam quaedam animae quibusdam locis magis conveniunt, sicut animae spiritualiter illuminatae cum corporibus luminosis; animae vero obtenebratae per culpam cum locis tenebrosis.
Pages 28, *80*

7.8

d. 49, *q.* 2, *a.* 1, *ad* 2:
. . . Quae est proportio cognitionis nostrae ad entia creata, ea est proportio cognitionis divinae ad suam essentiam.

7.9

d. 49, *q.* 2, *a.* 1, *arg.* 6 *et ad* 6:
Praeterea, cum intelligibile sit perfectio intellectus, oportet esse proportionem aliquam inter intellectum et intelligibile, visibile et visum. Sed non est accipere proportionem aliquam inter intellectum nostrum et essentiam divinam, cum in infinitum distent. Ergo intellectus noster non potest pertingere ad essentiam divinam videndam.

Ad sextum dicendum quod quamvis finiti ad infinitum non possit esse proportio, quia excessus infiniti supra finitum non est determinatus, potest tamen esse inter ea proportionalitas quae est similitudo proportionum; sicut enim finitum aequatur alicui finito, ita infinito infinitum. Ad hoc autem quod aliquid totaliter cognoscatur, quandoque oportet esse proportionem inter cognoscens et cognitum; quia oportet virtutem cognoscentis adaequari cognoscibilitati rei cognitae; aequalitas autem proportio quaedam est. Sed quandoque cognoscibilitas rei excedit virtutem cognoscentis; sicut cum nos cognoscimus Deum, aut e converso, sicut cum ipse cognoscit creaturas; et tunc non oportet esse proportionem inter cog-

noscentem et cognitum, sed proportionalitatem tantum; ut scilicet
sicut se habet cognoscens ad cognoscendum, ita se habeat cognoscibile ad hoc quod cognoscatur; et talis proportionalitas sufficit ad
hoc quod infinitum cognoscatur a finito, et e converso. Vel dicendum quod proportio secundum primam nominis institutionem significat habitudinem quantitatis ad quantitatem secundum aliquem
determinatum excessum vel adaequationem; sed ulterius est translatum ad significandum omnem habitudinem cuiuscumque ad aliud;
et per hunc modum dicimus quod materia debet esse proportionata
ad formam, et hoc modo nihil prohibet intellectum nostrum, quamvis sit finitus, dici proportionatum ad videndum essentiam infinitam; non tamen ad comprehendendum eam; et hoc propter suam
immensitatem.

Pages 32, 48, **87-88**

8.1 Quaestiones quodlibetales, Group I, VII-XI (1256-1259)

IX, (q. 2) a. 3, c.:

Dicendum quod esse dupliciter dicitur, ut patet per Philosophum in
V *Metaphys.* et in quadam Glossa Origenis super principium *Joan.*
Uno modo, secundum quod est copula verbalis significans compo-
sitionem cuiuslibet enuntiationis quam anima facit. . . . Alio modo
esse dicitur actus entis in quantum est ens; idest quo denominatur
aliquid ens actu in rerum natura. . . . Sed hoc esse attribuitur alicui
dupliciter. Uno modo sicut ei quod proprie et vere habet esse vel
est. Et sic attribuitur soli substantiae per se subsistenti: unde quod
vere est, dicitur substantia in I *Phys.* Omnia vero quae non per
se subsistunt, sed in alio et cum alio, sive sunt accidentia, sive
formae substantiales, aut quaelibet partes, non habent esse ita ut
ipsa vere sint, sed attribuitur eis esse alio modo, idest ut quo aliquid est; sicut albedo dicitur esse, non quia ipsa in se subsistat,
sed quia ea aliquid habet esse album.

Pages 40, 65, 70

8.2

X, (q. 8) a. 17, ad 1:

Dicendum quod proportio dupliciter dicitur. Uno modo, proprie,
secundum quod importat quemdam determinatum excessum, et sic
proportio requiritur inter intellectum et intelligibile ad hoc quod
sit cognitio cum comprehensione, qualiter divina essentia nunquam
videbitur ab intellectu creato. Alio modo dicitur communiter pro

qualibet habitudine; et sic infinitum potest habere proportionem ad finitum, si sit perfectio eius, vel aliquam huiusmodi habitudinem habeat ad ipsum. Et talis proportio sufficit ad hoc quod intellectus noster videat divinam essentiam attingendo, non comprehendendo.

Pages 32, 48

9.1 De veritate (1256-1259)

I, 1, *c.*:

Sed enti non potest addi aliquid quasi extranea natura, per modum quo differentia additur generi vel accidens subiecto, quia quaelibet natura essentialiter est ens; unde etiam probat Philosophus in III *Metaphys.* quod ens non potest esse genus, sed secundum hoc aliqua dicuntur "addere" supra ens, in quantum exprimunt ipsius modum qui nomine ipsius "entis" non exprimitur.

9.2

I, 2, *c.*:

Dicendum quod in illis quae dicuntur per prius et posterius de multis, non semper oportet quod id quod per prius recipit praedicationem communis, sit ut causa aliorum, sed illud in quo primo ratio illius communis completa invenitur; sicut sanum per prius dicitur de animali, in quo primo perfecta ratio sanitatis invenitur, quamvis medicina dicatur sana ut effectiva sanitatis. Et ideo, cum verum dicatur de pluribus per prius et posterius, oportet quod de illo per prius dicatur in quo invenitur perfecta ratio veritatis.

Page 69

9.3

I, 4, *sed contra* 5:

Praeterea, Deus comparatur ad res in habitudine triplicis causae: scilicet efficientis, exemplaris et finalis; et propter quamdam appropriationem entitas rerum refertur ad Deum ut ad causam efficientem, veritas ut ad causam exemplarem, bonitas ut ad causam finalem, quamvis etiam singula possint ad singula referri secundum locutionis proprietatem.

Page 54

9.4

I, 4, *c.*:

Dicendum quod sicut ex praedictis [art. 2], patet, veritas proprie invenitur in intellectu humano vel divino, sicut sanitas in animali.

In rebus autem aliis invenitur per relationem ad intellectum, sicut et sanitas dicitur de quibusdam aliis in quantum sunt effectiva vel conservativa sanitatis animalis. Ergo est in intellectu divino quidem veritas proprie et primo; in intellectu vero humano proprie quidem et secundario; in rebus autem improprie et secundario, quia non nisi in respectu ad alterutram duarum veritatum. . . . Si ergo accipiatur veritas proprie dicta secundum quam omnia principaliter vera sunt, sic omnia sunt vera una veritate, id est veritate intellectus divini. . . . Si autem accipiatur veritas proprie dicta, secundum quam res secundario verae dicuntur, sic sunt plurium verorum plures veritates in animabus diversis. Si autem accipiatur veritas improprie dicta, secundum quam omnia dicuntur vera, sic sunt plurium verorum plures veritates; sed unius rei una est tantum veritas.

Denominantur autem res verae a veritate quae est in intellectu divino vel in intellectu humano, sicut denominatur cibus sanus a sanitate quae est in animali, et non sicut a forma inhaerente; sed a veritate quae est in ipsa re (quae nihil est aliud quam entitas intellectui adaequata, vel intellectum sibi adaequans) sicut a forma inhaerente, sicut cibus denominatur sanus a qualitate sua, a qua sanus dicitur.

Page 45

9.5

I, 5, *c*.:

Unde et potest aliquid denominari verum dupliciter: uno modo a veritate inhaerente; alio modo ab extrinseca veritate: et sic denominantur omnes res verae a prima veritate. Et quia veritas quae est in intellectu, mensuratur a rebus ipsis; sequitur quod non solum veritas rei, sed etiam veritas intellectus, vel enuntiationis, quae intellectum significat, a veritate prima denominetur.

Pages 45, 95

9.6

II, 3, *ad* 4:

Dicendum quod aliquid dicitur proportionatum alicui dupliciter. Uno modo quia inter ea attenditur proportio; sicut dicimus quatuor proportionari duobus, quia se habet in dupla proportione ad duo. Alio modo per modum proportionalitatis; ut si dicamus sex et octo esse proportionata, quia sicut sex est duplum ad tria, ita et octo ad quatuor: est enim proportionalitas similitudo proportionum. Et quia in omni proportione attenditur habitudo ad invicem eorum quae proportionari dicuntur secundum aliquem determinatum excessum unius super alterum, ideo impossibile est infinitum aliquod proportionari finito per modum proportionis. Sed in his quae proportionata dicuntur per modum proportionalitatis, non attenditur habitudo eorum ad invicem, sed similis habitudo aliquorum duorum ad alia duo; et sic nihil prohibet proportionatum esse infinitum infinito: quia sicut quoddam finitum est aequale cuidam finito, ita infinitum est aequale alteri infinito. Et secundum hunc modum oportet esse proportionatum medium ei quod per ipsum cognoscitur; ut, scilicet sicut se habet ad aliquid demonstrandum, ita se habeat quod per ipsum cognoscitur ad hoc quod demonstretur; et sic nihil prohibet essentiam divinam esse medium quo creatura cognoscitur.

Pages 31, *86-87*

9.7

II, 3, *ad* 9:

Dicendum quod similitudo aliquorum duorum ad invicem potest dupliciter attendi. Uno modo secundum convenientiam in ipsa natura; et talis similitudo non requiritur inter cognoscens et cognitum; immo videmus quandoque quod, quanto talis similitudo est minor, tanto cognitio est perspicacior; sicut minor est similitudo similitudinis quae est in intellectu ad lapidem, quam illius quae est in sensu, cum sit a materia magis remota; et tamen intellectus perspicacius cognoscit quam sensus. Alio modo quantum ad repraesentationem; et haec similitudo requiritur cognoscentis ad cognitum. Quamvis igitur sit minima similitudo creaturae ad Deum secundum convenientiam in natura; est tamen maxima similitudo secundum quod expressissime divina essentia repraesentat creaturam; et ideo intellectus divinus optime rem cognoscit.

Page 26

9.8

II, 3, *ad* 16:

Unde quantum creatura accedit ad Deum, tantum habet de esse; quantum vero ab eo recedit, tantum habet de non esse. Et quia non accedit ad Deum nisi secundum quod esse finitum participat, distat autem in infinitum.

Pages 28, 59

9.9

II, 11, *c.*:

Unde dicendum est quod nec omnino univoce nec pure aequivoce nomen scientiae de scientia Dei et nostra praedicatur; sed secundum analogiam, quod nihil est aliud dictu quam secundum proportionem. Convenientia enim secundum proportionem potest esse duplex: et secundum hoc duplex attenditur analogiae communitas. Est enim quaedam convenientia inter ipsa quorum est ad invicem proportio, eo quod habent determinatam distantiam vel aliam habitudinem ad invicem, sicut binarius cum unitate, eo quod est eius duplum; convenientia etiam quandoque attenditur duorum ad invicem inter quae non sit proportio, sed magis similitudo duarum ad invicem proportionum, sicut senarius convenit cum quaternario ex hoc quod sicut senarius est duplum ternarii, ita quaternarius binarii. Prima ergo convenientia est proportionis, secunda autem proportionalitatis; unde et secundum modum primae convenientiae invenimus aliquid analogice dictum de duobus quorum unum ad alterum habitudinem habet: sicut ens dicitur de substantia et accidente ex habitudine quam substantia et accidens habent; et sanum dicitur de urina et animali, ex eo quod urina habet aliquam similitudinem ad sanitatem animalis. Quandoque vero dicitur aliquid analogice secundo modo convenientiae; sicut nomen visus dicitur de visu corporali et intellectu, eo quod sicut visus est in oculo, ita intellectus est in mente. Quia ergo in his quae primo modo analogice dicuntur, oportet esse aliquam determinatam habitudinem inter ea quibus est aliquid per analogiam commune, impossibile est aliquid per hunc modum analogiae dici de Deo et creatura; quia nulla creatura habet talem habitudinem ad Deum per quam possit divina perfectio determinari. Sed in alio modo analogiae nulla determinata habitudo attenditur inter ea quibus est aliquid per analogiam commune; et ideo secundum illum modum nihil prohibet aliquod nomen analogice dici de Deo et creatura.

Pages **8-9, 9, 11, 12, 13, 14, 27**, *31*, 47, 84, *89-90*, 112, 126, 131

9.10

II, 11, *ad* 1:

Dicendum quod sicut Dionysius dicit, XI cap. *De div. nomin.*, Deus nullo modo similis creaturis dicendus est, sed creaturae similes possunt dici Deo aliquo modo. Quod enim ad imitationem alicuius

fit, si perfecte id imitetur, simpliciter potest ei simile dici; sed non
e converso, quia homo non dicitur suae imagini similis, sed e converso: si autem imperfecte imitetur, tunc potest dici simile et dissimile id quod imitatur ei ad cuius imitationem fit: simile, secundum quod repraesentat; sed non simile, inquantum a perfecta
repraesentatione deficit. Et ideo sacra Scriptura Deum creaturis esse
similem omnibus modis negat, sed creaturam esse similem Deo
quandoque quidem concedit, quandoque autem negat: concedit,
cum dicit hominem ad similitudinem Dei factum; sed negat, cum
dicit: *Deus, quis similis erit tibi?*

Page 49

9.11

II, 11, *ad* 2:

Dicendum quod Philosophus, in II *Topic.*, ponit duplicem modum
similitudinis. Unum quod invenitur in diversis generibus; et hic
attenditur secundum proportionem vel proportionalitatem, ut
quando alterum se habet ad alterum sicut aliud ad aliud, ut ipse
ibidem dicit. Alium modum in his quae sunt eiusdem generis, ut
quando idem diversis inest. Similitudo autem non requirit comparationem secundum determinatam habitudinem quae primo modo
dicitur, sed solum quae secundo modo; unde non oportet quod
primus modus similitudinis a Deo removeatur respectu creaturae.

Pages **27**, 31, 47, *90*

9.12

II, 11, *ad* 4:

Dicendum quod similitudo quae attenditur ex eo quod aliqua duo
participant unum, vel ex eo quod unum habet aptitudinem determinatam ad aliud, ex qua scilicet ex uno alterum comprehendi
possit per intellectum, diminuit distantiam; non autem similitudo
quae est secundum convenientiam proportionum. Talis enim similitudo similiter invenitur in multum vel parum distantibus; non
enim est maior similitudo proportionalitatis inter duo et unum et
sex et tria, quam inter duo et unum et centum et quinquaginta. Et
ideo infinita distantia creaturae ad Deum similitudinem praedictam
non tollit.

Pages **27**, 28, 31, 47, *58, 90*

9.13

II, 11, *ad* 5:

Dicendum quod enti et non enti aliquid secundum analogiam convenit, quia ipsum non ens, ens dicitur analogice, ut patet in IV *Metaphys.*; unde naturae distantia quae est inter creaturam et Deum, communitatem analogiae impedire non potest.

Page 70

9.14

II, 11, *ad* 6:

Dicendum quod ratio illa procedit de communitate analogiae quae accipitur secundum determinatam habitudinem unius ad alterum: tunc enim oportet quod unum in definitione alterius ponatur, sicut substantia in definitione accidentis; vel aliquid unum in definitione duorum, ex eo quod utraque dicuntur per habitudinem ad unum, sicut substantia in definitione quantitatis et qualitatis.

Page 33

9.15

II, 11, *ad* 7:

Dicendum quod quamvis inter duas species substantiae sit maior convenientia quam inter accidens et substantiam, tamen possibile est ut nomen non imponatur illis speciebus diversis secundum considerationem alicuius convenientiae quae sit inter ea; et tunc erit nomen pure aequivocum; nomen vero quod convenit substantiae et accidenti, potest esse impositum secundum considerationem alicuius convenientiae inter ea, unde non erit aequivocum, sed analogum.

9.16

II, 11, *ad* 8:

Dicendum quod hoc nomen *animal* imponitur non ad significandum figuram exteriorem, in qua pictura imitatur animal verum, sed ad significandum naturam, in qua pictura non imitatur; et ideo nomen animalis de vero et picto aequivoce dicitur; sed nomen scientiae convenit creaturae et Creatori secundum id in quo creatura Creatorem imitatur; et ideo non omnino aequivoce praedicatur de utroque.

Page 52

9.17

III, 1, *c.*:

. . . Tertio modo dicitur forma alicuius illud ad quod aliquid formatur; et haec est forma exemplaris, ad cuius similitudinem aliquid constituitur; et in hac significatione consuetum est nomen ideae accipi, ut idem sit idea quod forma quam aliquid imitatur.

Page 53

9.18

III, 2, *c.*:

Dico ergo quod Deus per intellectum omnia operans, omnia ad similitudinem essentiae suae producit; unde essentia sua est idea rerum; non quidem ut essentia, sed ut est intellecta. Res autem creatae non perfecte imitantur divinam essentiam; unde essentia non accipitur absolute ab intellectu divino ut idea rerum, sed cum proportione creaturae fiendae ad ipsam divinam essentiam, secundum quod deficit ab ea, vel imitatur eam.

Page 26

9.19

III, 6, *ad* 2:

Dicendum quod aliud est esse in Deo, et aliud in cognitione Dei: malum enim non est in Deo, sed est in scientia Dei.

9.20

IV, 1, *c.*:

Dicendum quod nomina imponuntur secundum quod cognitionem de rebus accipimus; et quia ea quae sunt posteriora in natura, sunt ut plurimum prius nota nobis; inde est quod frequenter secundum nominis impositionem aliquando nomen prius in aliquo duorum invenitur in quorum altero res significata per nomen prius existit; sicut patet de nominibus quae dicuntur de Deo et creaturis, ut ens, et bonum, et huiusmodi, quae prius fuerint creaturis imposita, et ex his ad divinam praedicationem translata; quamvis esse et bonum prius inveniantur in Deo.

Page 67

9.21

IV, 1, *ad* 10:

Dicendum quod de his quae dicuntur de Deo et creaturis, quaedam sunt quorum res significatae per prius inveniuntur in Deo quam in creaturis, quamvis nomina prius fuerint creaturis imposita; et talia proprie dicuntur de Deo, ut bonitas et sapientia, et huiusmodi. Quaedam vero sunt quorum res significatae Deo non conveniunt sed aliquid simile illis rebus; et huiusmodi dicuntur metaphorice de Deo, sicut dicimus Deum leonem vel ambulantem.

Page 67

9.22

IV, 4, *ad* 2:

Sed in his quae se habent per modum causae et causati, non invenitur, proprie loquendo, reciprocatio similitudinis: dicimus enim quod imago Herculis similatur Herculi sed non e converso.

Page *49*

9.23

IV, 6, *c.*:

Dicendum quod sicut dicit Dionysius causata deficiunt ab imitatione suarum causarum, quae eis supercollocantur. Et propter istam distantiam causae a causato, aliquid vere praedicatur de causato quod non praedicatur de causa, sicut patet quod delectationes non dicuntur delectari, quamvis sint nobis causae delectandi: quod quidem non contingit nisi quia modus causarum est sublimior quam ea quae de effectibus praedicantur. Et hoc invenimus in omnibus causis aequivoce agentibus; sicut sol non potest dici calidus, quamvis ab eo alia calefiant, quod est propter ipsius solis eminentiam ad ea quae calida dicuntur.

Pages 51, 52, 73, 74

9.24

IV, 6, *ad* 1:

Dicendum quod si intelligatur de veritate praedicationis, simpliciter verum est quod verius est aliquid ubi est per essentiam quam ubi est per similitudinem.

9.25

VII, 7, ad 1:

Dicendum quod quaedam causae sunt nobiliores his quorum sunt causae, scilicet efficiens, formalis, et finalis; et ideo quod est in talibus causis, nobilius est in eis quam in his quorum sunt causae. Sed materia est imperfectior eo cuius est causa; et ideo aliquid est in materia minus nobiliter quam sit in materiato; in materia enim est incomplete et in potentia, et in materiato est actu. Omnis autem dispositio quae praeparat subiectum ad aliquam formam vel perfectionem recipiendam, reducitur ad causam materialem.

Page 74

9.26

VIII, 1, c.:

In omni enim cognitione quae est per similitudinem, modus cognitionis est secundum convenientiam similitudinis ad illud cuius est similitudo; et dico convenientiam secundum repraesentationem. . . . Si autem deficiat etiam a repraesentatione generis, repraesentaret autem secundum convenientiam analogiae tantum; tunc nec etiam secundum rationem generis cognosceretur, sicut si cognosceretur substantia per similitudinem accidentis. Omnis autem similitudo divinae essentiae in intellectu recepta, non potest habere aliquam convenientiam cum essentia divina nisi analogice tantum. Et ideo cognitio quae esset per talem similitudinem non esset ipsius Dei per essentiam, sed multo imperfectior quam si cognosceretur substantia per similitudinem accidentis.

Page 49

9.27

VIII, 1, ad 6:

Dicendum quod proportio, proprie loquendo, nihil est aliud quam habitudo quantitatis ad quantitatem, sicut quod aequalis sit una alteri, vel tripla; et exinde translatum est nomen proportionis, ut habitudo cuiuslibet ad rem alteram proportio nominetur; sicut dicitur materia esse proportionata formae inquantum se habet ad formam ut materia eius, non considerata aliqua habitudine quantitatis. Et similiter intellectus creatus est proportionatus ad videndum divinam essentiam, inquantum se habet ad ipsam quodammodo ut ad formam intelligibilem; quamvis secundum quantitatem virtutis nulla possit esse proportio, propter distantiam infinitam.

Pages 32, 48, 140

9.28

X, 5, *ad* 1:

Cognitio qua cognoscitur materia secundum analogiam quam habet ad formam, non sufficit ad cognitionem rei singularis.

Page *79*

9.29

X, 7, *c.*:

In illa cognitione qua mens temporalia cognoscit, non invenitur expressa similitudo Trinitatis increatae neque secundum conformationem, quia res materiales sunt magis Deo dissimiles quam ipsa mens, unde per hoc quod mens earum scientia informatur, non efficitur Deo magis conformis; similiter neque secundum analogiam, eo quod res temporalis, quae sui notitiam parit in anima, vel intelligentiam actualem, non est eiusdem substantiae cum mente, sed extraneum a natura eius; et sic non potest per hoc increatae Trinitatis consubstantialitas repraesentari.

Sed in cognitione qua mens nostra cognoscit seipsam, est repraesentatio Trinitatis Increatae secundum analogiam. . . . Maior autem est similitudo quae est per conformitatem, ut visus ad colorem, quam quae est per analogiam, ut visus ad intellectum, qui similiter ad sua obiecta comparatur.

9.30

XXI, 4, *c.*:

Specialiter tamen quantum ad propositum pertinet, apparet falsitas praedictae positionis ex hoc quod omne agens invenitur sibi simile agere; unde si prima bonitas sit effectiva omnium bonorum, oportet quod similitudinem suam imprimat in rebus effectis; et sic unumquodque dicetur bonum sicut forma inhaerente per similitudinem summi boni sibi inditam, et ulterius per bonitatem primam, sicut per exemplar et effectivum omnis bonitatis creatae. Quantum ad hoc opinio Platonis sustineri potest.

Pages 28, 45, *55*, **97**

9.31

XXI, 4, *ad* 2:

Dicendum quod dupliciter denominatur aliquid per respectum ad alterum. Uno modo quando ipse respectus est ratio denominationis, sicut urina dicitur sana per respectum ad sanitatem animalis. Ratio enim sani, secundum quod de urina praedicatur, est esse signum sanitatis animalis. Et in talibus, quod denominatur per respectum ad alterum, non denominatur ab aliqua forma sibi inhaerente, sed ab aliquo extrinseco ad quod refertur. Alio modo denominatur aliquid per respectum ad alterum, quando respectus non est ratio denominationis, sed causa sicut si aer dicatur lucens a sole: non quod ipsum referri aerem ad solem sit lucere aeris, sed quia directa oppositio aeris ad solem est causa quod luceat. Et hoc modo creatura dicitur bona per respectum ad bonum; unde ratio non sequitur.

Pages *45-46*

9.32

XXI, 4, *ad* 3:

Dicendum quod Augustinus in multis opinionem Platonis sequitur, quantum fieri potest secundum fidei veritatem; et ideo verba sua sic sunt intelligenda, ut ipsa divina bonitas dicatur esse bonum omnis boni, in quantum est causa efficiens prima et exemplaris omnis boni, sine hoc quod excludatur bonitas creata, qua creaturae denominantur bonae sicut forma inhaerente.

Pages 45, 55

9.33

XXI, 4, *ad* 5:

Dicendum quod similiter distinguendum est de veritate; scilicet quod omnia sunt vera veritate prima sicut exemplari primo, cum tamen sint vera veritate creata sicut forma inhaerente.

Pages 45, 54

9.34

XXI, 5, *c.*:

Ipsa autem natura vel essentia divina est eius esse; natura autem vel essentia cuiuslibet rei creatae non est suum esse, sed esse participans ab alio. Et sic in Deo est esse purum, quia ipse Deus est suum esse subsistens; in creatura autem est esse receptum vel participatum. Unde dico, quod si bonitas absoluta diceretur de re

creata secundum suum esse substantiale, nihilominus adhuc rema-
neret habere bonitatem per participationem, sicut et habet esse participatum.

Pages 28, 61

9.35

XXIII, 7, *ad* 9:
Dicendum quod homo conformatur Deo, cum sit ad imaginem et
similitudinem Dei factus. Quamvis autem propter hoc quod a Deo
in infinitum distat, non possit esse ipsius ad Deum proportio, secundum quod proportio proprie in quantitatibus invenitur, comprehendens duarum quantitatum ad invicem comparatarum certam
mensuram; secundum tamen quod nomen proportionis translatum
est ad quamlibet habitudinem significandam unius rei ad rem
aliam, utpote cum dicimus hic esse proportionum similitudinem,
sicut se habet princeps ad civitatem ita gubernator ad navim, nihil
prohibet dicere aliquam proportionem hominis ad Deum, cum in
aliqua habitudine ipsum ad se habeat, utpote ab eo effectus, et
ei subiectus.

Vel potest dici, quod finiti ad infinitum quamvis non possit
esse proportio proprie accepta, tamen potest esse proportionalitas,
quae est duarum proportionum similitudo: dicimus enim quatuor
esse proportionata duobus, quia sunt eorum dupla; sex vero esse
quatuor proportionabilia, quia sicut se habeat sex ad tria, ita quatuor ad duo. Similiter finitum et infinitum, quamvis non possint
esse proportionata, possunt tamen esse proportionabilia; quia sicut
infinitum est aequale infinito, ita finitum finito. Et per hunc modum
est similitudo inter creaturam et Deum, quia sicut se habet ad ea
quae ei competunt, ita creatura ad sua propria.

Pages **27**, *32*, 47, 48, *91*, 92

9.36

XXIII, 7, *ad* 10:
Dicendum quod creatura non dicitur conformari Deo quasi parti-
cipanti eamdem formam quam ipsa participat, sed quia Deus est
substantialiter ipsa forma, cuius creatura per quamdam imitationem est participativa.

Pages 28, *58*, 64

9.37

XXIII, 7, *ad* 11:

. . . Sed quando forma est in uno principaliter, in altero vero quasi secundario, non recipitur similitudinis reciprocatio; sicut dicimus statuam Herculis similem Herculi, sed non e converso; non enim potest dici quod Hercules habeat formam statuae, sed solum quod statua habeat Herculis formam. Et per hunc modum creaturae dicuntur esse Deo similes et conformes, non tamen e contra. Sed conformatio, cum sit motus ad conformitatem, non importat aequiparantiae relationem, sed praesupponit aliquid ad cuius conformitatem alterum moveatur; unde posteriora prioribus conformantur, sed non e converso.

Pages 49, 70

9.38

XXIV, 10, *ad* 18:

Anselmus venatur communem rationem liberi arbitrii in Deo, angelis et hominibus, secundum quamdam communissimam analogiam; unde non oportet quod quantum ad omnes speciales conditiones similitudo inveniatur.

10.1 In librum Boethii De hebdomadibus (1256-1261)

lectio 2:

Non enim ens dicitur proprie et per se, nisi de substantia, cuius est subsistere. Accidentia enim non dicuntur entia quasi ipsa sint, sed inquantum eis subest aliquid, ut postea dicetur. . . . Est autem participare quasi partem capere; et ideo quando aliquid particulariter recipit id quod ad alterum pertinet, universaliter dicitur participare illud; sicut homo dicitur participare animal, quia non habet rationem animalis secundum totam communitatem; et eadem ratione Socrates participat hominem; similiter etiam subiectum participat accidens, et materia formam, quia forma substantialis vel accidentalis, quae de sui ratione communis est, determinatur ad hoc vel ad illud subiectum; et similiter effectus dicitur participare suam causam, et praecipue quando non adaequat virtutem suae causae; puta, si dicamus quod aer participat lucem solis, quia non recipit eam in ea claritate qua est in sole.

Pages **56**, 65, 131

11.1 Super librum Boethii De Trinitate (1256-1261)
Ed. Decker

q. 1, *a.* 2, *c.*:

Unde relinquitur quod solummodo per effectus formam cognoscatur. Effectus autem est duplex: quidam, qui adaequatur virtuti suae causae, et per talem effectum cognoscitur plenarie virtus causae, et per consequens quidditas ipsius; alius effectus est, qui deficit a praedicta aequalitate, et per talem effectum non potest comprehendi virtus agentis et per consequens nec essentia eius; sed cognoscitur tantum de causa quod est. Et sic se habet cognitio effectus ut principium ad cognoscendum de causa an est, sicut se habet quidditas ipsius causae, cum per suam formam cognoscitur. Hoc autem modo se habet omnis effectus ad Deum. Et ideo non possumus in statu viae pertingere ad cognoscendum de ipso nisi quia est. Et tamen unus cognoscentium quia est alio perfectius cognoscit, quia causa tanto ex effectu perfectius cognoscitur, quanto per effectum magis apprehenditur habitudo causae ad effectum. Quae quidem habitudo in effectu non pertingente ad aequalitatem suae causae attenditur secundum tria, scilicet secundum progressionem effectus a causa et secundum hoc quod effectus consequitur de similitudine suae causae et secundum hoc quod deficit ab eius perfecta consecutione. Et sic tripliciter mens humana proficit in cognitione Dei, quamvis ad cognoscendum quid est non pertingat, sed an est solum. Primo, secundum quod perfectius cognoscitur eius efficacia in producendo res. Secundo, prout nobiliorum effectuum causa cognoscitur, qui cum eius similitudinem aliquam gerant, magis eminentiam eius commendant. Tertio in hoc quod magis ac magis cognoscitur elongatus ab omnibus his, quae in effectibus apparent.

Pages 72, 74

11.2

q. 1, *a.* 2, *ad* 3:

Dicendum quod proportio nihil aliud est quam quaedam habitudo duorum ad invicem convenientium in aliquo, secundum hoc quod conveniunt aut differunt. Possunt autem intelligi esse convenientia dupliciter. Uno modo ex hoc quod conveniunt in eodem genere quantitatis aut qualitatis, sicut habitudo superficiei ad superficiem aut numeri ad numerum, in quantum unum excedit aliud aut aequatur ei, vel etiam caloris ad calorem, et sic nullo modo potest esse proportio inter Deum et creaturam, cum non conveniant in aliquo

genere. Alio modo possunt intelligi convenientia ita quod conveniant in aliquo ordine, et sic attenditur proportio inter materiam et
formam, faciens et factum et alia huiusmodi, et talis proportio requiritur inter potentiam cognoscentem et cognoscibile, cum cognoscibile sit quasi actus potentiae cognoscentis. Et sic etiam est
proportio creaturae ad Deum ut causati ad causam et cognoscentis
ad cognoscibile, sed propter infinitum excessum creatoris super
creaturam non est proportio creaturae ad creatorem, ut recipiat influentiam ipsius secundum totam virtutem eius, neque ut ipsum perfecte cognoscat, sicut ipse se ipsum perfecte cognoscit.

   Pages 32, 47, 48, 70

11.3

q. 1, a. 4, c.:

Quod patet ex hoc quod Deum non cognoscimus in statu viae nisi
ex effectibus, ut ex praedictis patere potest. Et ideo naturali ratione
de Deo cognoscere non possumus nisi hoc quod percipitur de ipso
ex habitudine effectuum ad ipsum, sicut illa quae designant causalitatem ipsius et eminentiam super causata et quae removent ab ipso
imperfectas condiciones effectuum.

   Page 74

11.4

q. 1, a. 4, ad 4:

Dicendum quod quamvis omne aequivocum reducatur ad univocum,
non tamen oportet quod generatio aequivoca reducatur ad generationem univocam, sed ad generans quod est in se univocum. In
rebus enim naturalibus videmus quod generationes aequivocae sunt
priores generationibus univocis, eo quod causae aequivocae habent
influentiam supra totam speciem, non autem causae univocae, sed
solum supra unum individuum, unde sunt quasi instrumenta causarum aequivocarum, sicut corpora inferiora corporum caelestium.

   Page 25

11.5

q. 4, a. 2, c.:

Cum autem genus sit principium cognoscendi, utpote prima diffini-
tionis pars, materia autem secundum se sit ignota, non potest secundum se ex ea accipi diversitas generis, sed solum illo modo, quo
cognoscibilis est. Est autem cognoscibilis dupliciter. Uno modo per

analogiam sive per proportionem, ut dicitur in I *Phys.* Hoc est, ut dicamus illud esse materiam quod hoc modo se habet ad res naturales sicut lignum ad lectum. Alio modo cognoscitur per formam, per quam habet esse in actu.

Page 79

11.6

q. 5, a. 4, c.:

Sicut autem uniuscuiusque determinati generis sunt quaedam communia principia quae se extendunt ad omnia principia illius generis, ita etiam et omnia entia, secundum quod in ente communicant, habent quaedam principia quae sunt principia omnium entium. . . . Omnium autem entium sunt principia communia non solum secundum primum modum, quod appellat Philosophus in XI *Metaphys.* omnia entia habere eadem principia secundum analogiam, sed etiam secundum modum secundum, ut sint quaedam res eaedem numero exsistentes omnium rerum principia.

[See autograph first draft: Unde cum omnia entia conveniant in ente communitate analogiae, oportet quod et principia communia secundum analogiam habeant. Et sic quodammodo sunt eadem omnium principia secundum analogiam, in quantum in unoquoque genere entium est invenire aliquid, quod se habet ad alterum per modum causae efficientis, formalis, finalis, et materialis.]

Page 85

11.7

q. 6, a. 3, c.:

Ad hoc autem quod de aliqua re sciamus quid est, oportet quod intellectus noster feratur in ipsius rei quidditatem sive essentiam vel immediate vel mediantibus aliquibus quae sufficienter eius quidditatem demonstrent. Immediate quidem intellectus noster ferri non potest secundum statum viae in essentiam dei et in alias essentias separatas, quia immediate extenditur ad phantasmata. . . . Unde dicit Dionysius 2 c. *Caelestis hierarchiae* quod "nostra analogia non valet immediate extendi in invisibiles contemplationes." . . . Sensibiles autem naturae intellectae non sufficienter exprimunt essentiam divinam neque etiam alias essentias separatas, cum non sint unius generis naturaliter loquendo et quidditas et omnia huiusmodi nomina fere aequivoce dicantur de sensibilibus et de illis substantiis. . . . Et sic per viam similitudinis non sufficienter illae substantiae ex his innotescunt. Neque etiam per viam causalitatis, quia ea, quae ab illis substantiis inveniuntur effecta in his inferioribus, non sunt effectus adaequantes earum virtutes, ut sic perveniri possit ad sciendum quod quid est de causa. . . . Aliae autem substantiae immateriales creatae sunt quidem in genere, et quamvis logice considerando conveniant cum istis substantiis sensibilibus in genere remoto quod est substantia, naturaliter tamen loquendo non conveniunt in eodem genere, sicut nec etiam corpora caelestia cum istis inferioribus. Corruptibile enim et incorruptibile non sunt unius generis, ut dicitur in X *Metaphys*. Logicus enim considerat absolute intentiones, secundum quas nihil prohibet convenire immaterialia materialibus, et incorruptibilia corruptibilibus. Sed naturalis et philosophus primus considerant essentias secundum quod habent esse in rebus, et ideo ubi inveniunt diversum modum potentiae et actus et per hoc diversum modum essendi, dicunt esse diversa genera.

Pages 101, 102

11.8

q. 6, a. 4, ad 2:

Quaedam vero res sunt, quae non sunt nobis cognoscibiles ex se ipsis, sed per effectus suos. Et si quidem effectus sit adaequans causam, ipsa quidditas effectus accipitur ut principium ad demonstrandum causam esse et ad investigandum quidditatem eius, ex qua iterum proprietates eius ostenduntur. Si autem sit effectus non adaequans causam, tunc effectus accipitur ut principium ad demonstrandum causam esse et aliquas condiciones eius, quamvis quidditas causae sit semper ignota, et ita accidit in substantiis separatis.

Page 72

12.1 In S. Pauli epistolas, lectura (from *In I Corinthians*, cap. 10 on) (1259-1265)

I Cor., cap. 11, *lectio* 1:

Circa primum considerandum est quod ita se habet naturalis ordo rerum quod ea quae sunt inferiora in entibus imitantur ea quae sunt superiora secundum suum posse. Unde etiam naturale agens tamquam superius assimilat sibi patiens.

Page 50

12.2

I Cor., cap. 13, *lectio* 4:

Tertio vero modo cognoscimus nos Deum in vita ista, inquantum
invisibilia Dei per creaturas cognoscimus, ut dicitur *Rom.* c. 1. Et
ita tota creatura est nobis sicut speculum quoddam: quia ex ordine,
et bonitate, et magnitudine quae in rebus a Deo causata sunt, veni-
mus in cognitionem sapientiae, bonitatis, et eminentiae divinae. Et
haec cognitio dicitur visio in speculo. . . .

Inquantum ergo invisibilia Dei per creaturas cognoscimus, dicimur videre per speculum. Inquantum vero illa invisibilia sunt nobis
occulta, videmus in aenigmate.

Page 73

12.3

Ephesios, cap. 3, *lectio* 4:

Nomen alicuius rei nominatae a nobis, dupliciter potest accipi:
quia vel est expressivum aut significativum conceptus intellectus . . .
et sic nomen prius est in creaturis quam in Deo: aut inquantum est
manifestativum quidditatis rei nominatae exterius et sic est prius in
Deo. Unde hoc nomen paternitas secundum quod significat concep-
tionem intellectus nominantis rem, sic per prius invenitur in creaturis quam in Deo; quia per prius creatura innotescit nobis quam
Deus; secundum autem quod significat ipsam rem nominatam, sic
per prius est in Deo quam in nobis; quia certe omnis virtus generativa in nobis est a Deo.

Page 67

12.4

Coloss., cap. 1, *lectio* 4:

. . . Cuius ratio accipitur ex dictis Platonicorum: quia omne quod
convenit alicui convenit tripliciter: quia aut essentialiter, aut participative, aut causaliter. Essentialiter quidem quod convenit rei
secundum proportionem suae naturae; sicut homini rationale. Participative autem quod excedit suam naturam, sed tamen aliquid de
illo participat, sed imperfecte; sicut intellectuale homini, quod est
supra rationale, et est essentiale Angelorum, et idem aliquid participat homo. Causaliter vero quod convenit rei supervenienter, sicut
homini artificialia, quia in eo non sunt sicut in materia, sed per
modum artis. Unumquodque autem denominatur solum ab eo quod

convenit ei essentialiter. Unde homo non dicitur intellectualis nec artificialis, sed rationalis.

Page 63

13.1 Super primam et secundam decretalem (possibly 1259-1268)

1st:

. . . Deus autem excedit magnitudine suae dignitatis omnem creaturam in infinitum; et ideo dicitur immensus, quia nulla est commensuratio vel proportio alicuius creaturae ad ipsum.

13.2

2nd:

Non tamen est idem modus perfectionis humanae et divinae, quia non potest esse tanta similitudo inter Creatorem et creaturam, quin major inveniatur ibi dissimilitudo, propter hoc quod creatura in infinitum distat a Deo.

14.1 De potentia (1259-1268)

II, 5, *ad* 6:

Dicendum quod generatio Filii et productio creaturarum non sunt unius rationis secundum univocationem, sed secundum analogiam tantum.

14.2

III, 4, *ad* 9:

Dicendum quod quamvis inter Deum et creaturam non possit esse similitudo generis vel speciei; potest tamen esse similitudo quaedam analogiae, sicut inter potentiam et actum, et substantiam et accidens. Et hoc dicitur uno modo in quantum res creatae imitantur suo modo ideam divinae mentis, sicut artificiata formam quae est in mente artificis. Alio modo secundum quod res creatae ipsi naturae divinae quodammodo similantur, prout a primo ente alia sunt entia, et a bono bona, et sic de aliis.

Page 26

14.3

III, 5, *c.*:

Secunda ratio est quia, cum aliquid invenitur a pluribus diversimode participatum oportet quod ab eo in quo perfectissime invenitur, attribuatur omnibus illis in quibus imperfectius invenitur. . . .

. . . Unde oportet quod ab uno illo ente omnia alia sint, quaecumque non sunt suum esse, sed habent esse per modum participationis.
Pages *61*, 63, 66

14.4

III, 5, *ad* 1:
Dicendum quod licet causa prima, quae Deus est, non intret essentiam rerum creaturarum; tamen esse, quod rebus creatis inest, non
potest intelligi nisi ut deductum ab esse divino; sicut nec proprius
effectus potest intelligi nisi ut deductus a causa propria.
Page 33

14.5

III, 16, *ad* 12:
Creaturae vero non perfecte imitantur suum exemplar. Unde diver-
simode possunt ipsum imitari, et sic esse diversa exemplata.
Page 54

14.6

III, 16, *ad* 13:
Intelliguntur creaturae diversimode formam divini intellectus imi-
tari.
Page 52

14.7

VI, 6, *ad* 5:
Dicendum quod secundum Philosophum etiam in causis formalibus
prius et posterius invenitur; unde nihil prohibet unam formam per
alterius formae participationem formari; et sic ipse Deus, qui est
esse tantum, est quodammodo species omnium formarum subsisten-
tium quae esse participant et non sunt suum esse.
Page 61

14.8

VII, 1, *ad* 8:
Dicendum quod forma effectus invenitur aliter in agente naturali,
et aliter in agente per artem. In agente namque per naturam, invenitur forma effectus secundum quod agens in sua natura assimilat sibi
effectum, eo quod omne agens agit sibi simile. Quod quidem contingit dupliciter: quando enim effectus perfecte assimilatur agenti,

utpote adaequans agentis virtutem, tunc forma effectus est in agente
secundum eamdem rationem, ut patet in agentibus univocis, ut cum
ignis generat ignem; quando vero effectus non perfecte assimilatur
agenti, utpote non adaequans agentis virtutem, tunc forma effectus
est in agente non secundum eamdem rationem, sed sublimiori
modo; ut patet in agentibus aequivocis, ut cum sol generat ignem.

In agentibus autem per artem, formae effectuum praeexistunt
secundum eamdem rationem, non autem eodem modo essendi, nam
in effectibus habent esse materiale, in mente vero artificis habent
esse intelligibile.

Pages 72, 74

14.9

VII, 3, *ad* 4:

Ens enim non potest esse alicuius genus, ut probat Philosophus cum
nihil possit addi ad ens quod non participet ipsum; differentia vero
non debet participare genus.

14.10

VII, 5, *sed contra* 3:

Praeterea, omne quod dicitur per participationem, reducitur ad aliquid per se et essentialiter dictum. Sed praedicta nomina de creaturis dicuntur per participationem. Ergo cum reducantur in Deum
sicut in causam primam, oportet quod de Deo dicantur essentialiter;
et ita sequitur quod significent eius substantiam.

Page 60

14.11

VII, 5, *c.*:

Cum omne agens agat in quantum actu est, et per consequens agat
aliqualiter simile, oportet formam facti aliquo modo esse in agente:
diversimode tamen: quia quando effectus adaequat virtutem agentis,
oportet quod secundum eamdem rationem sit illa forma in faciente
et in facto; tunc enim faciens et factum coincidunt in idem specie,
quod contingit in omnibus univocis: homo enim generat hominem,
et ignis ignem. Quando vero effectus non adaequat virtutem agentis,
forma non est secundum eamdem rationem in agente et facto, sed
in agente eminentius; secundum enim quod est in agente habet
agens virtutem ad producendum effectum. Unde si tota virtus
agentis non exprimitur in facto, relinquitur quod modus quo forma

est in agente excedit modum quo est in facto. Et hoc videmus in omnibus agentibus aequivocis, sicut cum sol generat ignem.

. . . Nulla ergo forma alicuius effectus divini est per eamdem rationem, qua est in effectu, in Deo: nihilominus oportet quod sit ibi per quemdam modum altiorem; et inde est quod omnes formae quae sunt in diversis effectibus distinctae et divisae ad invicem, in eo uniuntur sicut in una virtute communi, sicut etiam omnes formae per virtutem solis in istis inferioribus productae, sunt in sole secundum unicam eius virtutem, cui omnia generata per actionem solis secundum suas formas similantur.

Et similiter perfectiones rerum creatarum assimilantur Deo secundum unicam et simplicem essentiam eius.

Pages 71-72, 74

14.12

VII, 5, ad 2:
[Ea nomina] Deo autem conveniunt sublimiori modo. . . . Rursum quia sapientia non negatur de Deo quia ipse deficiat a sapientia, sed quia supereminentius est in ipso.

Pages 73, 74

14.13

VII, 5, ad 8:
[Esse, vivere, et intelligere et huiusmodi] dicuntur de Deo, immo per prius de ipso et eminentius quam de creaturis.

Pages 67, 73

14.14

VII, 6, c.:
Sed illa virtus (causandi) est quaedam supereminens similitudo sui effectus, sicut et quaelibet virtus agentis aequivoci.

Pages 71, 73

14.15

VII, 7, ar. 7:
Praeterea, omne agens aequivocum reducitur ad aliquid univocum.

14.16

VII, 7, sed contra 1:
Est quod Philosophus dicit quod aeterno et temporali nihil est commune nisi nomen. Sed Deus est aeternus, et creaturae temporales.

Ergo Deo et creaturis nihil potest esse commune nisi nomen; et sic praedicantur aequivoce pure nomina de Deo et creaturis.

Pages 101, 102

14.17

VII, 7, sed contra 2:

Praeterea, cum genus sit prima pars definitionis, ablato genere removetur significata ratio per nomen; unde si aliquod nomen imponatur ad significandum id quod est in alio, erit nomen aequivocum. Sed sapientia dicta de creatura est in genere qualitatis. Cum ergo sapientia dicta de Deo non sit qualitas, ut supra ostensum est, videtur quod hoc nomen sapientia aequivoce praedicetur de Deo et creaturis.

14.18

VII, 7, sed contra 3:

Praeterea, ubi nulla est similitudo, ibi non potest aliquid communiter praedicari, nisi aequivoce. Sed inter creaturam et Deum nulla est similitudo.

14.19

VII, 7, sed contra 4:

Sed dicendum quod licet Deus non possit dici similis creaturae, creatura tamen potest dici similis Deo.

Page 49

14.20

VII, 7, c.:

Et praeterea ens non dicitur univoce de substantia et accidente, propter hoc quod substantia est ens tamquam per se habens esse, accidens vero tamquam cuius esse est inesse. Ex quo patet quod diversa habitudo ad esse impedit univocam praedicationem entis. Deus autem alio modo se habet ad esse quam aliqua alia creatura; nam ipse est suum esse, quod nulli alii creaturae competit. Unde nullo modo univoce de Deo et creatura dicitur. . . .

. . . Et praeterea oportet causatum esse aliqualiter simile causae; unde oportet de causato et causa nihil pure aequivoce praedicari, sicut sanum de medicina et animali.

Et ideo aliter dicendum est, quod de Deo et creatura nihil praedicetur univoce; non tamen ea quae communiter praedicantur, pure aequivoce praedicantur, sed analogice. Huius autem praedicationis duplex est modus. Unus quo aliquid praedicatur de duobus per respectum ad aliquod tertium, sicut ens de qualitate et quantitate per respectum ad substantiam. Alius modus est quo aliquid praedicatur de duobus per respectum unius ad alterum, sicut ens de substantia et quantitate.

In primo autem modo praedicationis oportet esse aliquid prius duobus, ad quod ambo respectum habent, sicut substantia ad quantitatem et qualitatem; in secundo autem non, sed necesse est unum esse prius altero. Et ideo cum Deo nihil sit prius, sed ipse sit prior creatura, competit in divina praedicatione secundus modus analogiae, et non primus.

Pages 75, 96, 126

14.21

VII, 7, *ad* 2:
Dicendum quod similitudo creaturae ad Deum deficit a similitudine univocorum in duobus. Primo, quia non est per participationem unius formae, sicut duo calida secundum participationem unius caloris; hoc enim quod de Deo et creaturis dicitur, praedicatur de Deo per essentiam, de creatura vero per participationem; ut sic talis similitudo creaturae ad Deum intelligatur, qualis est calidi ad calorem, non qualis calidi ad calidius. Secundo, quia ipsa forma in creatura participata deficit a ratione eius quod Deus est, sicut calor ignis deficit a ratione virtutis solaris, per quam calorem generat.

Pages 62, 74

14.22

VII, 7, *ad* 3:
Dicendum quod magis et minus tripliciter potest considerari, et sic praedicari. Uno modo secundum solam quantitatem participati; sicut nix dicitur albior pariete, quia perfectior est albedo in nive quam in pariete, sed tamen unius rationis; unde talis diversitas secundum magis et minus non diversificat speciem. Alio modo secundum quod unum participatur, et aliud per essentiam dicitur; sicut diceremus, quod bonitas est melior quam bonum. Tertio modo secundum quod modo eminentiori competit idem aliquid uni quam alteri, sicut calor soli quam igni; et hi duo modi impediunt unitatem speciei et univocam praedicationem; et secundum hoc aliquid praedicatur magis et minus de Deo et creatura, ut ex dictis patet.

Pages 22, 62-63, 73

14.23

VII, 7, ad 5:

Dicendum quod quanto species intelligibilis eminentior est in aliquo, tanto ex ea relinquitur perfectior cognitio; sicut ex specie lapidis in intellectu quam in sensu. Unde per hoc Deus perfectissime potest cognoscere res per suam essentiam, inquantum sua essentia est supereminens similitudo rerum, et non adaequata.

Pages 49, 73

14.24

VII, 7, ad 6:

Dicendum quod inter creaturam et Deum est duplex similitudo. Una creaturae ad intellectum divinum; et sic forma intellecta per Deum est unius rationis cum re intellecta, licet non habeat eumdem modum essendi; quia forma intellecta est tantum in intellectu, forma autem creaturae est etiam in re. Alio modo secundum quod ipsa divina essentia est omnium rerum similitudo superexcellens, et non unius rationis. Et ex hoc modo similitudinis contingit quod bonum et huiusmodi praedicantur communiter de Deo et creaturis, non autem ex primo. Non enim haec est ratio Dei cum dicitur, Deus est bonus, quia bonitatem creaturae intelligit, cum iam ex dictis pateat quod nec etiam domus quae est in mente artificis cum domo quae est in materia univoce dicatur domus.

Pages 49, 74

14.25

VII, 7, ad 7:

Dicendum quod agens aequivocum oportet esse prius quam agens univocum, quia agens univocum non habet causalitatem super totam speciem, alias esset causa sui ipsius, sed solum super aliquod individuum speciei; agens autem aequivocum habet causalitatem super totam speciem; unde oportet primum agens esse aequivocum.

Page 25

14.26

VII, 7, ad 1 *in contraria*:

Dicendum quod Philosophus loquitur de communitate naturaliter et non logice. Ea vero quae habent diversum modum essendi, non communicant in aliquo secundum esse quod considerat naturalis; possunt tamen communicare in aliqua intentione quam considerat

logicus. Et praeterea etiam secundum naturalem corpus elementare
et caeleste non sunt unius generis; sed secundum logicum sunt. Ni·
hilominus tamen Philosophus non intendit excludere analogicam
communitatem, sed solum univocam. Vult enim ostendere quod corruptibile et incorruptibile non communicant in genere.

Pages *101*, 102, 112

14.27

VII, 7, ad 2 in contrarium:
Dicendum quod licet diversitas generis tollat univocationem, non
tamen tollit analogiam. Quod sic patet. Sanum enim, secundum
quod dicitur de urina, est in genere signi; secundum vero quod
dicitur de medicina, est in genere causae.

14.28

VII, 7, ad 3 in contrarium:
Dicendum quod Deus nullo modo dicitur esse similis creaturae, sed
e contrario, quia, ut dicit Dionysius, in causa et causatis non recipi-
mus similitudinis conversionem, sed solum in coordinatis; homo
enim non dicitur similis suae imagini, sed e contrario, propter hoc
quod forma illa secundum quam attenditur similitudo, per prius est
in homine quam in imagine. Et ideo Deum creaturis similem non
dicimus, sed e contrario.

Page 49

14.29

VII, 7, ad 4 in contrarium:
Dicendum quod cum dicitur, nulla creatura est similis Deo, ut
eodem cap. dicit Dionysius, hoc intelligendum est secundum quod
causata minus habent a sua causa, ab ipsa incomparabiliter defi-
cientia. Quod non est intelligendum secundum quantitatem participati, sed aliis duobus modis, sicut supra dictum est.

Page 74

14.30

IX, 7, c.:
Sapientia et vita et alia huiusmodi non removentur a Deo quasi ei
desint, sed quia excellentius habet ea quam intellectus humanus
capere, vel sermo significare possit; et ex illa perfectione divina
descendunt perfectiones creatae, secundum quamdam similitudinem
imperfectam. Et ideo de Deo, secundum Dionysium, non solum dici-

tur aliquid per modum negationis et per modum causae, sed etiam
per modum eminentiae.

Page 74

14.31

IX, 7, ad 2:

Dicendum quod licet in remotione quorumdam a Deo, sit cointel-
ligenda praedicatio eorumdem de Deo per eminentiam et per causam, tamen quaedam solummodo negantur de Deo et nullo modo
praedicantur.

Page 74

14.32

X, 2, ad 10:

Dicendum quod cum dicitur in divinis processio per modum naturae vel voluntatis, non ponitur in Deo modus qui sit qualitas divinae substantiae superaddita, sed ostenditur similitudinis cuiusdam
comparatio inter processiones divinas et processiones quae sunt in
rebus creatis.

Page 84

15.1 Summa contra gentiles (1261-1264) Ed. Leonine

I, cap. 22:

Amplius. Omnis res est per hoc quod habet esse. Nulla igitur res
cuius essentia non est suum esse, est per essentiam suam, sed participatione alicuius, scilicet ipsius esse. Quod autem est per participationem alicuius, non potest esse primum ens: quia id quod aliquid
participat ad hoc quod sit, est eo prius. Deus autem est primum ens,
quo nihil est prius. Dei igitur essentia est suum esse.

Page 60

15.2

I, cap. 29:

Effectus enim a suis causis deficientes non conveniunt cum eis in
nomine et ratione, necesse est tamen aliquam inter ea similitudinem
inveniri: de natura enim actionis est ut agens sibi simile agat, cum
unumquodque agat secundum quod actu est. Unde forma effectus in
causa excedente invenitur quidem aliqualiter, sed secundum alium
modum et aliam rationem, ratione cuius causa aequivoca dicitur.
Sol enim in corporibus inferioribus calorem causat agendo secundum quod actu est; unde oportet quod calor a sole generatus ali-

qualem similitudinem obtineat ad virtutem activam solis, per quam
calor in istis inferioribus causatur, ratione cuius sol calidus dicitur,
quamvis non una ratione. Et sic sol omnibus illis similis aliqualiter
dicitur in quibus suos effectus efficaciter inducit: a quibus tamen
rursus omnibus dissimilis est, inquantum huiusmodi effectus non
eodem modo possident calorem et huiusmodi quo in sole invenitur.
Ita etiam et Deus omnes perfectiones rebus tribuit, ac per hoc cum
omnibus similitudinem habet et dissimilitudinem simul. . . .

Secundum tamen hanc similitudinem convenientius dicitur Deo
creatura similis quam e converso. Simile enim alicui dicitur quod
eius possidet qualitatem vel formam. Quia igitur id quod in Deo
perfecte est, in rebus aliis per quandam deficientem participationem
invenitur, illud secundum quod similitudo attenditur, Dei quidem
simpliciter est, non autem creaturae. Et sic creatura habet quod Dei
est: unde et Deo recte similis dicitur. Non autem sic potest dici
Deum habere quod creaturae est.

Pages 49, *61*, 70, 71, 74

15.3

I, cap. 30:

Quia enim omnem perfectionem creaturae est in Deo invenire sed
per alium modum eminentiorem, quaecumque nomina absolute per·
fectionem absque defectu designant, de Deo praedicantur et de aliis
rebus: sicut est bonitas, sapientia, esse, et huiusmodi. . . .

Modus autem supereminentiae quo in Deo dictae perfectiones
inveniuntur, per nomina a nobis imposita significari non potest nisi
vel per negationem, sicut cum dicimus Deum aeternum vel infini·
tum; vel etiam per relationem ipsius ad alia, ut cum dicitur prima
causa, vel summum bonum.

Page 73

15.4

I, cap. 31:

Sic enim omnes perfectiones in rebus aliis inventas Deo attribui
diximus sicut effectus in suis causis aequivocis inveniuntur. Qui
quidem effectus in suis causis sunt virtute, ut calor in sole. Virtus
autem huiusmodi nisi aliqualiter esset de genere caloris, sol per eam
agens non sibi simile generaret. Ex hac igitur virtute sol calidus
dicitur, non solum quia calorem facit, sed quia virtus per quam
hoc facit, est aliquid conforme calori. Per eandem autem virtutem

per quam sol facit calorem, facit et multos alios effectus in inferioribus corporibus, utpote siccitatem. Et sic calor et siccitas, quae in igne sunt qualitates diversae, soli attribuuntur per unam virtutem. Ita et omnium perfectiones, quae rebus aliis secundum diversas formas conveniunt, Deo secundum unam eius virtutem attribui est necesse. Quae item virtus non est aliud a sua essentia: cum ei nihil accidere possit, ut probatum est. Sic igitur sapiens Deus dicitur non solum secundum hoc quod sapientiam efficit, sed quia, secundum quod sapientes sumus, virtutem eius, qua sapientes nos facit, aliquatenus imitamur.—Non autem dicitur lapis, quamvis lapides fecerit, quia in nomine lapidis intelligitur modus determinatus essendi, secundum quem lapis a Deo distinguitur. Imitatur autem lapis Deum ut causam secundum esse, secundum bonitatem, et alia huiusmodi, sicut et aliae creaturae.

Pages 52, 71

15.5

I, cap. 32:

Amplius. Omne quod de pluribus praedicatur univoce, secundum participationem cuilibet eorum convenit de quo praedicatur: nam species participare dicitur genus, et individuum speciem. De Deo autem nihil dicitur per participationem; nam omne quod participatur determinatur ad modum participati, et sic partialiter habetur et non secundum omnem perfectionis modum. Oportet igitur nihil de Deo et rebus aliis univoce praedicari.

Adhuc. Quod praedicatur de aliquibus secundum prius et posterius, certum est univoce non praedicari: nam prius in definitione posterioris includitur; sicut substantia in definitione accidentis secundum quod est ens. Si igitur diceretur univoce ens de substantia et accidente, oporteret quod substantia etiam poneretur in definitione entis secundum quod de substantia praedicatur. Quod patet esse impossibile. Nihil autem de Deo et rebus aliis praedicatur eodem ordine, sed secundum prius et posterius: cum de Deo omnia praedicentur essentialiter, dicitur enim ens quasi ipsa essentia, et bonus quasi ipsa bonitas; de aliis autem praedicationes fiunt per participationem, sicut Socrates dicitur homo non quia sit ipsa humanitas, sed humanitatem habens.

Pages *33*, 58, 60, 61, 63, *66*

15.6

I, cap. 33:

Nam in his quae sunt a casu aequivoca, nullus ordo aut respectus attenditur unius ad alterum sed omnino per accidens est quod unum nomen diversis rebus attribuitur; non enim nomen impositum uni significat ipsum habere ordinem ad aliud. Sic autem non est de nominibus quae de Deo dicuntur et creaturis. Consideratur enim in huiusmodi nominum communitate ordo causae et causati, ut ex dictis patet. . . .

Rerum autem ad Deum est aliquis modus similitudinis, ut ex supra dictis patet.

15.7

I, cap. 34:

Sic igitur ex dictis relinquitur quod ea quae de Deo et rebus aliis dicuntur, praedicantur neque univoce neque aequivoce, sed analogice: hoc est, secundum ordinem vel respectum ad aliquid unum.

Quod quidem dupliciter contingit. Uno modo, secundum quod multa habent respectum ad aliquid unum: sicut secundum respectum ad unam sanitatem animal dicitur sanum ut eius subiectum, medicina ut eius effectivum, cibus ut conservativum, urina ut signum.

Alio modo, secundum quod duorum attenditur ordo vel respectus, non ad aliquid alterum, sed ad unum ipsorum: sicut ens de substantia et accidente dicitur secundum quod accidens ad substantiam respectum habet, non quod substantia et accidens ad aliquid tertium referantur.

Huiusmodi igitur nomina de Deo et rebus aliis non dicuntur analogice secundum primum modum, oporteret enim aliquid Deo ponere prius: sed modo secundo.

In huiusmodi autem analogica praedicatione ordo attenditur idem secundum nomen et secundum rem quandoque, quandoque vero non idem. Nam ordo nominis sequitur ordinem cognitionis: quia est signum intelligibilis conceptionis. Quando igitur id quod est prius secundum rem, invenitur etiam cognitione prius, idem invenitur prius et secundum nominis rationem et secundum rei naturam: sicut substantia est prior accidente et natura, inquantum substantia est causa accidentis; et cognitione, inquantum substantia in definitione accidentis ponitur. Et ideo ens dicitur prius de substantia quam de accidente et secundum rei naturam et secundum

nominis rationem.—Quando vero id quod est prius secundum naturam, est posterius secundum cognitionem, tunc in analogicis non
est idem ordo secundum rem et secundum nominis rationem: sicut
virtus sanandi quae est in sanativis, prior est naturaliter sanitate
quae est in animali, sicut causa effectu; sed quia hanc virtutem per
effectum cognoscimus, ideo etiam ex effectu nominamus. Et inde est
quod sanativum est prius ordine rei, sed animal dicitur per prius
sanum secundum nominis rationem.

Sic igitur, quia ex rebus aliis in Dei cognitionem pervenimus,
res nominum de Deo et rebus aliis dictorum per prius est in Deo
secundum suum modum, sed ratio nominis per posterius. Unde et
nominari dicitur a suis causatis.

Pages **11, 15**, 96, 126

15.8

I, cap. 38:

Id quod est participare aliquid potest, ipsum autem esse nihil: quod
enim participat potentia est, esse autem actus est. Sed Deus est
ipsum esse, ut probatum est. Non est igitur bonus participative, sed
essentialiter.

Page 60

15.9

I, cap. 40:

Item. Quod per participationem dicitur aliquale, non dicitur tale
nisi inquantum habet quandam similitudinem eius quod per essentiam dicitur; sicut ferrum dicitur ignitum inquantum quandam
similitudinem ignis participat. Sed Deus est bonus per essentiam,
omnia vero alia per participationem, ut ostensum est. Igitur nihil
dicetur bonum nisi inquantum habet aliquam similitudinem divinae
bonitatis. Est igitur ipse bonum omnis boni.

See I, cap. 75:

Omne autem aliud esse est quaedam sui esse secundum similitudinem participatio, ut ex praedictis aliquatenus patet.

Pages 60, 64

15.10

I, cap. 43:

Omnis actus alteri inhaerens terminationem recipit ex eo in quo
est: quia quod est in altero, est in eo per modum recipientis. Actus

igitur in nullo existens nullo terminatur: puta, si albedo esset per se existens, perfectio albedinis in ea non terminaretur, quominus haberet quicquid de perfectione albedinis haberi potest. Deus autem est actus nullo modo in alio existens: quia nec est forma in materia, ut probatum est; nec esse suum inhaeret alicui formae vel naturae, cum ipse sit suum esse, ut supra ostensum est. Relinquitur igitur ipsum esse infinitum. . . .

Ipsum esse absolute consideratum infinitum est: nam ab infinitis et infinitis modis participari possibile est. Si igitur alicuius esse sit finitum, oportet quod limitetur esse illud per aliquid aliud quod sit aliqualiter causa illius esse. . . .

Omne quod habet aliquam perfectionem, tanto est perfectius quanto illam perfectionem plenius participat. Sed non potest esse aliquis modus, nec etiam cogitari, quo plenius habeatur aliqua perfectio quam ab eo quod per suam essentiam est perfectum et cuius esse est sua bonitas. Hoc autem Deus est.

Pages **28**, 59, 64, 75

15.11

I, cap. 80:
Omnia, inquantum sunt, assimilantur Deo, qui est primo et maxime ens.

Pages 50, 138

15.12

I, cap. 84:
Sicut supra ostensum est, Deus, volendo suum esse, quod est sua bonitas, vult omnia alia inquantum habent eius similitudinem. Secundum hoc autem quod aliquid repugnat rationi entis inquantum huiusmodi, non potest in eo salvari similitudo primi esse, scilicet divini, quod est fons essendi.

15.13

I, cap. 93:
Omnia quae a Deo esse accipiunt, necesse est ut ipsius similitudinem gerant, inquantum sunt, et bona sunt, et proprias rationes in divino intellectu habent, ut supra ostensum est.

15.14

II, cap. 15:

. . . Oportet igitur quod ab illo cui nihil est causa essendi, sit omne illud quod quocumque modo est. Deum autem supra ostendimus huiusmodi ens esse, cui nihil sit causa essendi. Ab eo igitur est omne quod quocumque modo est.—Si autem dicatur quod ens non est praedicatum univocum, nihil minus praedicta conclusio sequitur. Non enim de multis aequivoce dicitur, sed per analogiam: et sic oportet fieri reductionem in unum. . . .

Item. Quod per essentiam dicitur, est causa omnium quae per participationem dicuntur: sicut ignis est causa omnium ignitorum inquantum huiusmodi. Deus autem est ens per essentiam suam: quia est ipsum esse. Omne autem aliud ens est ens per participationem: quia ens quod sit suum esse, non potest esse nisi unum, ut in Primo ostensum est.

Page 60

15.15

II, cap. 46:

Ostensum est autem quod Deus in se omnes creaturas comprehendit. Et hoc repraesentatur in corporalibus creaturis, licet per alium modum: semper enim invenitur superius corpus comprehendens et continens inferius; tamen secundum extensionem quantitatis; cum Deus omnes creaturas simplici modo, et non quantitatis extensione, contineat. Ut igitur nec in hoc modo continendi Dei imitatio creaturis deesset, factae sunt creaturae intellectuales.

Page 52

15.16

II, cap. 53:

Omne participans aliquid comparatur ad ipsum quod participatur ut potentia ad actum: per id enim quod participatur fit participans actu tale. Ostensum autem est supra quod solus Deus est essentialiter ens, omnia autem alia participant ipsum esse. Comparatur igitur substantia omnis creata ad suum esse sicut potentia ad actum.

Page 60

15.17

II, cap. 98:

In causis autem non univocis similitudo effectus est in causa eminentius, causae autem in effectu inferiori modo.

Pages *71*, 73, 75

15.18

III, cap. 19:

Secundum hoc autem esse habent omnia quod Deo assimilantur, qui
est ipsum esse subsistens: cum omnia sint solum quasi esse participantia.

. . . Res omnes creatae sunt quaedam imagines primi agentis,
scilicet Dei: agens enim agit sibi simile. Perfectio autem imaginis
est ut repraesentet suum exemplar per similitudinem ad ipsum: ad
hoc enim imago constituitur.

Pages *53*, 61

15.19

III, cap. 20:

Ostensum est enim in Secundo quod nulla substantia creata est
ipsum suum esse. Unde, si secundum quod res quaelibet est, bona
est; non est autem earum aliqua suum esse: nulla earum est sua
bonitas, sed earum quaelibet bonitatis participatione bona est, sicut
et ipsius esse participatione est ens. . . . Divina igitur substantia sua
bonitas est; substantia vero simplex bonitatem participat secundum
id quod est; substantia autem composita secundum aliquid sui.

Page 61

15.20

III, cap. 54:

Proportio autem intellectus creati est quidem ad Deum intelligendum, non secundum commensurationem aliquam proportione exis-
tente, sed secundum quod proportio significat quamcumque habitudinem unius ad alterum, ut materiae ad formam, vel causae ad
effectum. Sic autem nihil prohibet esse proportionem creaturae ad
Deum secundum habitudinem intelligentis ad intellectum, sicut et
secundum habitudinem effectus ad causam.

Pages 32, *48*, 66, 140

15.21

III, cap. 66:

Praeterea. Quod est per essentiam tale, est propria causa eius quod est per participationem tale: sicut ignis est causa omnium ignitorum. Deus autem solus est ens per essentiam suam, omnia autem alia sunt entia per participationem: nam in solo Deo esse est sua essentia.

Page *60*

15.22

III, cap. 97:

Quia vero omnem creatam substantiam a perfectione divinae bonitatis deficere necesse est, ut perfectius divinae bonitatis similitudo rebus communicaretur, oportuit esse diversitatem in rebus, ut quod perfecte ab uno aliquo repraesentari non potest, per diversa diversimode perfectiori modo repraesentaretur.

Pages 50, *64,* 74

15.23

IV, cap. 21:

Sciendum tamen est quod ea quae a Deo in nobis sunt, reducuntur in Deum sicut in causam efficientem et exemplarem. In causam quidem efficientem, inquantum virtute operativa divina aliquid in nobis efficitur. In causam quidem exemplarem, secundum quod id quod in nobis a Deo est, aliquo modo Deum imitatur.

Page 54

16.1 Responsio ad Joannem Vercellensem (1264-1266)

q. 1:

Intellectus autem noster Deum comprehendere non potest, nec ipsum in essentia sua videre in statu viae, sed aliqualiter ex rebus creatis ipsum cognoscit. Diversae autem perfectiones rerum creatarum, puta sapientia, voluntas, et huiusmodi, repraesentant quidem imperfecte divinam perfectionem: ex hoc enim quod aliqua creatura est sapiens, aliqualiter accedit ad divinam similitudinem; similiter ex hoc quod est potens, et ex hoc quod est volens; ita tamen quod quidquid perfectionis seu nobilitatis competit creaturae, etiam Deo competit, qui est creaturarum causa effectiva aequivoca. Sed tamen haec diversa eminentius competunt Deo secundum simplicem essentiam suam. Et similiter intellectus noster ex rebus creatis scientiam accipiens per diversas conceptiones assimilatur uni divinae essentiae, licet imperfecte.

Pages *49-50*, 71, *73*

17.1 Summa theologiae, prima pars (1266-1268) Ed. Leonine

1, 10 *ad* 2:

Analogia vero est, cum veritas unius Scripturae ostenditur veritati alterius non repugnare.

Page *78*

17.2

3, 2 *c.*:

Primum autem quod est bonum et optimum, quod Deus est, non est bonum per participationem, quia bonum per essentiam prius est bono per participationem.

17.3

3, 3 *ad* 2:

Dicendum quod effectus Dei imitantur ipsum non perfecte, sed secundum quod possunt. Et hoc ad defectum imitationis pertinet, quod id quod est simplex et unum, non potest repraesentari nisi per multa.

Page 51

17.4

3, 4 *c.*:

. . . illud quod habet esse et non est esse, est ens per participationem. Deus autem est sua essentia, ut ostensum est. Si igitur non sit suum esse, erit ens per participationem, et non per essentiam. Non ergo erit primum ens, quod absurdum est dicere.

Pages 59, 60

17.5

3, 8 *c.*:

Sicut autem participans est posterius eo quod est per essentiam, ita et ipsum participatum; sicut ignis in ignitis est posterior eo quod est per essentiam. Ostensum est autem quod Deus est primum ens simpliciter.

Pages 63, 66

17.6

3, 8 *ad* 1:

Dicendum quod deitas dicitur esse omnium effective et exemplariter, non autem per essentiam. [See also: q. 15, a. 2; q. 18, a. 4 ad 2; q. 93, a. 5 ad 4.]

Page 54

17.7

4, 2 *c.*:

Quidquid perfectionis est in effectu, oportet inveniri in causa effectiva; vel secundum eamdem rationem, si sit agens univocum, ut homo generat hominem; vel eminentiori modo, si sit agens aequivocum, sicut in sole est similitudo eorum quae generantur per virtutem solis. Manifestum est enim quod effectus praeexistit virtute in causa agente; praeexistere autem in virtute causae agentis, non est existere imperfectiori modo, sed perfectiori, licet praeexistere in potentia causae materialis, sit praeexistere imperfectiori modo, eo quod materia, inquantum huiusmodi, est imperfecta; agens vero, inquantum huiusmodi, est perfectum. Cum ergo Deus sit prima causa effectiva rerum, oportet omnium rerum perfectiones praeexistere in Deo secundum eminentiorem modum. . . .

Manifestum est enim quod, si aliquod calidum non habeat totam perfectionem calidi, hoc ideo est, quia calor non participatur secundum perfectam rationem; sed si calor esset per se subsistens, non posset ei aliquid deesse de virtute caloris. Unde cum Deus sit ipsum esse subsistens, nihil de perfectione essendi potest ei deesse. Omnium autem perfectiones pertinent ad perfectionem essendi; secundum hoc enim aliqua perfecta sunt, quod aliquo modo esse habent.

Pages 62, 71, 73, 75, 133

17.8

4, 3 *c.*:

Tertio modo dicuntur aliqua similia, quae communicant in eadem forma, sed non secundum eandem rationem; ut patet in agentibus non univocis. Cum enim omne agens agat sibi simile inquantum est agens, agit autem unumquodque secundum suam formam, necesse est quod in effectu sit similitudo formae agentis. Si ergo agens sit contentum in eadem specie cum suo effectu, erit similitudo inter faciens et factum in forma secundum eandem rationem speciei;

sicut homo generat hominem. Si autem agens non sit contentum in eadem specie, erit similitudo, sed non secundum eandem rationem speciei; sicut ea quae generantur ex virtute solis, accedunt quidem ad aliquam similitudinem solis, non tamen ut recipiant formam solis secundum similitudinem speciei, sed secundum similitudinem generis. Si igitur sit aliquod agens, quod non in genere contineatur, effectus eius adhuc magis accedent remote ad similitudinem formae agentis; non tamen ita quod participent similitudinem formae agentis secundum eandem rationem speciei aut generis, sed secundum aliqualem analogiam, sicut ipsum esse est commune omnibus. Et hoc modo illa quae sunt a Deo, assimilantur ei inquantum sunt entia, ut primo et universali principio totius esse.

Pages *50*, 59, 72, 138

17.9

4, 3 *ad* 3:

Dicendum quod non dicitur esse similitudo creaturae ad Deum propter communicantiam in forma secundum eandem rationem generis et speciei, sed secundum analogiam tantum, prout scilicet Deus est ens per essentiam, et alia per participationem.

Page 64

17.10

4, 3 *ad* 4:

Dicendum quod licet aliquo modo concedatur quod creatura sit similis Deo, nullo tamen modo concedendum est quod Deus sit similis creaturae.

Page 49

17.11

5, 6 *ad* 3:

Dicendum quod bonum non dividitur in ista tria sicut univocum aequaliter de his praedicatum, sed sicut analogum, quod praedicatur secundum prius et posterius. Per prius enim praedicatur de honesto, et secundario de delectabili; tertio de utili.

Pages 65, 112

17.12

6, 2 *c.*:

Similitudo autem effectus in causa quidem univoca invenitur uniformiter, in causa autem aequivoca invenitur excellentius, sicut calor excellentiori modo est in sole quam in igne. Sic ergo oportet quod, cum bonum sit in Deo sicut in prima causa omnium non univoca, quod sit in eo excellentissimo modo. Et propter hoc dicitur summum bonum.

Pages 25, 71, 74, 133

17.13

6, 2 *ad* 3:

De Deo autem negatur esse in eodem genere cum aliis bonis, non quod ipse sit in quodam alio genere, sed quia ipse est extra genus, et principium omnis generis. Et sic comparatur ad alia per excessum.

Page 74

17.14

6, 3 *c.*:

Haec autem triplex perfectio nulli creato competit secundum suam essentiam, sed soli Deo: cuius solius essentia est suum esse, et cui non adveniunt aliqua accidentia; sed quae de aliis dicuntur accidentaliter, sibi conveniunt essentialiter, ut esse potentem, sapientem, et huiusmodi, sicut ex dictis patet.

Page 61

17.15

6, 4 *c.*:

A primo igitur per suam essentiam ente et bono, unumquodque potest dici bonum et ens, inquantum participat ipsum per modum cuiusdam assimilationis, licet remote et deficienter, ut ex superioribus patet. Sic ergo unumquodque dicitur bonum bonitate divina, sicut primo principio exemplari, effectivo et finali totius bonitatis. Nihilominus tamen unumquodque dicitur bonum similitudine divinae bonitatis sibi inhaerente, quae est formaliter sua bonitas denominans ipsum. Et sic est bonitas una omnium; et etiam multae bonitates.

Pages 45, 55, 62, 64, 134, *142*

17.16

9, 1 *ad* 2:

Nihil enim esse potest, quod non procedat a divina sapientia per quandam imitationem, sicut a primo principio effectivo et formali. . . . Sic igitur inquantum similitudo divinae sapientiae gradatim procedit a supremis, quae magis participant de eius similitudine, usque ad infima rerum, quae minus participant, dicitur esse quidam processus et motus divinae sapientiae in res.

Pages 52, 54, 64

17.17

10, 2 *ad* 2; 10, 3 *c. et ad* 1; 10, 5 *ad* 1:

Nam Deus dicitur esse ante aeternitatem prout participatur a substantiis immaterialibus.

Quaedam autem amplius participant de ratione aeternitatis . . . multi participantes aeternitatem. . . .

Sed quantum ad visionem gloriae, participant aeternitatem.

Page 63

17.18

12, 1 *ad* 4:

Dicendum quod proportio dicitur dupliciter. Uno modo, certa habitudo unius quantitatis ad alteram; secundum quod duplum, triplum et aequale, sunt species proportionis. Alio modo, quaelibet habitudo unius ad alterum proportio dicitur. Et sic potest esse proportio creaturae ad Deum, inquantum se habet ad ipsum ut effectus ad causam, et ut potentia ad actum. Et secundum hoc, intellectus creatus proportionatus esse potest ad cognoscendum Deum.

Pages 32, 48, 140

17.19

12, 2 *c.*:

Et cum ipsa intellectiva virtus creaturae non sit Dei essentia, relinquitur quod sit aliqua participata similitudo ipsius, qui est primus intellectus. Unde et virtus intellectualis creaturae lumen quoddam intelligibile dicitur, quasi a prima luce derivatum; sive hoc intelligatur de virtute naturali, sive de aliqua perfectione superaddita gratiae vel gloriae. . . .

. . . divina essentia est aliquod incircumscriptum, continens in se supereminenter quidquid potest significari vel intelligi ab intellectu creato.

17.20

12, 3 c.:

Actus autem proportionatur ei cuius est actus.

"Proportion" is used in the same sense in:

21, 4	25, 6 ad 3	84, 8
23, 1	46, 1 ad 6	97, 1
23, 7 ad 3	77, 3	103, 5
25, 5	84, 7	

Page *80*

17.21

12, 4 c.:

Relinquitur ergo quod cognoscere ipsum esse subsistens sit connaturale soli intellectui divino, et quod sit supra facultatem naturalem cuiuslibet intellectus creati, quia nulla creatura est suum esse, sed habet esse participatum.

Page 59

17.22

12, 6 c. *et ad* 3:

Unde intellectus plus participans de lumine gloriae, perfectius Deum videbit. Plus autem participabit de lumine gloriae, qui plus habet de caritate.

. . . diversitas videndi non erit ex parte obiecti, quia idem obiectum omnibus praesentabitur, scilicet Dei essentia; nec ex diversa participatione obiecti per differentes similitudines, sed erit per diversam facultatem intellectus.

Page 63

17.23

12, 11 *ad* 3:

. . . omnia dicimur in Deo videre, et secundum ipsum de omnibus iudicare, inquantum per participationem sui luminis omnia cognoscimus, et diiudicamus; nam et ipsum lumen naturale rationis participatio quaedam est divini luminis.

Page 63

17.24

12, 12 c.:

Sed quia sunt eius effectus a causa dependentes, ex eis in hoc perduci possumus ut cognoscamus de Deo an est; et ut cognoscamus de ipso ea quae necesse est ei convenire secundum quod est prima omnium causa, excedens omnia sua causata. Unde cognoscimus de ipso habitudinem ipsius ad creaturas, quod scilicet omnium est causa; et differentiam creaturarum ab ipso, quod scilicet ipse non est aliquid eorum quae ab eo causantur; et quod haec non removentur ab eo propter eius defectum, sed quia superexcedit.

Pages 46, 74

17.25

13, 1 c.:

Ostensum est autem supra quod Deus in hac vita non potest a nobis videri per suam essentiam; sed cognoscitur a nobis ex creaturis secundum habitudinem principii, et per modum excellentiae, et remotionis.

Pages 46, 74

17.26

13, 2 c.:

Secundo, quia sequeretur quod omnia nomina dicta de Deo, per posterius dicerentur de ipso; sicut sanum per posterius dicitur de medicina, eo quod significat hoc tantum quod sit causa sanitatis in animali, quod per prius dicitur sanum.

. . . Unde quaelibet creatura intantum eum repraesentat, et est ei similis, inquantum perfectionem aliquam habet; non tamen ita quod repraesentet eum sicut aliquid eiusdem speciei vel generis, sed sicut excellens principium, a cuius forma effectus deficiunt, cuius tamen aliqualem similitudinem effectus consequuntur; sicut formae corporum inferiorum repraesentant virtutem solarem. . . .

Id quod bonitatem dicimus in creaturis, praeexistit in Deo, et hoc quidem secundum modum altiorem.

Pages 50, 67, 74

17.27

13, 2 *ad* 2:

. . . Secundum diversos processus perfectionum, creaturae Deum repraesentant, licet imperfecte; ita intellectus noster secundum unumquemque processum Deum cognoscit et nominat. Sed tamen haec nomina non imponit ad significandum ipsos processus, ut cum dicitur: Deus est vivens, sit sensus: ab eo procedit vita; sed ad significandum ipsum rerum principium, prout in eo praeexistit vita, licet eminentiori modo quam intelligatur vel significetur.

Page 73

17.28

13, 3 c.:

. . . Deum cognoscimus ex perfectionibus procedentibus in creaturas ab ipso; quae quidem perfectiones in Deo sunt secundum eminentiorem modum quam in creaturis. . . . Quantum igitur ad id quod significant huiusmodi nomina, proprie competunt Deo, et magis proprie quam ipsis creaturis, et per prius dicuntur de eo. Quantum vero ad modum significandi, non proprie dicuntur de Deo; habent enim modum significandi qui creaturis competit.

Pages 67, 73

17.29

13, 3 ad 1:

Dicendum quod quaedam nomina significant huiusmodi perfectiones a Deo procedentes in res creatas, hoc modo quod ipse modus imperfectus quo a creatura participatur divina perfectio, in ipso nominis significato includitur, sicut lapis significat aliquid materialiter ens; et huiusmodi nomina non possunt attribui Deo nisi metaphorice. Quaedam vero nomina significant ipsas perfectiones absolute, absque hoc quod aliquis modus participandi claudatur in eorum significatione, ut ens, bonum, vivens, et huiusmodi; et talia proprie dicuntur de Deo.

17.30

13, 4 c.:

Sed secundum quod dictum est huiusmodi nomina substantiam divinam significare, licet imperfecte, etiam plane apparet, secundum praemissa, quod habent rationes diversas. . . . Intellectus . . . format ad intelligendum Deum conceptiones proportionatas perfectionibus procedentibus a Deo in creaturas. Quae quidem perfectiones in Deo praeexistunt unite et simpliciter, in creaturis vero recipiuntur divise et multipliciter. Sicut igitur diversis perfectionibus creaturarum respondet unum simplex principium, repraesentatum per diversas perfectiones creaturarum varie et multipliciter; ita variis et multi-

plicibus conceptibus intellectus nostri respondet unum omnino simplex, secundum huiusmodi conceptiones imperfecte intellectum.

See 14, 1 ad 2.

Page 61

17.31

13, 5 *c.*:

Dicendum est igitur quod huiusmodi nomina dicuntur de Deo et
creaturis secundum analogiam, idest proportionem. Quod quidem
dupliciter contingit in nominibus: vel quia multa habent proportionem ad unum, sicut sanum dicitur de medicina et urina, inquantum utrumque habet ordinem et proportionem ad sanitatem
animalis, cuius hoc quidem signum est, illud vero causa; vel ex eo
quod unum habet proportionem ad alterum, sicut sanum dicitur
de medicina et animali, inquantum medicina est causa sanitatis
quae est in animali. Et hoc modo aliqua dicuntur de Deo et creaturis analogice, et non aequivoce pure, neque univoce. Non enim
possumus nominare Deum nisi ex creaturis, ut supra dictum est. Et
sic quidquid dicitur de Deo et creaturis, dicitur secundum quod est
aliquis ordo creaturae ad Deum, ut ad principium et causam, in
qua praeexistunt excellenter omnes rerum perfectiones.

Et iste modus communitatis medius est inter puram aequivocationem et simplicem univocationem. Neque enim in his quae analogice dicuntur, est una ratio, sicut est in univocis; nec totaliter
diversa, sicut in aequivocis; sed nomen quod sic multipliciter dicitur significat diversas proportiones ad aliquid unum; sicut sanum,
de urina dictum significat signum sanitatis animalis, de medicina
vero dictum significat causam eiusdem sanitatis.

Pages 11, *24, 36,* 74, 96, 112, 126

17.32

13, 5 *ad* 1:

Causa igitur universalis totius speciei non est agens univocum.
Causa autem universalis est prior particulari. Hoc autem agens universale, licet non sit univocum, non tamen est omnino aequivocum,
quia sic non faceret sibi simile; sed potest dici agens analogicum;
sicut in praedicationibus omnia univoca reducuntur ad unum primum, non univocum, sed analogicum, quod est ens.

Page *25*

17.33

13, 5 *ad* 3:

Dicendum quod Deus non est mensura proportionata mensuratis. Unde non oportet quod Deus et creatura sub uno genere contineantur.

17.34

13, 6 *arg.* 3:

Omnia nomina quae communiter de Deo et creaturis dicuntur, "dicuntur de Deo sicut de causa omnium," ut dicit Dionysius. Sed quod dicitur de aliquo per causam, per posterius de illo dicitur; per prius enim dicitur animal sanum quam medicina, quae est causa sanitatis. Ergo huiusmodi nomina per prius dicuntur de creaturis quam de Deo.

17.35

13, 6 *c.*:

Dicendum quod in omnibus nominibus quae de pluribus analogice dicuntur, necesse est quod omnia dicantur per respectum ad unum; et ideo illud unum oportet quod ponatur in definitione omnium. Et quia "ratio quam significat nomen, est definitio," ut dicitur in IV *Metaphys.*, necesse est quod illud nomen per prius dicatur de eo quod ponitur in definitione aliorum, et per posterius de aliis, secundum ordinem quo appropinquant ad illud primum vel magis vel minus; sicut sanum quod dicitur de animali, cadit in definitione sani quod dicitur de medicina; quae dicitur sana inquantum causat sanitatem in animali; et in definitione sani quod dicitur de urina, quae dicitur sana inquantum est signum sanitatis animalis.

Sic ergo omnia nomina quae metaphorice de Deo dicuntur, per prius de creaturis dicuntur quam de Deo, quia dicta de Deo nihil aliud significant quam similitudines ad tales creaturas. Sicut enim ridere dictum de prato nihil aliud significat quam quod pratum similiter se habet in decore cum floret, sicut homo cum ridet, secumdum similitudinem proportionis; sicut nomen leonis dictum de Deo nihil aliud significat quam quod Deus similiter se habet ut fortiter operetur in suis operibus, sicut leo in suis. Et sic patet quod secundum quod dicuntur de Deo, eorum significatio definiri non potest, nisi per illud quod de creaturis dicitur.

De aliis autem nominibus, quae non metaphorice dicuntur de Deo, esset etiam eadem ratio, si dicerentur de Deo causaliter tantum, ut quidam posuerunt. Sic enim cum dicitur Deus est bonus, nihil aliud esset quam Deus est causa bonitatis creaturae; et sic hoc nomen bonum, dictum de Deo, clauderet in suo intellectu bonitatem creaturae. Unde bonum per prius diceretur de creatura quam de Deo. Sed supra ostensum est quod huiusmodi nomina non solum dicuntur de Deo causaliter, sed etiam essentialiter. Cum enim dicitur Deus est bonus, vel sapiens, non solum significatur quod ipse sit causa sapientiae vel bonitatis, sed quod haec in eo eminentius praeexistunt. Unde, secundum hoc, dicendum est quod quantum ad rem significatam per nomen, per prius dicuntur de Deo quam de creaturis, quia a Deo huiusmodi perfectiones in creaturas manant. Sed quantum ad impositionem nominis, per prius a nobis imponuntur creaturis, quas prius cognoscimus. Unde et modum significandi habent qui competit creaturis, ut supra dictum est.

Pages **10, 15**, *33, 68-69,* 73, 80, 133

17.36

13, 6 *ad* 3:

Dicendum quod obiectio illa procederet, si huiusmodi nomina solum de Deo causaliter dicerentur et non essentialiter, sicut sanum de medicina.

17.37

13, 8 *ad* 2:

Sed ex effectibus divinis divinam naturam non possumus cognoscere secundum quod in se est, ut sciamus de ea quid est; sed per modum eminentiae et causalitatis et negationis, ut supra dictum est.

Page 74

17.38

13, 9 *c.*:

Dicendum quod aliquod nomen potest esse communicabile dupliciter: uno modo, proprie; alio modo, per similitudinem. Proprie quidem communicabile est quod secundum totam significationem nominis est communicabile multis. Per similitudinem autem communicabile est quod est communicabile secundum aliquid eorum quae includuntur in nominis significatione. Hoc enim nomen "leo" proprie communicatur omnibus illis in quibus invenitur natura quam significat hoc nomen "leo"; per similitudinem vero communicabile est illis qui participant aliquid leoninum, ut puta auda-

ciam vel fortitudinem, qui metaphorice leones dicuntur. . . . . Unde
cum hoc nomen Deus impositum sit ad significandum naturam divinam, ut dictum est; natura autem divina multiplicabilis non est,
ut supra ostensum est; sequitur quod hoc nomen "Deus" incommu-
nicabile quidem sit secundum rem, sed communicabile quidem sit
secundum opinionem. . . . Est nihilominus communicabile hoc
nomen "Deus," non secundum suam totam significationem, sed secundum aliquid eius per quandam similitudinem; ut "dii" dicantur
qui participant aliquid divinum per similitudinem, secundum illud
"Ego dixi, dii estis."

Page 64

17.39

13, 9 *ad* 1:

Dicendum quod natura divina non est communicabilis, nisi secundum similitudinis participationem.

Page 64

17.40

13, 9 *ad* 3:

Dicendum quod haec nomina "bonus," "sapiens," et huiusmodi
similia, imposita quidem sunt a perfectionibus procedentibus a Deo
in creaturas; non tamen sunt imposita ad significandum divinam
naturam, sed ad significandum ipsas perfectiones absolute. Et ideo
etiam secundum rei veritatem sunt communicabilia multis. Sed hoc
nomen "Deus" impositum est ab operatione propria Dei, quam ex-
perimur continue, ad significandum divinam naturam.

Pages 64, 125

17.41

13, 10 *c.*:

Dicendum quod hoc nomen Deus in praemissis tribus significationi-
bus non accipitur neque univoce neque aequivoce, sed analogice.
Quod ex hoc patet. Quia univocorum est omnino eadem ratio,
aequivocorum est omnino ratio diversa; in analogicis vero oportet
quod nomen, secundum unam significationem acceptum, ponatur in
definitione eiusdem nominis secundum alias significationes accepti.
Sicut ens de substantia dictum ponitur in definitione entis secundum
quod de accidente dicitur; et sanum dictum de animali ponitur in
definitione sani secundum quod dicitur de urina et de medicina;

huius enim sani quod est in animali, urina est significativa, et medicina factiva.

Sic accidit in proposito. Nam hoc nomen Deus, secundum quod pro Deo vero sumitur, in ratione Dei sumitur secundum quod dicitur Deus secundum opinionem vel participationem. Unde manifestum est quod analogice dicitur.

Pages *24, 33, 36,* **37, 38**

17.42

13, 10 *ad* 4:

Dicendum quod animal dictum de animali vero et de picto, non dicitur pure aequivoce; sed Philosophus largo modo accipit aequivoca, secundum quod includunt in se analoga. Quia et ens, quod analogice dicitur, aliquando dicitur aequivoce praedicari de diversis praedicamentis.

17.43

14, 3 *ad* 2:

. . . cum dicitur "Deus est finitus sibi," intelligendum est secundum quandam similitudinem proportionis; quia sic se habet in non excedendo intellectum suum, sicut se habet aliquid finitum in non excedendo intellectum finitum.

Page 84

17.44

14, 6 *c.*:

Supra enim ostensum est quod quidquid perfectionis est in quacumque creatura, totum praeexistit et continetur in Deo, secundum modum excellentem. Non solum autem id in quo creaturae communicant, scilicet ipsum esse, ad perfectionem pertinet; sed etiam ea per quae creaturae ad invicem distinguuntur, sicut vivere, et intelligere, et huiusmodi, quibus viventia a non viventibus, et intelligentia a non intelligentibus distinguuntur. . . . Propria enim natura uniuscuiusque consistit secundum quod per aliquem modum divinam perfectionem participat. Non autem Deus perfecte seipsum cognosceret, nisi cognosceret quomodocumque participabilis est ab aliis sua perfectio; nec etiam ipsam naturam essendi perfecte sciret, nisi cognosceret omnes modos essendi.

Pages 62, 74, 75

17.45

14, 6 *ad* 2:

Dicendum quod essentia creaturae comparatur ad essentiam Dei, ut actus imperfectus ad perfectum.

17.46

14, 9 *ad* 2:

Dicendum quod, cum Deus sit ipsum esse, intantum unumquodque est, inquantum participat de Dei similitudine; sicut unumquodque intantum est calidum, inquantum participat calorem.

Pages *59*, 64

17.47

14, 11 *c.*:

Omnes enim perfectiones in creaturis inventae, in Deo praeexistunt secundum altiorem modum. . . . Cum enim sciat alia a se per essen-tiam suam, inquantum est similitudo rerum velut principium ac-tivum earum, necesse est quod essentia sua sit principium sufficiens cognoscendi omnia quae per ipsum fiunt.

Page 74

17.48

16, 1 *c.*:

Sicut autem bonum est in re inquantum habet ordinem ad appe-titum, et propter hoc ratio bonitatis derivatur a re appetibili in appetitum, secundum quod appetitus dicitur bonus prout est boni; ita, cum verum sit in intellectu secundum quod conformatur rei intellectae, necesse est quod ratio veri ab intellectu ad rem intellec-tam derivetur, ut res etiam intellecta vera dicatur, secundum quod habet aliquem ordinem ad intellectum. . . . Sic ergo veritas prin-cipaliter est in intellectu; secundario vero in rebus secundum quod comparantur ad intellectum ut ad principium.

Page 65

17.49

16, 3 *ad* 1:

. . . ens est in rebus et in intellectu, sicut et verum; licet verum principaliter in intellectu, ens vero principaliter in rebus.

Fuller text on twofold meaning of *ens*: 48, 2 ad 2.

Pages 65, 70

17.50

16, 1 *ad* 3:

Dicendum quod, licet veritas intellectus nostri a re causetur, non
tamen oportet quod in re per prius inveniatur ratio veritatis, sicut
neque in medicina per prius invenitur ratio sanitatis quam in animali; virtus enim medicinae, non sanitas eius, causat sanitatem,
cum non sit agens univocum. Et similiter esse rei, non veritas eius,
causat veritatem intellectus.

17.51

16, 6 *c.*:

Quando aliquid praedicatur univoce de multis, illud in quolibet
eorum secundum propriam rationem invenitur, sicut animal in qualibet specie animalis. Sed quando aliquid dicitur analogice de
multis, illud invenitur secundum propriam rationem in uno eorum
tantum, a quo alia denominantur. Sicut sanum dicitur de animali
et urina et medicina, non quod sanitas sit nisi in animali tantum,
sed a sanitate animalis denominatur medicina sana, inquantum est
illius sanitatis effectiva, et urina, inquantum est illius sanitatis significativa. Et quamvis sanitas non sit in medicina neque in urina,
tamen in utroque est aliquid per quod hoc quidem facit, illud
autem significat sanitatem.

Dictum est autem quod veritas per prius est in intellectu et per
posterius in rebus, secundum quod ordinantur ad intellectum divinum. . . . Et sic, licet plures sint essentiae vel formae rerum,
tamen una est veritas divini intellectus, secundum quam omnes res
denominantur verae.

Pages *36*, **38**, 40, *41*, 45, 65, 69, 133, 134

17.52

16, 7 *c.*:

. . . sicut urina dicitur sana, non a sanitate quae in ipsa sit, sed a
sanitate animalis, quam significat. Similiter etiam supra dictum est
quod res denominantur verae a veritate intellectus.

17.53

18, 3 *c.*:

. . . quanto perfectiorem sensum habent, tanto perfectius movent
seipsa. . . . Unde perfectior modus vivendi est eorum quae habent
intellectum; haec enim perfectius movent seipsa. . . . Illud igitur

cuius sua natura est ipsum eius intelligere, et cui id quod naturaliter habet non determinatur ab alio, hoc est quod obtinet summum
gradum vitae. Tale autem est Deus. Unde in Deo maxime est vita.
Page 73

17.54

19, 1 *c.*:

. . . et hoc pertinet ad rationem voluntatis, ut bonum quod quis
habet, aliis communicet secundum quod possibile est. Et hoc praecipue pertinet ad voluntatem divinam, a qua per quandam similitudinem derivatur omnis perfectio. Unde si res naturales, inquantum perfectae sunt, suum bonum aliis communicant, multo magis
pertinet ad voluntatem divinam, ut bonum suum aliis per similitudinem communicet, secundum quod possibile est. Sic igitur vult
et se esse et alia. Sed se ut finem, alia vero ut ad finem, inquantum
condecet divinam bonitatem etiam alia ipsam participare.
Pages 50, 64

17.55

19, 4 *c.*:

. . . esse divinum non sit determinatum, sed contineat in se totam
perfectionem essendi.
Page 73

17.56

21, 3 *c.*:

. . . elargiri perfectiones rebus, pertinet quidem et ad bonitatem divinam, et ad iustitiam, et ad liberalitatem, et misericordiam, tamen
secundum aliam et aliam rationem. Communicatio enim perfectionum, absolute considerata, pertinet ad bonitatem, ut supra ostensum
est. Sed inquantum perfectiones rebus a Deo dantur secundum
earum proportionem, pertinet ad iustitiam, ut dictum est supra. Inquantum vero non attribuit rebus perfectiones propter utilitatem
suam, sed solum propter suam bonitatem, pertinet ad liberalitatem.
Inquantum vero perfectiones datae rebus a Deo omnem defectum
expellunt pertinet ad misericordiam.
Page *144*

17.57

22, 4 c.:

. . . principale bonum in ipsis rebus existens est perfectio universi;
quae quidem non esset, si non omnes gradus essendi invenirentur
in rebus.

Page 73

17.58

23, 4 *ad* 1:

. . . si consideretur communicatio bonitatis divinae in communi,
absque electione bonitatem suam communicat; inquantum scilicet
nihil est quod non participet aliquid de bonitate eius.

Page 59

17.59

23, 5 *ad* 1:

Necesse est autem quod divina bonitas, quae in se est una et simplex, multiformiter repraesentetur in rebus; propter hoc quod res
creatae ad simplicitatem divinam attingere non possunt. Et inde est
quod ad completionem universi requiruntur diversi gradus rerum,
quarum quaedam altum, et quaedam infimum locum teneant in
universo.

On *diversi gradus*, see also:

48, 2	75, 7 ad 2
50, 2 ad 1	76, 3
50, 4 ad 1 and 2	76, 4 ad 3
Page 61	

17.60

25, 1 c.:

. . . Deus est purus actus, et simpliciter et universaliter perfectus.

Page 61

17.61

25, 2 *ad* 2:

Sed potentia agentis non univoci non tota manifestatur in sui ef·
fectus productione; sicut potentia solis non tota manifestatur in
productione alicuius animalis ex putrefactione generati. Manifestum est autem quod Deus non est agens univocum; nihil enim aliud
potest cum eo convenire neque in specie, neque in genere, ut supra

ostensum est. Unde relinquitur quod effectus eius semper est minor quam potentia eius.

Page 25

17.62

26, 3 *ad* 1:

. . . beatitudo, quantum ad obiectum, est summum bonum simpliciter; sed quantum ad actum, in creaturis beatis, est summum bonum, non simpliciter, sed in genere bonorum participabilium a creatura.

Page 59

17.63

26, 4 *c. et ad* 1:

. . . quidquid est desiderabile in quacumque beatitudine, vel vera vel falsa, totum eminentius in divina beatitudine praeexistit.

. . . beatitudo aliqua secundum hoc est falsa, secundum quod deficit a ratione verae beatitudinis, et sic non est in Deo. Sed quidquid habet de similitudine, quantumcumque tenuis, beatitudinis, totum praeexistit in divina beatitudine.

Page 73

17.64

27, 1 *c. et ad* 2:

Cum autem Deus sit super omnia, ea quae in Deo dicuntur, non sunt intelligenda secundum modum infimarum creaturarum, quae sunt corpora; sed secundum similitudinem supremarum creaturarum, quae sunt intellectuales substantiae, a quibus etiam similitudo accepta deficit a repraesentatione divinorum. . . .

Unde cum divinum intelligere sit in fine perfectionis, ut supra dictum est, necesse est quod verbum divinum sit perfecte unum cum eo a quo procedit, absque omni diversitate.

Page 50

17.65

29, 3 *c. et ad* 1:

. . . persona significat id quod est perfectissimum in tota natura, scilicet subsistens in rationali natura. Unde cum omne illud quod est perfectionis Deo sit attribuendum, eo quod eius essentia continet in se omnem perfectionem, conveniens est ut hoc nomen persona de Deo dicatur. Non tamen eodem modo quo dicitur de creaturis, sed excellentiori modo; sicut et alia nomina, quae creaturis a nobis imposita Deo attribuuntur. . . .

. . . dignitas divinae naturae excedit omnem dignitatem, et secundum hoc maxime competit Deo nomen personae.

Pages 62, 73, 74

17.66

29, 4 *ad* 4:

. . . diversa ratio minus communium non facit aequivocationem in magis communi. Licet enim sit alia propria definitio equi et asini, tamen univocantur in nomine animalis, quia communis definitio animalis convenit utrique. Unde non sequitur quod, licet in significatione personae divinae contineatur relatio, non autem in significatione angelicae personae vel humanae, quod nomen personae aequivoce dicatur. Licet nec etiam dicatur univoce, cum nihil univoce de Deo dici possit et de creaturis, ut supra ostensum est.

Page 103

17.67

33, 2 *ad* 4:

Dicendum quod nomen generationis et paternitatis, sicut et alia nomina quae proprie dicuntur in divinis, per prius dicuntur de Deo quam de creaturis, quantum ad rem significatam, licet non quantum ad modum significandi. . . . Generatio, et per consequens paternitas, per prius sit in Deo quam in creaturis.

Page 67

17.68

33, 3 *c.*:

Dicendum quod per prius dicitur nomen de illo in quo salvatur tota ratio nominis perfecte, quam de illo in quo salvatur secundum aliquid; de hoc enim dicitur quasi per similitudinem ad id in quo perfecte salvatur, quia omnia imperfecta sumuntur a perfectis. . . . Sic igitur patet quod per prius paternitas dicitur in divinis secundum quod importatur respectus Personae ad Personam, quam secundum quod importatur respectus Dei ad creaturam.

Page 66

17.69

34, 1 c.:

Sicut igitur primo et principaliter interior mentis conceptus verbum dicitur; secundario vero ipsa vox interioris conceptus significativa; tertio vero ipsa imaginatio vocis verbum dicitur. . . . Dicitur autem figurative quarto modo verbum id quod verbo significatur vel efficitur.

Page 65

17.70

41, 3 *ad* 4:

. . . sapientia creata est participatio quaedam Sapientiae increatae.

Page 59

17.71

42, 1 *ad* 1:

Dicendum quod duplex est quantitas. Una scilicet quae dicitur quantitas molis vel quantitas dimensiva, quae in solis rebus corporalibus est, unde in divinis personis locum non habet. Sed alia est quantitas virtutis, quae attenditur secundum perfectionem alicuius naturae vel formae, quae quidem quantitas designatur secundum quod dicitur aliquid magis vel minus calidum, inquantum est perfectius vel minus perfectum in tali caliditate. Huiusmodi autem quantitas virtualis attenditur primo quidem in radice, idest in ipsa perfectione formae vel naturae, et sic dicitur magnitudo spiritualis, sicut dicitur magnus calor propter suam intensionem et perfectionem. Et ideo dicit Augustinus, VI *De Trin.*, quod "in his quae non mole magna sunt, hoc est maius esse, quod est melius esse," nam melius dicitur quod perfectius est. Secundo autem attenditur quantitas virtualis in effectibus formae. Primus autem effectus formae est esse, nam omnis res habet esse secundum suam formam. Secundus autem effectus est operatio, nam omne agens agit per suam formam. Attenditur igitur quantitas virtualis et secundum esse, et secundum operationem; secundum esse quidem, inquantum ea quae sunt perfectioris naturae, sunt maioris durationis; secundum operationem vero, inquantum ea quae sunt perfectioris naturae, sunt magis potentia ad agendum.

See 48, 5.

Page 70

17.72

42, 1 *ad* 2:

Quaecumque enim communicant in una forma, possunt dici similia, etiamsi inaequaliter illam formam participant, sicut si dicatur aer esse similis igni in calore; sed non possunt dici aequalia, si unum altero perfectius formam illam participet.

Page 59

17.73

44, 1 *c.*:

Ostensum est autem supra, cum de divina simplicitate ageretur, quod Deus est ipsum esse per se subsistens. . . . Relinquitur ergo quod omnia alia a Deo non sint suum esse, sed participant esse. Necesse est igitur quod omnia quae diversificantur secundum diversam participationem essendi, ut sint perfectius vel minus perfecte, causari ab uno primo ente, quod perfectissime est.

Pages *61, 66*

17.74

44, 1 *ad* 1:

Dicendum quod licet habitudo ad causam non intret definitionem entis quod est causatum, tamen sequitur ad ea quae sunt de eius ratione; quia ex hoc quod aliquid per participationem est ens, sequitur quod sit causatum ab alio. Unde huiusmodi ens non potest esse, quin sit causatum.

Page *33*

17.75

44, 3 *c.*:

Dicendum quod Deus est prima causa exemplaris omnium rerum. Ad cuius evidentiam, considerandum est quod ad productionem alicuius rei ideo necessarium est exemplar, ut effectus determinatam formam consequatur; artifex enim producit determinatam formam in materia, propter exemplar ad quod inspicit, sive illud sit exemplar ad quod extra intuetur, sive sit exemplar interius mente conceptum. Manifestum est autem quod ea quae naturaliter fiunt, determinatas formas consequuntur. Haec autem formarum determinatio oportet quod reducatur, sicut in primum principium, in divinam sapientiam, quae ordinem universi excogitavit, qui in rerum distinctione consistit. Et ideo oportet dicere quod in divina sapientia sunt rationes omnium rerum, quas supra diximus ideas, id est formas exemplares in mente divina existentes. . . . Sic igitur ipse Deus est primum exemplar omnium. Possunt etiam in rebus creatis quaedam aliorum exemplaria dici, secundum quod quaedam sunt ad similitudinem aliorum, vel secundum eandem speciem, vel secundum analogiam alicuius imitationis.

17.76

45, 4 *c.*:

Illi enim proprie convenit esse, quod habet esse, et quod est subsistens in suo esse. Formae autem et accidentia, et alia huiusmodi, non dicuntur entia quasi ipsa sint, sed quia eis aliquid est; ut albedo ea ratione dicitur ens, quia ea subiectum est album. Unde, secundum Philosophum, accidens magis proprie dicitur entis quam ens. Sicut igitur accidentia et formae, et huiusmodi quae non subsistunt, magis sunt coexistentia quam entia, ita magis debent dici concreata quam creata. See 90, 2; 104, 4 ad 3; 110, 2.

Pages 40, 65

17.77

45, 5 *et ad* 1:

Inter omnes autem effectus universalissimum est ipsum esse. Unde oportet quod sit proprius effectus primae et universalissimae causae, quae est Deus. . . . Contingit autem quod aliquid participet actionem propriam alicuius alterius non virtute propria, sed instrumentaliter, inquantum agit in virtute alterius. . . . Illud autem quod est proprius effectus Dei creantis, est illud quod praesupponitur omnibus aliis, scilicet esse absolute. Unde non potest aliquid operari dispositive et instrumentaliter ad hunc effectum, cum creatio non sit ex aliquo praesupposito. . . .

Sed sicut hic homo participat humanam naturam, ita quodcumque ens creatum participat, ut ita dixerim, naturam essendi, quia solus Deus est suum esse. . . . Nullum igitur ens creatum potest producere aliquod ens absolute, nisi inquantum esse causat in hoc.

Page 140

17.78

45, 7 *c.*:

Dicendum quod omnis effectus aliqualiter repraesentat suam causam, sed diversimode. Nam aliquis effectus repraesentat solam causalitatem causae, non autem formam eius, sicut fumus repraesentat ignem; et talis repraesentatio dicitur esse repraesentatio vestigii; vestigium autem demonstrat motum alicuius transeuntis, sed non qualis sit. Aliquis autem effectus repraesentat causam quantum ad similitudinem formae eius, sicut ignis generatus ignem generantem, et statua Mercurii Mercurium; et haec est repraesentatio imaginis.

Page 55

17.79

45, 8 *ad* 3:

Dicendum quod ad generationem animalium imperfectorum sufficit agens universale, quod est virtus caelestis, cui assimilantur non secundum speciem, sed secundum analogiam quandam; neque oportet dicere quod eorum formae creantur ab agente separato. Ad generationem vero animalium perfectorum non sufficit agens universale, sed requiritur agens proprium, quod est generans univocum.

17.80

47, 1 *c.*:

Nam bonitas quae in Deo est simpliciter et uniformiter, in creaturis est multipliciter et divisim. Unde perfectius participat divinam bonitatem et repraesentat eam totum universum, quam alia quaecumque creatura.

Pages 50, 59, *61*, 64

17.81

48, 3 *c.*:

Subiectum autem privationis et formae est unum et idem, scilicet ens in potentia; sive sit ens in potentia simpliciter, sicut materia prima, quae est subiectum formae substantialis et privationis oppositae; sive sit ens in potentia secundum quid et in actu simpliciter. ... Manifestum est autem quod forma per quam aliquid est actu, perfectio quaedam est, et bonum quoddam; et sic omne ens in actu bonum quoddam est. Et similiter omne ens in potentia, inquantum huiusmodi, bonum quoddam est, secundum quod habet ordinem ad bonum; sicut enim est ens in potentia, ita et bonum in potentia.

Page 65

17.82

48, 6 c. *et ad* 1:

. . . cum bonum simpliciter consistat in actu et non in potentia, ultimus autem actus est operatio vel usus quarumcumque rerum habitarum; bonum hominis simpliciter consideratur in bona operatione vel bono usu rerum habitarum . . . perfectius habet rationem mali culpa quam poena . . . malum vero culpae . . . contrariatur enim impletioni divinae voluntatis et divino amore quo bonum divinum in seipso amatur, et non solum secundum quod participatur a creatura.

. . . ordo actionis, qui tollitur per culpam, est perfectius bonum agentis, cum sit perfectio secunda, quam bonum quod tollitur per poenam, quod est perfectio prima. [See 48, 5.]

Page 59

17.83

49, 3 *ad* 4:

. . . nullum ens dicitur malum per participationem, sed per privationem participationis. Unde non oportet fieri reductionem ad aliquid quod sit per essentiam malum.

Page 59

17.84

50, 4, *sed contra*:

. . . in his quae sunt unius speciei, non est invenire prius et posterius, ut dicitur in III *Metaphys.*

Page 138

17.85

51, 1 c.:

In quocumque autem genere invenitur aliquid imperfectum, oportet praeexistere aliquid perfectum in genere illo.

Pages 63, 73

17.86

54, 1, *sed contra, et c.*:

Sed contra. Plus differt actio rei a substantia eius quam ipsum esse eius. . . .

Actio enim est proprie actualitas virtutis; sicut esse est actualitas substantiae vel essentiae. . . . Si etiam angelus ipse esset suum intelligere, non possent esse gradus in intelligendo perfectius et minus perfecte, cum hoc contingat propter diversam participationem ipsius intelligere.

Page 59

17.87

55, 3 c.:

In Deo autem tota plenitudo intellectualis cognitionis continetur in uno, scilicet in essentia divina, per quam Deus omnia cognoscit. Quae quidem intelligibilis plenitudo in intellectibus creatis inferiori modo et minus simpliciter invenitur.

Page 75

17.88

55, 3 *ad* 3:

. . . idem non potest esse plurium propria ratio adaequata. Sed si sit excellens, potest idem accipi ut propria ratio et similitudo diversorum.

Pages 73, 74

17.89

57, 1 c.:

. . . talis est ordo in rebus, quod superiora in entibus sunt perfectiora inferioribus, et quod in inferioribus continetur deficienter et partialiter et multipliciter, in superioribus continetur eminenter et per quandam totalitatem et simplicitatem. Et ideo in Deo, sicut in summo rerum vertice, omnia supersubstantialiter praeexistunt secundum ipsum suum simplex esse, ut Dionysius dicit in libro *De div. nomin.* Angeli autem inter ceteras creaturas sunt Deo propinquiores et similiores; unde et plura participant ex bonitate divina, et perfectius.

Page 61

17.90

57, 2 *c. et ad* 2:

Hoc enim rerum ordo habet, quod quanto aliquid est superius, tanto habeat virtutem magis unitam et ad plura se extendentem. . . .

. . . secundum suam naturam angeli non assimilantur rebus materialibus sicut assimilatur aliquid alicui secundum convenientiam in genere vel in specie, aut in accidente, sed sicut superius habet similitudinem cum inferiori, ut sol cum igne. Et per hunc etiam modum in Deo est similitudo omnium, et quantum ad formam et quantum ad materiam, inquantum in ipso praeexistit ut in causa quidquid in rebus invenitur. Et eadem ratione species intellectus angeli, quae sunt quaedam derivatae similitudines a divina essentia, sunt similitudines rerum.

Page 50

17.91

61, 1 c.:

. . . Et ex hoc manifestum est quod solus Deus est ens per suam essentiam; omnia vero alia sunt entia per participationem. Omne autem quod est per participationem, causatur ab eo quod est per essentiam, sicut omne ignitum causatur ab igne.

Page 60

17.92

61, 3 ad 2:

. . . Deus non est aliqua pars universi, sed est supra totum universum, praehabens in se eminentiori modo totam universi perfectionem.

Page 73

17.93

63, 3 c.:

. . . cum nulla creatura esse possit nisi per hoc quod sub Deo esse participat.

Page 59

17.94

65, 2 c.:

Ulterius autem, totum universum cum singulis suis partibus, ordinatur in Deum sicut in finem, inquantum in eis per quandam imitationem divina bonitas repraesentatur ad gloriam Dei.

Page 50

17.95

66, 2 c.:

. . . non est eadem materia corporis caelestis et elementorum, nisi secundum analogiam, secundum quod conveniunt in ratione potentiae.

Pages 79, 84

17.96

66, 2 *ad* 2:

Dicendum quod si genus consideretur physice, "corruptibilia et incorruptibilia non sunt in eodem genere," propter diversum modum potentiae in eis, ut dicitur X *Metaphys*. Secundum autem logicam considerationem, est unum genus omnium corporum, propter unam rationem corporeitatis.

Page 101

17.97

68, 4 *c.*:

Secundo dicitur caelum per participationem alicuius proprietatis ·caelestis corporis, scilicet sublimitatis et luminositatis actu vel potentia.

Page 59

17.98

75, 5 *ad* 1:

. . . primus actus est universale principium omnium actuum, quia est infinitum, virtualiter "in se omnia praehabens," ut dicit Dionysius. Unde participatur a rebus, non sicut pars, sed secundum diffusionem processionis ipsius. Potentia autem, cum sit receptiva actus, oportet quod actui proportionetur. Actus vero recepti, qui procedunt a primo actu infinito et sunt quaedam participationes eius, sunt diversi. Unde non potest esse potentia una quae recipiat omnes actus, sicut est unus actus influens omnes actus participatos.

Page 62

17.99

75, 5 *ad* 4:

. . . omne participatum comparatur ad participans ut actus eius. Quaecumque autem forma creata per se subsistens ponatur, oportet quod participet esse; quia etiam ipsa vita, vel quidquid sic diceretur, "participat ipsum esse," ut dicit Dionysius, v cap. *De div. nomin.* Esse autem participatum finitur ad capacitatem participantis. Unde solus Deus, qui est ipsum suum esse, est actus purus et infinitus. In substantiis vero intellectualibus est compositio ex actu et potentia, non quidem ex materia et forma, sed ex forma et esse participato.

Page 60

17.100

77, 6 *c.*:

. . . forma substantialis et accidentalis . . . differunt . . . in duobus. Primo quidem, quia forma substantialis facit esse simpliciter, et eius subiectum est ens in potentia tantum. Forma autem accidentalis non facit esse simpliciter, sed esse tale, aut tantum, aut aliquo modo se habens; subiectum enim eius est ens in actu. Unde patet quod actualitas per prius invenitur in forma substantiali quam in eius subiecto; et quia primum est causa in quolibet genere, forma substantialis causat esse in actu in suo subiecto. Sed e converso, actualitas per prius invenitur in subiecto formae accidentalis quam in forma accidentali; unde actualitas formae accidentalis causatur ab actualitate subiecti.

Page 66

17.101

77, 7 *c.*:

Sensus etiam est quaedam deficiens participatio intellectus.

Page 63

17.102

79, 4 *c. et ad* 1, 5:

Semper enim quod participat aliquid, et quod est mobile, et quod est imperfectum, praeexigit ante se aliquid quod est per essentiam suam tale et quod est immobile et perfectum. Anima autem humana intellectiva dicitur per participationem intellectualis virtutis . . . oportet ponere in ipsa anima aliquam virtutem ab illo intellectu superiori participatam . . . aliqua virtus derivata a superiori intellectu. . . . Unde ab ipso [Deo] anima humana lumen intellectuale participat. . . .

. . . illa lux vera illuminat sicut causa universalis, a qua anima humana participat quandam particularem virtutem. . . .

. . . nihil prohibet virtutem quae a supremo intellectu participatur, per quam abstrahit a materia, ab essentia ipsius procedere.

Pages 60, 62

17.103

84, 1 *ad* 2:

. . . inferior virtus non se extendit ad ea quae sunt superioris virtutis, sed virtus superior ea quae sunt inferioris virtutis excellentiori modo operatur.

Pages 73, 74

17.104

84, 4 *arg.* 1 *et ad* 1:

Omne enim quod per participationem est tale, causatur ab eo quod est per essentiam tale. . . . Sed anima intellectiva, secundum quod est actu intelligens, participat ipsa intelligibilia. . . .

. . . species intelligibiles quas participat noster intellectus reducuntur sicut in primam causam in aliquod principium per suam essentiam intelligibile, scilicet in Deum. Sed ab illo principio procedunt mediantibus formis rerum sensibilium et materialium, a quibus scientiam colligimus.

Pages 62, 63

17.105

84, 5 *c.*:

. . . anima humana omnia cognoscat in rationibus aeternis, per quarum participationem omnia cognoscimus. Ipsum enim lumen intellectuale . . . nihil est aliud quam quaedam participata similitudo luminis increati in quo continentur rationes aeternae . . . praeter lumen intellectuale in nobis exiguntur species intelligibiles a rebus acceptae . . . non per solam participationem rationum aeternarum de rebus materialibus notitiam habemus.

Page 64

17.106

84, 7 *ad* 3:

Deum autem, ut Dionysius dicit, cognoscimus ut causam, et per excessum, et per remotionem; alias autem incorporeas substantias in statu praesentis vitae cognoscere non possumus nisi per remotionem, vel aliquam comparationem ad corporalia. [See 88, 2 ad 1.]

Page 46

17.107

88, 2 *ad* 4:

Dicendum quod substantiae immateriales creatae in genere quidem naturali non conveniunt cum substantiis materialibus, quia non est in eis eadem ratio potentiae et materiae; conveniunt tamen cum eis in genere logico, quia etiam substantiae immateriales sunt in praedicamento Substantiae, cum earum quidditas non sit earum esse. Sed Deus non convenit cum rebus materialibus neque secundum genus naturale, neque secundum genus logicum, quia Deus nullo modo est in genere, ut supra dictum est. Unde per similitudines rerum materialium aliquid affirmative potest cognosci de angelis secundum rationem communem, licet non secundum rationem speciei; de Deo autem nullo modo.

Pages 101, 102

17.108

89, 4 *c.*:

Sicut enim ipse Deus per suam essentiam, inquantum est causa universalium et individualium principiorum cognoscit omnia et universalia et singularia, ut supra dictum est; ita substantiae separatae per species, quae sunt quaedam participatae similitudines illius divinae essentiae, possunt singularia cognoscere.

Page 64

17.109

90, 1 *ad* 2:

. . . anima, etsi sit forma simplex secundum suam essentiam, non tamen est suum esse, sed est ens per participationem, ut ex supra dictis patet. Et ideo non est actus purus, sicut Deus.

Page 60

17.110

90, 2 *ad* 1:

. . . in anima est sicut materiale ipsa simplex essentia, formale autem in ipsa est esse participatum; quod quidem ex necessitate simul est cum essentia animae, quia esse per se consequitur ad formam.

Page 60

17.111

91, 3 *ad* 3:

Plantae vero habent superius sui versus inferius mundi, nam ra-dices sunt ori proportionales, inferius autem sui versus superius mundi.

Page 84

17.112

93, 1 *c.*:

Ex quo patet quod similitudo est de ratione imaginis, et imago ali-quid addit supra rationem similitudinis, scilicet quod sit ex alio expressum; imago enim dicitur ex eo quod agitur ad imitationem alterius. . . . Manifestum est autem quod in homine invenitur ali-qua Dei similitudo, quod deducitur a Deo sicut ab exemplari; non tamen est similitudo secundum aequalitatem, quia in infinitum ex-cedit exemplar hoc tale exemplatum.

Pages *51*, 52, 54

17.113

93, 1 *ad* 3:

Dicendum quod cum unum sit ens indivisum, eo modo dicitur spe-cies indifferens, quo una. Unum autem dicitur aliquid non solum numero aut specie aut genere, sed etiam secundum analogiam vel proportionem quandam; et sic est unitas vel convenientia creaturae ad Deum.

17.114

93, 2 *ad* 1, 4:

Ad primum. Ergo. Dicendum quod omne imperfectum est quaedam participatio perfecti. Et ideo etiam ea quae deficiunt a ratione imaginis, inquantum tamen aliqualem Dei similitudinem habent, participant aliquid de ratione imaginis.

Ad quartum. Dicendum quod imago accipitur a Boethio secun-dum rationem similitudinis qua artificiatum imitatur speciem artis quae est in mente artificis; sic autem quaelibet creatura est imago rationis exemplaris quam habet in mente divina. Sic autem non loquimur nunc de imagine, sed secundum quod attenditur secun-dum similitudinem in natura; prout scilicet primo enti assimilantur

omnia inquantum sunt entia; et primae vitae inquantum sunt viventia, et summae sapientiae inquantum sunt intelligentia.
Page 27

17.115

93, 4 c.:
Dicendum quod cum homo secundum intellectualem naturam ad imaginem Dei esse dicatur, secundum hoc est maxime ad imaginem Dei, secundum quod intellectualis natura Deum maxime imitari potest.
Page 52

17.116

94, 2 c. et ad 2:
. . . angelus non intelligat per conversionem ad phantasmata, sed longe eminentiori modo, ut supra dictum est . . . etiam ipsi angeli, per hoc quod cognoscunt seipsos, non possunt pertingere ad cognitionem divinae substantiae, propter eius excessum.
. . . anima primi hominis deficiebat ab intellectu substantiarum . . . non ex aggravatione corporis, sed ex hoc quod obiectum ei connaturale erat deficiens ab excellentia substantiarum separatarum. Nos autem deficimus propter utrumque.
Page 73

17.117

95, 4 c. et ad 2:
. . . quantitas proportionalis . . . magis enim excedit parvum opus potestatem eius qui cum difficultate operatur illud, quam opus magnum potestatem eius qui sine difficultate operatur . . . quantitatem operis proportionalem.
Page 78

17.118

96, 1 c.:
. . . Secundo apparet hoc ex ordine divinae providentiae, quae semper inferiora per superiora gubernat. . . . Omne autem quod est per participationem, subditur ei quod est per essentiam et universaliter. . . . [See ad 4; 113, 6 c.]
Pages 60, 61

17.119

103, 2 c.:

Bonum autem universale est quod est per se et per suam essentiam bonum, quod est ipsa essentia bonitatis; bonum autem particulare est quod est participative bonum. Manifestum est autem quod in tota universitate creaturarum nullum est bonum quod non sit participative bonum.

Page 61

17.120

103, 4 c.:

Finis autem gubernationis mundi est bonum essentiale, ad cuius participationem et assimilationem omnia tendunt.

17.121

104, 1 c.:

Sed aliquando effectus non est natus recipere impressionem agentis secundum eandem rationem secundum quam est in agente; sicut patet in omnibus agentibus quae non agunt simile secundum speciem. . . . Et tale agens potest esse causa formae secundum rationem talis formae, et non solum secundum quod acquiritur in hac materia; et ideo est causa non solum fiendi, sed essendi . . . nec esse rei potest permanere, cessante actione agentis quod est causa effectus non solum secundum fieri, sed etiam secundum esse . . . si autem imperfecte participet aliquid . . . non semper remanebit, sed ad tempus, propter debilem participationem principii. . . . Sicut enim sol est lucens per suam naturam, aer autem fit luminosus participando lumen a sole, non tamen participando naturam solis; ita solus Deus est ens per essentiam suam, quia eius essentia est suum esse; omnis autem creatura est ens participative, non quod sua essentia sit eius esse.

Pages 72, 74

17.122

105, 1 ad 1:

. . . effectus aliquis invenitur assimilari causae agenti dupliciter. Uno modo, secundum eandem speciem. . . Alio modo, secundum virtualem continentiam, prout scilicet forma effectus virtualiter continetur in causa.

Page 71

17.123

105, 5 *c.*:

. . . nihil autem est vel apparet bonum, nisi secundum quod participat aliquam similitudinem summi boni, quod est Deus.

Page 59

17.124

106, 4 *c.*:

. . . qui divinam bonitatem per gratiam participant . . . sancti angeli, qui sunt in plenissima participatione divinae bonitatis.

Page 59

17.125

107, 2 *c.*:

. . . voluntas creata non est lux, nec regula veritatis, sed participans lucem.

Page 59

17.126

108, 5 *c.*:

. . . Ad videndum autem quae sit proprietas cuiuslibet ordinis, considerare oportet quod in rebus ordinatis tripliciter aliquid esse contingit, scilicet per proprietatem, per excessum, et per participationem. . . . Per participationem autem, quando illud quod attribuitur alicui, non plenarie invenitur in eo, sed deficienter; sicut sancti homines participative dicuntur dii. . . . Sicut si quis velit proprie nominare hominem, dicet eum substantiam rationalem; non autem substantiam intellectualem, quod est proprium nomen angeli, quia simplex intelligentia convenit angelo per proprietatem, homini vero per participationem.

Pages 63, 74

17.127

108, 5 *ad* 2:

. . . nomen cuiuslibet ordinis significat participationem eius quod est in Deo, sicut nomen Virtutum significat participationem divinae virtutis.

Page 59

17.128

115, 1 c.:

Secundum enim quod participatur aliquid, secundum hoc est necessarium quod participetur id quod est proprium ei; sicut quantum participatur de lumine, tantum participatur de ratione visibilis.

Page 59

17.129

47, 2 *bis* c. *(Appendix ad Iam Partem)*:

Sed sicut creatura esse in actu participat a Deo, qui est actus purus, ita et virtutem agendi participat a Deo, et agit eius virtute, sicut causa secunda virtute causae primae.

Page 60

18.1 In Dionysium De divinis nominibus (before 1268)

cap. 1, *lectio* 3:

. . . Considerandum est quod cum effectus procedant per quamdam assimilationem a suis causis, secundum modum quo aliquid est causa, praehabet in se similitudinem sui effectus. Si enim aliquid est causa alterius secundum suam speciem vel naturam, effectus in se habet similitudinem secundum suam naturam: sicut homo generat hominem et equus equum. Si vero sit causa alterius secundum aliquam dispositionem superadditam, secundum hoc etiam habebit similitudinem sui effectus. Aedificator enim est causa domus, non secundum suam naturam, sed secundum suam artem, unde similitudo domus non est in natura aedificatoris, sed in eius arte. . . .

. . . Quia igitur Deus est bonus, non quidem bonus quasi bonitatem participans, sed sicut ipsa essentia bonitatis, non per aliquam dispositionem participatam est causa rerum, sed per ipsum esse suum est causa omnium existentium; nec per hoc excluditur quin agat per intellectum et voluntatem, quia intelligere Eius et velle est ipsum esse Eius. Sic igitur in Ipso sua causa praehabet similitudinem omnium suorum effectuum. Omnis autem causa intantum potest nominari ex nomine sui effectus, inquantum habet in se similitudinem eius. Si enim sit similitudo secundum identitatem rationis, nomen illud conveniet causae et causato, sicut nomen hominis, generanti et generato. Si vero non sit similitudo secundum eamdem rationem, sed sit supereminentius in causa, non dicetur nomen de utroque secundum unam rationem, sed supereminentius de causa, sicut calor de sole et igne. Sic igitur, quia similitudo

omnium rerum praeexistit in divina essentia non per eamdem rationem, sed eminentius, sequitur quod providentiam Deitatis, sicut
principem totius boni, idest, principaliter in se totum bonum haben-
tem, et aliis diffundentem, convenit laudare ex omnibus causatis;
non tamen univoce sed supereminenter, quod contingit propter convenientiam creaturarum cum ipsa; quam quidem convenientiam
designat cum subdit: quoniam et circa Ipsam sunt omnia. Effectus
enim dicuntur circa causam consistere, inquantum accedunt ad similitudinem ipsius, secundum similitudinem qua lineae egredientes e
centro circumstant ipsum, secundum quamdam similitudinem, ab
ipso derivatae.
   Pages 64, 73

18.2

cap. 2, lectio 4:

. . . per participationem divinae bonitatis omnia sunt bona, et per
participationem divini esse seu vitae, res dicuntur existentes seu
viventes. . . . Deus ita participatur a creaturis per similitudinem
quod tamen remanet imparticipatus super omnia per proprietatem
suae substantiae. . . . Dicit quod inter causas et causata, non potest
esse diligens, idest perfecta comparatio, quia causae excedunt sua
causata; sed est quaedam alia comparatio causatorum ad causas,
inquantum causata habent imagines, idest similitudines causarum.
Omnis enim causa producit suum effectum per aliquem modum
similitudinis, non tamen causata consequuntur perfectam similitudinem causae; contingentes, idest prout contingit secundum suam
proportionem. Sed ideo non est perfecta comparatio, quia causae
separantur a causatis, inquantum superponuntur eis, secundum rationem proprii principii, idest in illa ratione in qua sunt principia.
   Pages 52, 74

18.3

cap. 4, lectio 3:

Dictum est enim quod divina Bonitas dat esse omnibus rebus per
creationem, sed in hoc aliquam similitudinem Eius habet sol, qui
dat esse per generationem. Confert enim ad generationem sensibilium corporum, sicut quoddam universale agens et causa non
univoca.
   Page 25

18.4

cap. 4, lectio 9:

. . . Nam bonum dupliciter dicitur, sicut et ens: dicitur enim, uno modo ens proprie et vere, quod subsistit ut lapis et homo; alio modo quod non subsistit, sed eo aliquid est, sicut albedo non sub-sistit, sed ea aliquid album est.

Page 65

18.5

cap. 5, lectio 1:

Quidquid enim intellectus noster apprehendit, minus est quam Dei essentia, et quidquid lingua nostra loquitur, minus est quam esse divinum. . . . Omnis forma recepta in aliquo, limitatur et finitur secundum capacitatem recipientis; unde hoc corpus album non habet totam albedinem secundum totum posse albedinis. Sed si esset albedo separata, nihil deesset ei quod ad virtutem albedinis pertineret. Omnia autem alia, ut superius dictum est, habent esse receptum et participatum, et ideo non habent esse secundum totam virtutem essendi; sed solus Deus, qui est ipsum esse subsistens se-cundum totam virtutem essendi esse habet. . . .

Ipse [Deus] est principium effectivum et causa finalis omnis saeculi et temporis et cuiuslibet quocumque modo existentis: et iterum omnia ipso participant, sicut prima forma exemplari.

Pages 54, 59

18.6

cap. 9, lectio 3:

. . . Et quidquid dicitur simile in quibuscumque rebus creatis, dici-tur simile quodam vestigio, idest quadam repraesentatione divinae similitudinis, ex qua perficitur non solum similitudo, sed etiam omnis unitio quae est in rebus.

. . . Ne tamen aliquis intelligeret, per hoc quod dicitur minus, aliquam proportionem, sicut contingit in rebus quae sunt unius generis quorum unum est altero perfectius, subiungit quod crea-turae deficiunt a Deo, non secundum aliquam determinatam men-suram, sed infinite et incomparabiliter, et pro tanto dicuntur ei dissimilia.

Pages 50, 74

18.7

cap. 11, *lectio* 4:

. . . Dicit quod per se esse et per se vita et huiusmodi, dupliciter dicuntur: uno modo, dicuntur de Deo qui est unum supersubstantiale principium omnium et causa; et dicitur Deus per se vita vel per se ens, quia non vivit participatione alicuius vitae neque est per participationem alicuius esse, sed ipse est suum vivere et sua vita et excedens omne esse et omnem vitam quae participatur a creaturis et existens principium vivendi et essendi omnibus. [*Similiter*, see cap. 2, lectio 6.]

Pages 63, 74

19.1 In libros De anima (1267-1271) Ed. Pirotta

lectio 1, no. 220:

[Accipitur] hic large subiectum, non solum prout subiectum dicitur aliquid ens actu; per quem modum accidens dicitur esse in subiecto; sed etiam secundum quod materia prima, quae est ens in potentia, dicitur subiectum.

19.2

lectio 1, no. 224:

. . . forma accidentalis non facit ens actu simpliciter, sed ens actu tale vel tantum, utputa magnum vel album vel aliquid aliud huiusmodi. Forma autem substantialis facit esse actu simpliciter.

20.1 In libros Perihermeneias (1268-1271) Ed. Leonine

I, lectio 5, no. 19:

Ad probandum enim quod verba non significant rem esse vel non esse, assumpsit id quod est fons et origo ipsius esse, scilicet ipsum ens, de quo dicit quod nihil est (ut Alexander exponit), quia ens aequivoce dicitur de decem praedicamentis; omne autem aequivocum per se positum nihil significat, nisi aliquid addatur quod determinet eius significationem; unde nec ipsum EST per se dictum significat quod est vel non est. Sed haec expositio non videtur conveniens, tum quia ens non dicitur proprie aequivoce, sed secundum prius et posterius; unde simpliciter dictum intelligitur de eo, quod per prius dicitur: tum etiam, quia dictio aequivoca non nihil significat, sed multa significat.

Pages 65, 119

20.2

I, lectio 5, no. 22:

. . . Quia vero actualitas, quam principaliter significat, hoc verbum *est*, est communiter actualitas omnis formae, vel actus substantialis vel accidentalis.

20.3

I, lectio 8, no. 5:

. . . Genus enim univoce praedicatur de suis speciebus, non secundum prius et posterius: unde Aristoteles noluit quod ens esset genus commune omnium, quia per prius praedicatur de substantia, quam de novem generibus accidentium.

Page 65

20.4

I, lectio 8, no. 6:

Sed dicendum quod unum dividentium aliquod commune potest esse prius altero dupliciter: uno modo, secundum proprias rationes, aut naturas dividentium; alio modo, secundum participationem rationis illius communis quod in ea dividitur. Primum autem non tollit univocationem generis. . . . Sed secundum impedit univocationem generis. Et propter hoc ens non potest esse genus substantiae et accidentis: quia in ipsa ratione entis, substantia, quae est ens per se, prioritatem habet respectu accidentis, quod est ens per aliud et in alio.

Pages 58, 66, 112

20.5

I, lectio 8, no. 20:

. . . Id autem quod non univoce praedicatur de multis (quia scilicet non significat aliquid unum, quod sit commune multis), non potest notificari nisi per illa multa quae significantur. Et inde est quod quia unum non dicitur aequivoce de simplici et composito, sed per prius et posterius, Aristoteles in praecedentibus semper ad notificandum unitatem enunciationis usus est utroque.

Page 65

21.1 In libros Posteriorum analyticorum (1268-1271)
Ed. Leonine

I, lectio 12, no. 8:

. . . Circa primum sciendum est quod proportio est habitudo unius quantitatis ad alteram; sicut sex ad tria se habent in proportione dupla. Proportionalitas vero est collatio duarum proportionum. Quae, si sit disiuncta, habet quatuor terminos.

Pages *83*, 99

21.2

II, lectio 19, no. 3:

. . . Si vero non accipiantur per accidens causa et causatum, oportet quod medium quod accipitur pro causa, similiter se habeat cum effectu cuius demonstratio quaeritur. Utpote si aliqua sint aequivoca, et medium commune quod accipitur, erit aequivocum. Si autem non sint aequivoca, sed conveniunt quasi in genere, et medium erit commune secundum genus, sicut vicissim analogum, idest communitatim proportionari, univoce in multis invenitur, puta in numeris et in lineis, in quibus habet quodammodo aliam causam, et quodammodo eamdem. Aliam quidem secundum speciem, in quantum scilicet alii sunt numeri et aliae lineae: sed est genere eadem, in quantum scilicet tam lineae quam numeri conveniunt in hoc quod habent tale augmentum, ex quo in eis commutata proportio demonstratur. Aliud autem exemplum subiungit in aequivocis; et dicit quod eius quod est esse simile, alia causa est in coloribus et in figuris, quia aequivoce dicitur utrobique. In figuris enim nihil est aliud esse simile, quam quod latera habeant analogiam, idest quod sint ad invicem proportionalia et quod anguli sint aequales. Sed in coloribus esse simile est quod faciant eamdem immutationem in sensu, vel aliquid aliud huiusmodi. Tertio autem dicit de his quae conveniunt secundum analogiam, quod in his etiam oportet esse medium unum secundum analogiam; sicut supra dictum est quod tam iris quam echo est quaedam repercussio.

Pages 83, *84*

22.1 In octo libros Physicorum (1268-1271) Ed. Leonine

I, lectio 6, no. 88:

. . . Parmenides assumit propositiones falsas, quia accepit quod *est*, idest ens, dici simpliciter, idest uno modo, cum tamen dicatur multipliciter. Dicitur enim ens uno modo substantia, alio modo accidens; et hoc multipliciter secundum diversa genera; potest etiam accipi ens prout est commune substantiae et accidenti.

22.2

I, lectio 7, no. 118:

. . . [Plato] ponebat enim, ens esse genus et univoce dictum de omnibus secundum participationem primi entis.

22.3

I, lectio 7, no. 119:

Ostendit autem Aristoteles quod hoc non sequitur: quia si ens sig- nificat principaliter unum quod est substantia, nihil prohibet dicere quod accidens, quod non est substantia, non sit simpliciter ens; sed tamen non propter hoc oportet quod illud quod non est aliquid, idest substantia, dicatur absolute non ens. Licet ergo accidens non sit ens simpliciter, non tamen potest dici absolute non ens.

Page 65

22.4

I, lectio 10, nos. 176-79:

. . . Ostendit quomodo in differentia praedictarum opinionum est etiam quaedam convenientia. . . . Eadem vero secundum analogiam, idest proportionem, quia principia accepta ab omnibus habent eandem proportionem. Et hoc tripliciter. . . . Primo quidem quia quaecumque principia accipiuntur ab eis, se habent ad invicem ut contraria. . . . Alius modus in quo conveniunt secundum analogiam est, quod quaecumque principia accipiuntur ab eis, unum eorum se habet ut melius et aliud ut peius. . . . Tertio modo conveniunt secundum analogiam in hoc quod omnes accipiunt principia noti- ora; sed quidam notiora secundum rationem, quidam vero secun- dum sensum.

Page 85

22.5

I, lectio 13, no. 237:

. . . Materia prima . . . scitur secundum analogiam, idest secundum proportionem.

Page *79*

22.6

I, lectio 15, no. 278:

. . . Materia prima scibilis est secundum proportionem.

Page 79

22.7

III, lectio 1, no. 553:

His autem generibus non est accipere aliquod commune univocum, quod non contineatur sub aliquo praedicamento ut sit genus eorum, sed ens est commune ad ea secundum analogiam, ut in IV *Metaphys.* ostendetur.

22.8

III, lectio 5, no. 617:

. . . Ens dividitur in decem praedicamenta, non univoce sicut genus in species, sed secundum diversum modum essendi. Modi autem essendi proportionales sunt modis praedicandi . . . unde et decem genera entis dicuntur decem praedicamenta.

22.9

VII, lectio 7, no. 1908:

Multa quidem secundum abstractam considerationem vel logici vel mathematici non sunt aequivoca, quae tamen secundum concretam rationem naturalis ad materiam applicantis, aequivoce quodammodo dicuntur.

Page 101

22.10

VII, lectio 8, nos. 1929, 1930:

Genus est unum logice sed non physice. . . . Quaedam vero [aequivocationes] sunt quae habent quandam similitudinem; sicut si hoc nomen *homo* dicatur de vero homine et de homine picto; inquantum habet similitudinem quandam veri hominis. Quaedam vero aequivocationes sunt proximae: aut propter convenientiam in genere (sicut si corpus dicatur de corpore caelesti et de corpore corruptibili, aequivoce dicitur; naturaliter loquendo, quia eorum non est materia una. Conveniunt tamen in genere logico: et propter hanc generis convenientiam videntur omnino non aequivoca esse) : aut etiam sunt propinquae secundum aliquam similitudinem; sicut ille qui docet in scholis dicitur magister, et similiter ille qui praeest domui dicitur magister domus, aequivoce et tamen propinqua aequivocatione, propter similitudinem; uterque enim est rector, hic quidem scholarum, ille vero domus.

Pages 84, 101

22.11

VII, lectio 9, no. 1950:

. . . eadem analogia, idest eadem proportio.

22.12

VIII, lectio 10, no. 2220:

Et similiter est in omnibus aliis in quibus movens est univocum, idest conveniens in nomine et ratione cum moto; sicut cum calidum facit calidum et homo generat hominem. Et hoc ideo dicit: quia sunt quaedam agentia non univoca, quae scilicet non conveniunt in nomine et ratione cum suis effectibus sicut sol generat hominem; in quibus tamen agentibus, etsi non sit species effectus secundum eandem rationem, est tamen quodam modo altiori et universaliori.

Pages 71, 74

23.1 De virtutibus in communi (1268-1272)

a. 12, *ad* 16:

. . . Ratio recta prudentiae non ponitur in definitione virtutis moralis, quasi aliquid de essentia eius existens; sed sicut causa quodammodo effectiva ipsius, vel per participationem. Nam virtus moralis nihil aliud est quam participatio quaedam rationis rectae in parte appetiva.

Page 63

24.1 De malo, qq. I-V, VII-XVI (probably before 1269)

I, a. 2, *ad* 4:

. . . Bonum autem non praedicatur univoce de omnibus bonis, sicut nec ens de omnibus entibus, cum utrumque circumeat omnia genera.

24.2

I, a. 3, *c.:*

. . . Omnis effectus per se habet aliqualiter similitudinem suae causae, vel secundum eamdem rationem, sicut in agentibus univocis, vel secundum deficientem rationem, sicut in agentibus aequivocis.

Pages 71, 74

24.3

I, a. 5, *arg.* 19:

Praeterea, quando aliquid secundum analogiam dicitur de pluribus, de illo videtur prius dici quod magis est famosum tale. Sed magis est famosum quod poena sit malum quam culpa, quia plures reputant poenam pro malo quam culpam.

24.4

I, a. 5, *ad* 19:

Dicendum quod aliquod nomen dicitur per prius de uno quam de alio dupliciter: uno modo quantum ad nominis impositionem; alio modo quantum ad rei naturam: sicut nomina dicta de Deo et creaturis quantum ad nominum impositionem per prius dicuntur de creaturis; quantum vero ad rei naturam per prius dicuntur de Deo, a quo in creaturis omnis perfectio derivatur.

Page *67*

24.5

II, a. 9, *ad* 16:

Dicendum quod omnia animalia sunt aequaliter animalia, non tamen sunt aequalia animalia, sed unum animal est altero maius et perfectius; et similiter non oportet quod omnia peccata propter hoc sint paria.

Page *103*

24.6

VII, a. 1, *ad* 1:

. . . Duplex est divisio: una qua dividitur genus univocum in suas species, quae ex aequo participant genus, sicut animal in bovem et equum; alia est divisio communis analogi in ea de quibus dicitur secundum prius et posterius; sicut ens dividitur per substantiam et accidens, et per potentiam et actum; et in talibus ratio communis perfecte salvatur in uno; in aliis autem secundum quid et per posterius, et talis est divisio peccati per veniale et mortale.

Pages 66, 69

25.1 Summa theologiae, pars prima secundae partis (1269-1271) Ed. Leonine

3, 5 *ad* 1:

Dicendum quod similitudo praedicta intellectus practici ad Deum est secundum proportionalitatem; quia scilicet habet se ad suum cognitum, sicut Deus ad suum.

Pages 84, **88**

25.2

17, 4 *c.*:

. . . Unum autem hoc modo dicitur sicut et ens. Ens autem simpliciter est substantia; sed ens secundum quid est accidens, vel etiam ens rationis.

Page 65

25.3

20, 3 *ad* 3:

Dicendum quod quando aliquid de uno derivatur in alterum sicut ex causa agente univoca, tunc aliud est quod est in utroque; sicut cum calidum calefacit, alius numero est calor calefacientis et calor calefacti, licet idem specie. Sed quando aliquid derivatur ab uno in alterum secundum analogiam vel proportionem, tunc est tantum unum numero; sicut a sano quod est in corpore animalis, derivatur sanum ad medicinam et urinam; nec alia sanitas est medicinae et urinae quam sanitas animalis, quam medicina facit et urina significat.

Page **41**

25.4

26, 4 *c.*:

. . . Haec autem divisio est secundum prius et posterius. Nam id quod amatur amore amicitiae, simpliciter et per se amatur; quod autem amatur amore concupiscentiae, non simpliciter et secundum se amatur, sed amatur alteri. Sicut enim ens per se simpliciter est quod habet esse, ens autem secundum quid quod est in alio; ita et bonum, quod convertitur cum ente, simpliciter quidem est quod ipsum habet bonitatem; quod autem est bonum alterius, est bonum secundum quid.

Page 65

25.5

60, 1 c.:

. . . Aliquando vero materia recipit formam ab agente non secundum eandem rationem, prout est in agente; sicut patet in generan-
tibus non univocis, ut animal generatur a sole. Et tunc formae re-
ceptae in materia ab eodem agente non sunt unius speciei, sed
diversificantur secundum diversam proportionem materiae ad recipiendum influxum agentis; sicut videmus quod ab una actione solis
generantur per putrefactionem animalia diversarum specierum, secundum diversam proportionem materiae.

Page 71

25.6

61, 1 ad 1:

Sed quando est divisio alicuius analogi, quod dicitur de pluribus
secundum prius et posterius; tunc nihil prohibet unum esse principalius altero, etiam secundum communem rationem, sicut substantia principalius dicitur ens quam accidens.

Pages 65, 112

25.7

88, 1 ad 1:

Dicendum quod divisio peccati in veniale et mortale non est divisio generis in species, quae aequaliter participant rationem generis, sed analogi in ea de quibus praedicatur secundum prius et
posterius. . . . Peccatum autem veniale dicitur peccatum secundum
rationem imperfectam, et in ordine ad peccatum mortale; sicut
accidens dicitur ens in ordine ad substantiam, secundum imperfectam rationem entis.

Page 65

25.8

114, 3 c.:

. . . Sed est ibi congruitas propter quandam aequalitatem proportionis; videtur enim congruum ut homini operanti secundum suam
virtutem, Deus recompenset secundum excellentiam suae virtutis.

Page 78

26.1 In evangelium Ioannis (1269-1272)

prologus:

. . . [Platonici] consideraverunt enim, quod omne illud quod est secundum participationem, reducitur ad aliquid quod sit illud per suam essentiam, sicut ad primum et ad summum; sicut omnia ignita per participationem reducuntur ad ignem, qui est per essentiam talis. Cum ergo omnia quae sunt, participant esse, et sint per participationem entia, necesse est esse aliquid in cacumine omnium rerum, quod sit ipsum esse per suam essentiam, idest quod sua essentia sit suum esse; et hoc est Deus, qui est sufficientissima et dignissima et perfectissima causa totius esse; a quo omnia quae sunt, participant esse.

Page *60*

27.1 De anima (possibly 1269-1272)

a. 18, *c.*:

. . . Ulterius autem quaecumque sunt in tota creatura, eminentius sunt in ipso Deo.

Page 73

28.1 Quaestiones quodlibetales, Group II (I-VI, XII) (1269-1272)

I, (*q.* 10) *a.* 22, *ad* 1:

Dicendum quod proportione commutata sic est utendum: sicut se habet primum ad secundum, ut duo ad tria, ita se habet tertium ad quartum; ergo commutatim, sicut se habet primum ad tertium, ita et secundum ad quartum, idest tria ad sex; et secundum hoc ratio sic deberet procedere.

Page 83

28.2

II, (*q.* 2) *a.* 3, *c.*:

Dicendum quod dupliciter aliquid de aliquo praedicatur: uno modo essentialiter, alio modo per participationem: lux enim praedicatur de corpore illuminato participative; sed si esset aliqua lux separata praedicaretur de ea essentialiter. Secundum ergo hoc dicendum est, quod ens praedicatur de solo Deo essentialiter, eo quod esse divinum est esse subsistens et absolutum; de qualibet autem creatura praedicatur per participationem: nulla enim creatura est suum esse, sed est habens esse. Sic et Deus dicitur bonus essentialiter,

quia est ipsa bonitas; creaturae autem dicuntur bonae per participationem, quia habent bonitatem. . . . Quandocumque autem aliquid praedicatur de altero per participationem oportet ibi aliquid
esse praeter id quod participatur; et ideo in qualibet creatura est
aliud ipsa creatura quae habet esse, et ipsum esse eius. Sed sciendum est quod aliquid participatur dupliciter. Uno modo quasi
existens de substantia participantis, sicut genus participatur a
specie. Hoc autem modo esse non participatur a creatura; id enim
est de substantia rei quod cadit in eius definitione. Ens autem non
ponitur in definitione creaturae, quia nec est genus nec differentia;
unde participatur sicut aliquid non existens de essentia rei; et ideo
alia quaestio est *an est* et *quid est.* . . . Sed verum est quod hoc
nomen ens, secundum quod importat rem cui competit huiusmodi
esse, sic significat essentiam rei, et dividitur per decem genera; non
tamen univoce; quia non eadem ratione competit omnibus esse; sed
substantiae quidem per se, aliis autem aliter.

[See also XII, q. 5, a. 1, c.]

Pages *34*, 58, *60*, 61

28.3

III, (*q*. 8) *a*. 20, *c*.:

. . . Manifestum est quod solus Deus est suum esse, quasi essentialiter existens, in quantum scilicet suum esse est eius substantia. Quod
de nullo alio dici potest: esse enim subsistens non potest esse nisi
unum, sicut nec albedo subsistens non potest esse nisi unum.

Oportet ergo quod quaelibet alia res sit ens participative, ita
quod aliud sit in eo substantia participans esse, et aliud ipsum esse
participatum. Omne autem participans se habet ad participatum
sicut potentia ad actum; unde substantia cuiuslibet rei creatae se
habet ad suum esse sicut potentia ad actum. Sic ergo omnis substantia creata est composita ex potentia et actu, id est ex eo quod
est et esse, ut Boetius dicit in lib. *de Hebd.*

Page 75

28.4

IV, (*q*. 1) *a*. 1, *c*.:

Duplex est pluralitas. Una quidem est pluralitas rerum; et secundum hoc non sunt plures ideae in Deo. Nominat enim idea formam
exemplarem. Est autem una res quae est omnium exemplar: scilicet
divina essentia, quam omnia imitantur, in quantum sunt et bona

sunt. Alia vero pluralitas est secundum intelligentiae rationem; et secundum hoc sunt plures ideae. Licet enim omnes res, in quantum sunt, divinam essentiam imitentur, non tamen uno et eodem modo omnia imitantur ipsam, sed diversimode, et secundum diversos gradus. Sic ergo divina essentia, secundum quod est imitabilis hoc modo ab hac creatura, est propria ratio et idea huiusmodi creaturae, et similiter de aliis.

Pages 53-54

29.1 In S. Pauli epistolas, ordinatio (to *In I Corinthians,* cap. 7) (1269-1272)

In Rom., cap. 1, *lectio* 3:

Manifestum est autem quod id quod est per se, est mensura et regula eorum quae dicuntur per aliud et per participationem. Unde praedestinatio Christi, qui est praedestinatus ut sit filius Dei per naturam, est mensura et regula vitae, et ita praedestinationis nostrae, qui praedestinamur in filiationem adoptivam, quae est quaedam participatio et imago naturalis filiationis.

Page 52

29.2

In Rom., cap. 1, *lectio* 6:

Fuit enim in eis quantum ad aliquid vera Dei cognitio, quia quod notum est Dei, idest, quod cognoscibile est de Deo ab homine per rationem, manifestum est in illis, idest, manifestum est eis ex eo quod in illis est, idest ex lumine intrinseco. Sciendum est ergo quod aliquid circa Deum est omnino ignotum homini in hac vita, scilicet quid est Deus. Unde et Paulus invenit Athenis aram inscriptam: *Ignoto Deo;* et hoc ideo quia cognitio hominis incipit ab his quae sunt ei connaturalia, scilicet a sensibilibus creaturis, quae non sunt proportionatae ad repraesentandum divinam essentiam.

Potest tamen homo ex huiusmodi creaturis Deum tripliciter cognoscere, ut Dionysius dicit. Uno quidem modo per causalitatem: quia enim huiusmodi creaturae sunt defectibiles et mutabiles, necesse est eas reducere ad aliquod principium immobile et perfectum: et secundum hoc cognoscitur de Deo, an est. Secundo, per viam excellentiae: non enim reducuntur omnia in primum principium sicuti in propriam causam et univocam, prout homo hominem generat, sed sicut in causam communem et excedentem; et ex hoc cognoscitur quod est super omnia. Tertio, per viam negationis:

quia, si est causa excedens, nihil eorum quae sunt in creaturis potest ei competere, sicut etiam neque corpus caeleste proprie dicitur grave vel leve, aut calidum aut frigidum. Et secundum hoc dicimus Deum immobilem, et infinitum, et si quid aliud huiusmodi dicitur. Huiusmodi autem cognitionem habuerunt per lumen rationis inditum. . . .

Est autem manifesta nobis per quasdam similitudines in creaturas repertas, quae id quod in Deo unum est multipliciter participant; et secundum hoc intellectus noster considerat unitatem divinae essentiae sub ratione bonitatis, sapientiae, virtutis, et huiusmodi quae in Deo non sunt. Haec ergo invisibilia Dei dixit, quia illud unum, quod his nominibus seu rationibus in Deo respondet, non videtur a nobis. . . .

Tertium cognitum est quod dicit: "Et divinitas." Ad quod pertinet, quod cognoverunt Deum sicut ultimum finem in quem omnia tendunt. Divinum enim bonum dicitur bonum commune, quod ab omnibus participatur: propter hoc potius dixit divinitatem, quae participationem significat, quam deitatem quae significat essentiam Dei. "Et in ipso habitat omnis plenitudo divinitatis." Haec autem tria referuntur ad tres modos cognoscendi supradictos. Nam invisibilia Dei cognoscuntur per viam negationis; sempiterna virtus per viam causalitatis; divinitas per viam excellentiae.

Pages 59, 74

29.3

In Rom., cap. 1, lectio 7:

Dupliciter autem Deum cognoverunt. Uno modo, sicut omnibus supereminentem; et sic ei debebant gloriam et honorem quae superexcellentibus debetur; isti ideo dicuntur inexcusabiles, quia cum cognovissent Deum, non sicut Deum glorificaverunt; vel quia ei debitum cultum non impenderunt; vel quia virtuti eius et scientiae terminum imposuerunt, aliqua eius potentiae et scientiae subtrahentes, contra id quod dicitur *Eccli.* xliii: "Glorificantes Dominum quantumcumque poteritis." Secundo cognoverunt eum sicut omnium bonorum causam.

29.4

In I Cor., cap. 2, lectio 2:

. . . Daemonia dicebant Christum esse sanctum Dei, quasi singulariter sanctum: ipse enim naturaliter est sanctus cuius participatione omnes alii sancti vocantur.

30.1 In libros Meteorologicorum (1269-1273) Ed. Leonine

I, lectio 3, no. 7:

. . . Manifestum est enim quod adhuc quantitas aeris multum excederet aequalitatem analogiae, idest proportionis, quae debet esse communis inter elementa, ad hoc quod elementa conserventur. [*Variant:* proportionalitatis.]

Page 78

31.1 De substantiis separatis (possibly 1270)

cap. 8:

Cum enim ens non univoce de omnibus praedicetur, non est requirendus idem modus essendi in omnibus quae esse dicuntur; sed quaedam perfectius, quaedam imperfectius esse participant. Accidentia enim entia dicuntur, non quia in se ipsis esse habeant, sed quia esse eorum est in hic quod insunt substantiae.

Pages 58, *66*

31.2

cap. 12:

Uniuscuiusque enim effectus perfectio in hoc consistit quod suae causae assimiletur. Quod enim secundum naturam generatur, tunc perfectum est quando contingit ad similitudinem generantis. Artificialia etiam per hoc perfecta redduntur quod artis formam consequuntur. In primo autem principio non solum consideratur quod ipsum est bonum et ens et unum, sed etiam quod hoc eminentius prae ceteris habet, et alia ad sui bonitatem participandam adducit.

Pages 62, 64, 73

31.3

cap. 13, 14:

Sicut causa est quodammodo in effectu per sui similitudinem participatam, ita omnis effectus est in sua causa excellentiori modo secundum virtutem ipsius. . . . Oportet igitur omnia quae quocumque modo sunt in rebus, in Deo intelligibiliter existere secundum eminentiam substantiae eius. . . . Primum ens est omnis esse principium. . . .

. . . Quod causae et effectui convenit, eminentius invenitur in causa quam in effectu; a causa enim in effectum derivatur. Quidquid igitur in inferioribus causis existens primae omnium causae attribuitur, excellentissime convenit ei.

Pages *61-62*, 64, 73, 74

32.1 Summa theologiae, secunda pars secundae partis (1270-1272) Ed. Leonine

23, 2 *ad* 1:

Unde sicut dicimur boni bonitate quae est Deus, et sapientes sapientia quae est Deus, quia bonitas qua formaliter boni sumus est participatio quaedam divinae bonitatis, et sapientia qua formaliter sapientes sumus est participatio quaedam divinae sapientiae; ita etiam caritas qua formaliter diligimus proximum est quaedam participatio divinae caritatis.

Pages 45, *59*

32.2

53, 2 *c.*:

Primo autem modo, potest dici aliquod vitium generale dupliciter. Uno modo, per essentiam, quia scilicet praedicatur de omnibus peccatis. Et hoc modo imprudentia non est generale peccatum. . . . Alio modo, per participationem. Et hoc modo imprudentia est generale peccatum.

Page 63

32.3

120, 2 *c.*:

Pars autem subiectiva est de qua essentialiter praedicatur totum, et est in minus. Quod quidem contingit dupliciter: quandoque enim aliquid praedicatur de pluribus secundum unam rationem, sicut animal de equo et bove; quandoque autem praedicatur secundum prius et posterius, sicut ens praedicatur de substantia et accidente.

Page 65

33.1 In Metaphysicorum Aristotelis (before 1272) Ed. Cathala

proemium:

. . . Unde oportet quod ad eamdem scientiam pertineat considerare substantias separatas, et ens commune, quod est genus, cuius sunt praedictae substantiae communes et universales causae.

33.2

I, lectio 14, no. 224:

Hoc autem ideo addidit Aristoteles quia posset aliquis dicere quod non omnino aequivoce aliquod nomen praedicatur de idea et de substantia sensibili, cum de idea praedicetur essentialiter, de substantia vero sensibili per participationem. Nam idea hominis secundum Platonem dicitur per se homo, hic autem homo sensibilis dicitur per participationem. Sed tamen talis aequivocatio non est pura; sed nomen quod per participationem praedicatur, dicitur per respectum ad illud quod praedicatur per se, quod non est pura aequivocatio, sed multiplicitas analogiae.

33.3

I, lectio 15, no. 233:

Sciendum autem quod illa ratio, etsi destruat exemplaria separata a Platone posita, non tamen removet divinam scientiam esse rerum omnium exemplarem. Cum enim res naturales naturaliter intendant similitudines in res generatas inducere, oportet quod ista intentio ad aliquod principium dirigens reducatur, quod est in finem ordinans unumquodque. Et hoc non potest esse nisi intellectus cuius sit cognoscere finem et proportionem rerum in finem. Et sic ista similitudo effectuum ad causas naturales reducitur, sicut in primum principium, in intellectum aliquem.

Page 55

33.4

II, lectio 2, nos. 293-94:

Facit autem mentionem de univocatione, quia quandoque contingit quod effectus non pervenit ad similitudinem causae secundum eamdem rationem speciei, propter excellentiam ipsius causae. Sicut sol est causa caloris in istis inferioribus; non tamen inferiora corpora possunt recipere impressionem solis aut aliorum caelestium corporum secundum eamdem rationem speciei, cum non communicent in materia. Et propter hoc non dicimus solem esse calidissimum sicut ignem, sed dicimus solem esse aliquid amplius quam calidissimum.

Nomen autem veritatis non est proprium alicui speciei, sed se habet communiter ad omnia entia. Unde, quia illud quod est causa veritatis, est causa communicans cum effectu in nomine et ratione communi, sequitur quod illud quod est posterioribus causa ut sint vera sit verissimum.

Page 74

33.5

II, lectio 2, no. 296:

Et hoc est necessarium: quia necesse est ut omnia composita et participantia reducantur in ea quae sunt per essentiam, sicut in causas.

Page 59

33.6

III, lectio 8, no. 433:

. . . Nulla autem differentia potest accipi de qua non praedicetur ens et unum, quia quaelibet differentia cuiuslibet generis est ens et est una, alioquin non posset constituere unam aliquam speciem entis. Ergo impossibile est quod unum et ens sint genera.

33.7

III, lectio 8, nos. 437-38:

. . . Quando aliquid unum de pluribus praedicatur non secundum prius et posterius, [Plato] posuit illud unum separatum, sicut hominem praeter omnes homines. Quando vero aliquid praedicatur de pluribus secundum prius et posterius, non ponebat illud separatum: Et hoc est quod [Aristoteles] dicit quod "in quibus prius et posterius est," scilicet quando unum eorum de quibus aliquid commune praedicatur est altero prius, non est possibile in his aliquid esse separatum, praeter haec multa de quibus praedicatur.... Et huius ratio esse potest, quia ideo aliquod commune ponitur separatum, ut sit quoddam primum quod omnia alia participent. Si igitur unum de multis sit primum, quod omnia alia participent, non oportet ponere aliquod separatum, quod omnia participant. Sed talia videntur omnia genera; quia omnes species generum inveniuntur differre secundum perfectius et minus perfectum. Et, per consequens, secundum prius et posterius secundum naturam.

33.8

III, lectio 10, no. 465:

Haec autem quaestio solvetur in duodecimo. Ibi enim ostendetur quod principia quae sunt intrinseca rebus, scilicet materia et forma, vel privatio, non sunt eadem numero omnium, sed analogia sive proportione.

Page *85*

33.9

IV, lectio 1, nos. 534-39:

. . . Quaecumque communiter unius recipiunt praedicationem, licet non univoce, sed analogice de his praedicetur, pertinent ad unius scientiae considerationem: sed ens hoc modo praedicatur de omnibus entibus; ergo omnia entia pertinent ad considerationem unius scientiae, quae considerat ens inquantum est ens, scilicet tam substantias quam accidentia.

. . . Dicit ergo primo, quod ens sive quod est, dicitur multipliciter. Sed sciendum quod aliquid praedicatur de diversis multipliciter: quandoque quidem secundum rationem omnino eamdem, et tunc dicitur de eis univoce praedicari, sicut animal de equo et bove. Quandoque vero secundum rationes omnino diversas; et tunc dicitur de eis aequivoce praedicari, sicut canis de sidere et animali. Quandoque vero secundum rationes quae partim sunt diversae et partim non diversae; diversae quidem secundum quod diversas habitudines important, unae autem secundum quod ad unum aliquid et idem istae diversae habitudines referuntur; et illud dicitur analogice praedicari, idest proportionaliter, prout unumquodque secundum suam habitudinem ad illud unum refertur.

Item sciendum quod illud unum ad quod diversae habitudines referuntur in analogicis, est unum numero, et non solum unum ratione, sicut est unum illud quod per nomen univocum designatur. Et ideo dicit quod ens etsi dicatur multipliciter, non tamen dicitur aequivoce, sed per respectum ad unum; non quidem ad unum quod sit solum ratione unum, sed quod est unum sicut una quaedam natura. Et hoc patet in exemplis infra positis.

Ponit enim primo unum exemplum, quando multa comparantur ad unum sicut ad finem, sicut patet de hoc nomine sanativum vel salubre. Sanativum enim non dicitur univoce de diaeta, medicina, urina et animali. Nam ratio sani secundum quod dicitur de diaeta, consistit in conservando sanitatem. Secundum vero quod dicitur de medicina, in faciendo sanitatem. Prout vero dicitur de urina, est signum sanitatis. Secundum vero quod dicitur de animali, ratio eius est, quoniam est receptivum vel susceptivum sanitatis. Sic igitur omne sanativum vel sanum dicitur ad sanitatem unam et eamdem. Eadem enim est sanitas quam animal suscipit, urina significat, medicina facit, et diaeta conservat.

Secundo ponit exemplum quando multa comparantur ad unum sicut ad principium efficiens. Aliquid enim dicitur medicativum, ut qui habet artem medicinae, sicut medicus peritus. Aliquid vero quia est bene aptum ad habendum artem medicinae, sicut homines qui sunt dispositi ut de facili artem medicinae acquirant. Ex quo contingit quod ingenio proprio quaedam medicinalia operantur. Aliquid vero dicitur medicativum vel medicinale, quia eo opus est ad medicinam, sicut instrumenta quibus medici utuntur, medicinalia dici possunt, et etiam medicinae quibus medici utuntur ad sanandum. Et similiter accipi possunt alia quae multipliciter dicuntur, sicut et ista.

Et sicut est de praedictis, ita etiam et ens multipliciter dicitur. Sed tamen omne ens dicitur per respectum ad unum primum. Sed hoc primum non est finis vel efficiens sicut in praemissis exemplis, sed subiectum. Alia enim dicuntur entia vel esse, quia per se habent esse sicut substantiae, quae principaliter et prius entia dicuntur. Alia vero quia sunt passiones sive proprietates substantiae, sicut per se accidentia uniuscuiusque substantiae. Quaedam autem dicuntur entia, quia sunt via ad substantiam, sicut generationes et motus. Alia autem entia dicuntur, quia sunt corruptiones substantiae. Corruptio enim est via ad non esse, sicut generatio via ad substantiam.

Et quia corruptio terminatur ad privationem, sicut generatio ad formam, convenienter ipsae etiam privationes formarum substantialium esse dicuntur. Et iterum qualitates vel accidentia quaedam dicuntur entia, quia sunt activa vel generativa substantiae, vel eorum quae secundum aliquam habitudinem praedictarum ad substantiam dicuntur, vel secundum quamque aliam. Item negationes eorum quae ad substantiam habitudinem habent, vel etiam ipsius substantiae esse dicuntur. Unde dicimus quod non ens est non ens. Quod non diceretur nisi negationi aliquo modo esse competeret.

Pages 22, *24*, *36*, **41**, 43, 65, 131, 132

33.10

IV, lectio 1, no. 543:

Quartum autem genus est quod est perfectissimum, quod scilicet habet esse in natura absque admixtione privationis, et habet esse firmum et solidum, quasi per se existens, sicut sunt substantiae. Et ad hoc sicut ad primum et principale omnia alia referuntur. Nam qualitates et quantitates dicuntur esse, inquantum insunt substantiae; motus et generationes, inquantum tendunt ad substantiam vel ad aliquid praedictorum; privationes autem et negationes, inquantum removent aliquid trium praedictorum.

Pages **41**, 65, 132

33.11

IV, lectio 3, no. 568:

. . . Non enim sequitur quod si aliquid dicitur multipliciter, quod propter hoc sit alterius scientiae vel diversae. Diversa enim significata si neque dicuntur secundum unum, idest secundum unam rationem, scilicet univoce, nec ratione diversa referuntur ad unum, sicut est in analogicis: tunc sequitur quod sit alterius, idest diversae scientiae de his considerare, vel ad minus unius per accidens.

Pages 24, 36, **41**

33.12

V, lectio 1, no. 749:

. . . Et quia ea quae in hac scientia considerantur, sunt omnibus communia, nec dicuntur univoce, sed secundum prius et posterius de diversis, ut in quarto libro est habitum; ideo prius distinguit intentiones nominum quae in huius scientiae consideratione cadunt.

Page 65

33.13

V, lectio 5, no. 824:

. . . Sciendum est autem quod reductio aliorum modorum ad unum primum fieri potest dupliciter. Uno modo secundum ordinem rerum. Alio modo secundum ordinem qui attenditur quantum ad nominis impositionem. Nomina enim imponuntur a nobis secundum quod nos intelligimus, quia nomina sunt intellectuum signa. Intelligimus autem quandoque priora ex posterioribus. Unde aliquid per

prius apud nos sortitur nomen, cui res nominis per posterius convenit.

Page 67

33.14

V, lectio 8, no. 879:

Proportione vero vel analogia sunt unum quaecumque in hoc conveniunt, quod hoc se habet ad illud sicut aliud ad aliud. Et hoc
quidem potest accipi duobus modis, vel in eo quod aliqua duo
habent diversas habitudines ad unum; sicut sanativum de urina dictum habitudinem significat signi sanitatis; de medicina vero, quia
significat habitudinem causae respectu eiusdem. Vel in eo quod est
eadem proportio duorum ad diversa, sicut tranquillitatis ad mare et
serenitatis ad aeram. Tranquillitas enim est quies maris et sereni-
tas aeris.

Pages **41**, 83, 84, 99

33.15

V, lectio 12, no. 916:

. . . aliqua duo quae . . . conveniant . . . in aliquo uno secundum
proportionem, sicut quantitas et qualitas in ente.

Page **42**

33.16

V, lectio 13, no. 951:

Secundus modus attenditur secundum ordinem substantiae ad accidens. Quia enim ens multipliciter dicitur, et non univoce, oportet
quod omnes significationes entis reducantur ad unam primam, secundum quam dicitur ens, quod est subiectum aliorum entium per
se existens. Et propter hoc primum subiectum dicitur esse prius:
unde substantia prius est accidente.

Pages **42**, 65, 132

33.17

VII, lectio 4, no. 1331:

. . . Primo ostendit quomodo definitio et quod quid est invenitur in
substantia et accidentibus. Secundo quomodo de utrisque praedicetur. . . . Sicut autem ens praedicatur de omnibus praedicamentis,
non autem similiter, sed primum de substantia, et per posterius de

aliis praedicamentis, ita et quod quid est, simpliciter convenit substantiae, aliis autem alio modo, idest secundum quid.
    Page 65

33.18

VII, lectio 4, nos. 1334-38, 1351:
Propter hoc enim quod omnia alia praedicamenta habent rationem
entis a substantia, ideo modus entitatis substantiae, scilicet esse
quid, participatur secundum quamdam similitudinem proportionis
in omnibus aliis praedicamentis; ut dicamus, quod sicut animal est
quid hominis, ita color albedinis, et numerus dualitatis; et ita dicimus qualitatem habere quid non simpliciter, sed huius. Sicut aliqui
dicunt logice de non ente loquentes, non ens est, non quia non ens
sit simpliciter, sed quia non ens est non ens. Et similiter qualitas
non habet quid simpliciter, sed quid qualitatis.
    . . . Non ea dicamus univoce praedicari quorum non est una
ratio in essendo.
    . . . Manifestum est enim quod oportet definitionem et quod
quid est vel aequivoce praedicari in substantia et accidentibus, vel
addentes et auferentes secundum magis et minus, sive secundum
prius et posterius, ut ens dicitur de substantia et accidente. . . .
    Non enim est rectum quod quod quid est et definitio dicatur de
substantia et de accidentibus, neque aequivoce, neque simpliciter et
eodem modo, idest univoce. Sed sicut medicabile dicitur de diversis
particularibus per respectum ad unum et idem, non tamen significat unum et idem de omnibus de quibus dicitur, nec etiam dicitur
aequivoce. Dicitur enim corpus medicabile, quia est subiectum
medicinae; et opus medicabile, quia exercetur medicina. . . . Et
sic patet quod non dicitur omnino aequivoce medicinale de his
tribus, cum in aequivocis non habeatur respectus ad aliquod unum.
Nec iterum univoce dicitur secundum unam rationem. Non enim
est eadem ratio secundum quam dicitur medicinale id quo utitur
medicina, et quod facit medicinam. Sed dicitur analogice per respectum ad unum, scilicet ad medicinam. Et similiter quod quid est
et definitio, non dicitur nec aequivoce nec univoce, de substantia et
accidente, sed per respectum ad unum. . . .
    . . . rationes non dicuntur "certe," idest certitudinaliter, quasi
ea quae dicuntur univoce, sed dicuntur secundum prius et posterius,
ut supra dictum est.
    Pages 24, **42**, 58, 66, 131, 132

33.19

VII, lectio 4, no. 1352:

. . . Substantia enim quae habet quidditatem absolutam, non dependet in sua quidditate ex alio. Accidens autem dependet a subiecto, licet subiectum non sit de essentia accidentis; sicut creatura dependet a creatore et tamen creator non est de essentia creaturae, ita quod oporteat exteriorem essentiam in eius definitione poni. Accidentia vero non habent esse nisi per hoc quod insunt subiecto: et ideo eorum quidditas est dependens a subiecto: et propter hoc oportet quod subiectum in accidentis definitione ponatur, quandoque quidem in recto, quandoque vero in obliquo.

Page *34*

33.20

IX, lectio 1, no. 1773:

. . . Dicit ergo primo, quod determinatum est in aliis, scilicet quinto huius, quod multipliciter dicitur potentia et posse. Sed ista multiplicitas quantum ad quosdam modos est multiplicitas aequivocationis, sed quantum ad quosdam analogiae.

Page 85

33.21

IX, lectio 1, no. 1780:

Unde manifestum est quod omnes isti modi potentiarum reducuntur ad unum primum, scilicet ad potentiam activam. Et inde patet quod haec multiplicitas non est secundum aequivocationem, sed secundum analogiam.

33.22

IX, lectio 5, no. 1828:

. . . Ad hanc diversitatem actus insinuandam dicit primo, quod non omnia dicimus similiter esse actu, sed hoc diversimode. Et haec diversitas considerari potest per diversas proportiones. Potest enim sic accipi proportio, ut dicamus, quod sicut hoc est in hoc, ita hoc in hoc. Utputa visus sicut est in oculo, ita auditus in aure. Et per hunc modum proportionis accipitur comparatio substantiae, idest formae, ad materiam; nam forma in materia dicitur esse.

Pages 84, 99

33.23

IX, lectio 5, no. 1829:

Alius modus proportionis est, ut dicamus quod sicut habet se hoc ad hoc, ita hoc ad hoc; puta sicut se habet visus ad videndum, ita auditus ad audiendum. Et per hunc modum proportionis accipitur comparatio motus ad potentiam motivam, vel cuiuscumque operationis ad potentiam operativam.

Pages *84, 99*

33.24

X, lectio 8, no. 2092:

Et non dicit quod sit simpliciter genus; quia sicut ens genus non est, proprie loquendo, ita nec unum quod convertitur cum ente, nec pluralitas ei opposita. Sed est quasi genus; quia habet aliquid de ratione generis, inquantum est communis.

33.25

X, lectio 12, no. 2142:

Nam corruptibilium et incorruptibilium non potest esse materia una. Genus autem, physice loquendo, a materia sumitur. Unde supradictum est, quod ea quae non communicant in materia, sunt genere diversa. Logice autem loquendo, nihil prohibet quod conveniant in genere, inquantum conveniunt in una communi ratione, vel substantiae, vel qualitatis, vel alicuius huiusmodi.

Page *101*

33.26

XI, lectio 3, no. 2197:

Manifestum est enim quod quae sic dicuntur, media sunt inter univoca et aequivoca. In univocis enim nomen unum praedicatur de diversis secundum rationem totaliter eamdem; sicut animal de equo et de bove dictum, significat substantiam animatam sensibilem. In aequivocis vero idem nomen praedicatur de diversis secundum rationem totaliter diversam. Sicut patet de hoc nomine, canis, prout dicitur de stella, et quadam specie animalis. In his vero quae praedicto modo dicuntur, idem nomen de diversis praedicatur secundum rationem partim eandem, partim diversam. Diversam quidem quantum ad diversos modos relationis. Eamdem vero quantum ad id ad quod fit relatio. Esse enim significativum, et esse effectivum, diversum est. Sed sanitas una est. Et propter hoc huiusmodi dicuntur ana-

loga, quia proportionantur ad unum. Et similiter est de multiplici-
tate entis. Nam ens simpliciter dicitur id quod in se habet esse,
scilicet substantia. Alia vero dicuntur entia, quia sunt huius quod
per se est, vel passio, vel habitus, vel aliquid huiusmodi. Non enim
qualitas dicitur ens, quia ipsa habeat esse, sed per eam substantia
dicitur esse disposita. Et similiter est de aliis accidentibus. Et propter hoc dicit quod sunt entis. Et sic patet quod multiplicitas entis
habet aliquid commune, ad quod fit reductio.
Pages *24, 36-37,* **42,** *65, 132*

33.27

XII, lectio 4, no. 2477:

. . . Ponit alium modum, secundum quem sunt eadem principia
omnium proportionaliter: et dicit, quod alio modo sunt eadem
principia omnium proportionaliter, ita quod dicamus quod actus
et potentia sunt principia omnium.
Page *85*

33.28

XII, lectio 4, no. 2480:

Et quia dixerat hunc modum, quo proportionaliter sunt principia
eadem omnium, esse alium modum a praesignato, consequenter
ostendit quomodo reducantur in idem. . . . Sic igitur manifestum
est, quod actus et potentia in idem redeunt cum materia et forma et
privatione; et quod actus et potentia in diversis uno modo differunt: quia non similiter est in omnibus, sed aliter et aliter.
Page 85

33.29

XII, lectio 4, nos. 2483-86:

. . . Sicut autem actus et potentia sunt universaliter principia omnium, quia consequuntur ens commune, ita oportet quod secundum
quod descendit communitas principiatorum, descendat communitas
principiorum. Eorum enim quae non sunt in eodem genere, puta
colorum, sonorum, substantiarum et quantitatis, sunt aliae causae
et elementa, ut dictum est, praeterquam quod proportionaliter sint
eadem omnium. . . . Omnium enim quodammodo sunt eadem principia, aut secundum proportionem; sicut si dicamus, quod in quolibet genere inveniuntur aliqua quae se habent ut materia et forma
et privatio et movens; aut eo quod causae substantiarum sunt

causae omnium, quia destructis eis, alia destruuntur. Aut quia principia sunt endelechia, idest actus et potentia. Istis autem tribus modis sunt eadem principia omnium . . . secundum analogiam.

Page 85

34.1 In decem libros Ethicorum (1271-1272)

I, lectio 6, no. 80:

. . . Sed in bonis invenitur prius et posterius. Quod manifestat ex hoc, quod bonum invenitur in eo quod quid est, idest substantia, et similiter in qualitate, et etiam in aliis generibus. Manifestum est autem, quod illud quod est ens per seipsum, scilicet substantia, est naturaliter prius omnibus his quae non habent esse nisi in comparatione ad substantiam, sicut est quantitas, quae est mensura substantiae, et qualitas quae est dispositio substantiae, et ad aliquid, quod est habitudo substantiae. Et idem est in aliis generibus, quae omnia assimilantur propagini entis, idest substantiae, quae est principaliter ens, a qua propaginantur et derivantur omnia alia genera. Quae etiam in tantum dicuntur entia, inquantum accidunt substantiae. Et ex hoc concludit quod non potest esse quaedam communis idea boni.

Page 65

34.2

I, lectio 7, nos. 95-96:

. . . Aliquid dici de multis secundum diversas rationes contingit dupliciter. Uno modo secundum rationes omnino diversas non habentes respectum ad unum. Et ista dicuntur aequivoca a casu, quia scilicet casu accidit quod unum nomen unus homo imposuit uni rei, et alius alii rei, ut praecipue patet in diversis hominibus uno nomine nominatis. Alio modo unum nomen dicitur de multis secundum rationes diversas non totaliter, sed in aliquo uno convenientes. Quandoque quidem in hoc, quod referuntur ad unum principium, sicut res aliqua dicitur militaris, vel quia est instrumentum militis, sicut gladius, vel quia est tegumentum eius sicut lorica, vel quia est vehiculum eius, sicut equus. Quandoque vero in hoc, quod referuntur ad unum finem sicut medicina dicitur sana, eo quod est factiva sanitatis, dieta vero eo quod est conservativa sanitatis, urina vero eo quod est sanitatis significativa. Quandoque secundum proportiones diversas ad idem subiectum, sicut qualitas dicitur esse ens, quia est dispositio per se entis, idest substantiae, quantitas vero eo quod est mensura eiusdem, et sic de aliis, vel secundum unam proportionem ad diversa subiecta. Eamdem enim habent proportionem visus quoad corpus, et intellectus ad animam. Unde sicut visus est potentia organi corporalis ita etiam intellectus est potentia animae absque participatione corporis.

Sic ergo dicit, quod bonum dicitur de multis, non secundum rationes penitus differentes, sicut accidit in his quae sunt a casu aequivoca, sed magis secundum analogiam, idest proportionem eamdem, inquantum omnia bona dependent ab uno primo bonitatis principio, vel inquantum ordinantur ad unum finem. Non enim voluit Aristoteles quod illud bonum separatum sit idea et ratio omnium bonorum, sed principium et finis. Vel etiam dicuntur omnia bona magis secundum analogiam, idest proportionem eamdem, sicut visus est bonum corporis, et intellectus est bonum animae. Ideo hunc tertium modum praefert, quia accipitur secundum bonitatem inhaerentem rebus. Primi autem duo modi secundum bonitatem separatam, a qua non ita proprie aliquid denominatur.

Pages 24, *37*, **42**, 84, **85**, 99, 131

34.3

I, lectio 20, no. 242:

. . . Et dicit, quod si oportet dicere illam partem animae, quae participat rationem, esse aliqualiter rationalem, duplex erit rationale. Unum quidem sicut principaliter et in seipso rationem habens, quod est essentialiter rationale. Aliud autem est, quod est natum obedire rationi, ut et patri. Et hoc dicimus rationale per participationem.

Page 63

34.4

V, lectio 5, nos. 939-45:

. . . proportionalitas nihil aliud est quam aequalitas proportionis; cum scilicet aequalem proportionem habet hoc ad hoc, et illud ad illud. Proportio autem nihil est aliud quam habitudo unius quantitatis ad aliam . . . omnis proportionalitas ad minus consistit in quatuor . . . sicut proportionalitas, ita et iustum ad minus in quatuor invenitur. . . . Proportionale enim est medium inter excessum et defectum; quia proportionalitas est aequalitas proportionis.

Pages 78, 99

34.5

IX, lectio 1, no. 1758:

. . . analogum, scilicet id quod est proportionale utrique.

Page 83

34.6

X, lectio 11, no. 2106:

Et ideo manifestans quod dictum est, subdit, quod homo sic vivens, scilicet vacando contemplationi, non vivit secundum quod homo, qui est compositus ex diversis, sed secundum quod aliquid divinum in ipso existit, prout scilicet secundum intellectum divinam similitudinem participat.

34.7

X, lectio 11, no. 2110:

. . . Non est enim secundum hominem quantum ad naturam compositam, est autem propriissime secundum hominem quantum ad id quod est principalissimum in homine: quod quidem perfectissime invenitur in substantiis superioribus, in homine autem imperfecte et quasi participative.

Page 63

35.1 Super librum De causis (1272) Ed. Saffrey

prop. 1:

. . . Quod causa prima plus influat quam secunda, sic probat: eminentius convenit aliquid causae quam causato.

Page 73

35.2

prop. 3:

. . . Effectus autem omnis participat aliquid de virtute suae causae . . . omnia ista [sc. per se bonitas, per se esse, etc.] sunt essentialiter ipsa prima omnium causa a qua res participant omnes huiusmodi perfectiones.

prop. 6:

. . . secundum rei veritatem, causa prima est supra ens in quantum est ipsum esse infinitum, ens autem dicitur id quod finite participat esse . . . causa excedens effectum non sufficienter cognosci potest per suum effectum.

Page 59

35.3

prop. 12:

Apponit autem Proclus probationem manifestam ad ea quae dicta sunt, distinguens quod tripliciter aliquid de aliquo dicitur: uno modo causaliter, sicut calor de sole, alio modo essentialiter sive naturaliter, sicut calor de igne, tertio modo secundum quamdam posthabitionem, id est consecutionem sive participationem, quando scilicet aliquid non plene habetur sed posteriori modo et particulariter, sicut calor invenitur in corporibus elementatis non in ea plenitudine secundum quam est in igne. Sic igitur illud quod est essentialiter in primo, est participative in secundo et tertio; quod autem est essentialiter in secundo, est in primo quidem causaliter et in ultimo participative; quod vero est in tertio essentialiter, est causaliter in primo et in secundo. Et per hunc modum omnia sunt in omnibus.

Pages 61, 63, 66

35.4

prop. 22:

. . . In omnibus enim quae sunt infra causam primam, quaedam inveniuntur perfecte existentia sive completa, quaedam imperfecta sive diminuta. Perfecta quidem videntur esse ea quae per se subsistunt in natura, quae a nobis significantur per nomina concreta ut homo, sapiens et huiusmodi; imperfecta autem sunt illa quae per se non subsistunt, sicut formae ut humanitas, sapientia, et huiusmodi, quae significantur apud nos nominibus abstractis.

Pages 66, 69

36.1 In libros De caelo et mundo (1272-1273) Ed. Leonine

II, lectio 13, no. 4:

. . . In caelestibus autem corporibus, si sunt animata, non est virtus animae sensitiva, sicut etiam neque nutritiva; unde non dicuntur animalia nisi aequivoce, ex eo scilicet quod habent animam intellectivam.

37.1 In libros De generatione et corruptione (1272-1273) Ed. Leonine

I, lectio 8, no. 5:

. . . Non est possibile quod idem in uno sit accidens et in alio forma substantialis, nisi aequivoce diceretur: calidum autem et frigidum in aliis corporibus sunt accidentia, de quibus tamen univoce dicuntur cum elementis, ex quorum commixtione in eis huiusmodi qualitates inveniuntur.

37.2

I, lectio 13, no. 4:

. . . Tertio, quando materia patientis non est proportionata ad recipiendum formam agentis, propter illius excellentiam, sed recipit aliquid minus; sicut patet in animalibus quae generantur sine semine ex virtute solis. Et inde est etiam quod effectus non assimilatur in specie agenti remoto, sed propinquo; ut homo homini, non autem soli, quamvis homo generat hominem et sol, ut dicitur in II *Physicorum.*

Page 74

37.3

I, lectio 6, no. 5:

. . . "simpliciter ens" potest intelligi dupliciter: uno modo ut significat id quod est primum inter omnia praedicamenta entis, prout scilicet "simpliciter ens" dicitur de substantia; alio modo secundum quod "simpliciter ens" dicitur ipsum ens universale quod omnia praedicamenta comprehendit.

38.1 Summa theologiae, tertia pars (1272-1273) Ed. Leonine

60, 1 *c.*:

Dicendum quod omnia quae habent ordinem ad unum aliquid, licet diversimode, ab illo denominari possunt; sicut a sanitate quae est in animali, denominatur sanum non solum animal, quod est sanitatis subiectum, sed dicitur medicina sana inquantum est sanitatis effectiva, diaeta vero inquantum est conservativa eiusdem, et urina inquantum est significativa ipsius. Sic igitur sacramentum potest aliquid dici, vel quia in se habet aliquam sanctitatem occultam.

Page 42

38.2

60, 1 *ad* 1:

Dicendum quod quia medicina se habet ut causa effectiva sanitatis, inde est quod omnia denominata a medicina dicuntur per ordinem ad unum primum agens; et propter hoc, medicamentum importat causalitatem quandam.

Page 42

38.3

62, 3 c.:

Dicendum quod multipliciter aliquid dicitur esse in alio; inter quos duplici modo gratia est in sacramentis. Uno modo, sicut in signo; nam sacramentum est signum gratiae. Alio modo, sicut in causa. Nam, sicut dictum est, sacramentum novae legis est instrumentalis gratiae causa. Unde gratia est in sacramento novae legis, non quidem secundum similitudinem speciei, sicut effectus est in causa univoca; neque etiam secundum aliquam formam propriam et permanentem proportionatam ad talem effectum sicut sunt effectus in causis non univocis, puta res generatae in sole; sed secundum quandam instrumentalem virtutem, quae est fluens et incompleta in esse naturae.

Page 71

39.1 Compendium theologiae (1273 or 1261-1269)

1ᵃ *pars, cap.* 21:

Unde etiam apparet quod omnes perfectiones in quibuscumque rebus inventas, necesse est originaliter et superabundanter in Deo esse. Nam omne quod movet aliquid ad perfectionem, prius habet in se perfectionem ad quam movet, sicut magister prius habet in se doctrinam quam aliis tradit. Cum igitur Deus sit primum movens, et omnia alia immoveat in suas perfectiones, necesse est omnes perfectiones rerum in ipso praeexistere superabundanter.

Page 67

39.2

1ᵃ *pars, cap.* 27:

Quod nomina de Deo et aliis, non omnino univoce, nec aequivoce dicuntur. Tertium est quod nomina de Deo et aliis rebus dicta, non omnino univoce, nec omnino aequivoce dicuntur. Univoce namque dici non possunt, cum definitio eius quod de creatura dicitur, non sit definitio eius quod dicitur de Deo: oportet autem univoce dictorum eamdem definitionem esse. Similiter autem nec omnino aequivoce. In his enim quae sunt a casu aequivoca, idem nomen imponitur uni rei, nullo habito respectu ad rem aliam: unde per unum non potest ratiocinari de alio. Haec autem nomina quae dicuntur de Deo et de aliis rebus, attribuuntur Deo secundum aliquem ordinem quem habet ad istas res, in quibus intellectus significata eorum considerat; unde et per alias res ratiocinari de Deo possumus. Non igitur omnino aequivoce dicuntur ista de Deo et de aliis rebus, sicut ea quae sunt a casu aequivoca. Dicuntur igitur secundum analogiam, idest secundum proportionem ad unum. Ex eo enim quod alias res comparamus ad Deum sicut ad suam primam originem, huiusmodi nomina quae significant perfectiones aliarum, Deo attribuimus. Ex quo patet quod licet quantum ad nominis impositionem huiusmodi nomina per prius de creaturis dicantur, eo quod ex creaturis intellectus nomina imponens ascendit in Deum; tamen secundum rem significatam per nomen, per prius dicuntur de Deo, a quo perfectiones descendunt in alias res.

Pages **42**, 67, 134

39.3

1ª *pars, cap.* 43:

Inveniuntur autem quaedam quae ex aliis procedunt, perfectam eorum speciem non consequi, ex quibus procedunt. Uno modo sicut in generationibus aequivocis: a sole enim non generatur sol, sed quoddam animal. . . . Alio modo quod procedit ex aliquo, differt ab eo propter defectum puritatis, dum scilicet ab eo quod est in se simplex et purum, per applicationem ad extraneam materiam aliquid producitur a prima specie deficiens: sicut ex domo quae est in mente artificis, fit domus quae est in materia; et a lumine recepto in corpore terminato, fit color; et ex igne adiuncto aliis elementis, fit mixtum; et ex radio per oppositionem corporis opaci, fit umbra. . . . Tertio modo quod ex aliquo procedit, non consequitur speciem eius propter defectum veritatis, quia scilicet non vere recipit eius naturam, sed quandam eius similitudinem tantum, sicut imago in speculo vel sculptura, aut etiam similitudo rei in intellectu vel sensu. Non enim imago hominis dicitur verus homo, sed similitudo; nec lapis est in anima, ut dicit Philosophus, sed species lapidis.

Pages 52, 71

39.4

1ª *pars, cap.* 68:

Omne quod habet aliquid per participationem, reducitur in id quod habet illud per essentiam, sicut in principium et causam.

Page 60

39.5

1ª *pars, cap.* 101:

. . . Finis generationis uniuscuiusque rei generatae est forma eiusdem, hac enim adepta generatio quiescit. Unumquodque enim generatum, sive per artem sive per naturam, secundum suam formam similatur aliquo modo agenti, nam omne agens agit aliqualiter sibi simile. Domus enim quae est in materia, procedit a domo quae est in mente artificis. In naturalibus etiam homo generat hominem; et si aliquid sit genitum vel factum secundum naturam, quod non sit simile generanti secundum speciem, similatur tamen suis agentibus sicut imperfectum perfecto. Ex hoc enim contingit quod generatum generanti secundum speciem non similatur, quia ad eius perfectam similitudinem non possit pervenire, sed aliqualiter eam imperfecte participat; sicut animalia et plantae quae generantur ex virtute solis. Omnium igitur quae fiunt, finis generationis sive perfectionis est forma facientis vel generantis, ut scilicet ad eius similitudinem perveniatur. Forma autem primi agentis, scilicet Dei, non est aliud quam eius bonitas. Propter hoc igitur omnia facta sunt ut divinae bonitati assimilentur.

Pages 22, 62, 64, 71

39.6

1ª *pars, cap.* 109:

Solus igitur Deus est sua bonitas et essentialiter bonus, alia vero dicuntur bona secundum participationem aliquam ipsius.

Page 59

39.7

2ª *pars, cap.* 8:

Indicat se quippe Deus aliqualiter hominibus naturali quadam cognitione cognoscendum per hoc quod hominibus lumen rationis infundit, et creaturas visibiles condidit, in quibus bonitatis et sapientiae ipsius aliqualiter relucent vestigia. . . . Ista tamen cognitio imperfecta est, quia nec ipsa creatura perfecte ab homine conspici potest; et etiam creatura deficit a perfecta Dei repraesentatione, quia virtus huius causae in infinitum excedit effectum.

Page 74

40.1 De immortalitate animae (undated) Ed. Gomez
ad 1:

. . . Et tamen sciendum est quod ens et ea quae sunt entis non univoce sed analogice praedicantur de rebus, et ideo in huiusmodi non oportet quaerere rationem omnino eandem. (f. 48ra)

41.1 De instantibus (authenticity uncertain) (undated)
cap. 4:

. . . Aevum autem non se habet ad tempus sicut aliquid eiusdem speciei, sed tamquam causa analoga: per prius enim invenitur ratio mensurae in aevo quam in tempore.

Page 65

42.1 De natura accidentis (authenticity uncertain) (undated)
cap. 1:

Sciendum est igitur quod ens non dicitur de accidente hoc nisi mediante substantia, de qua per prius dicitur. Haec enim est natura omnis analogi, quod illud de quo primo dicitur, erit in ratione omnium quae sunt post: sicut sanum, quod prius dicitur de animali quam de urina vel medicina, et ideo sanitas animalis cadit in definitione utriusque sanitatis: urina enim dicitur sana inquantum est signum sanitatis in animali; et similiter medicina quia est causa sanitatis animalis. Per quem modum cum ens dicatur per prius de substantia quam de accidente, ideo ratio entis in substantia necessario cadit in definitione entis in accidente. Dicitur enim quantitas ens, quia est mensura per se entis, idest substantiae; et qualitas quia est dispositio per se entis dicitur ens, et sic universaliter de aliis.

Pages 34, 65, 69, 88

43.1 De natura generis (authenticity uncertain) (undated)
cap. 1:

. . . In ente autem sic accepto duplex analogia reperitur. Dicitur enim ens de Deo et creatura, sed per prius de Deo, et per posterius de creatura; licet verius sit Deum esse super omne ens, quam esse ens, sicut dicit Dionysius et Damascenus. Propter hanc tamen analogiam non sequitur ens esse prius utroque, Deo scilicet et creatura, sicut prius est ens substantia et accidente, de quibus analogice dicitur. Ad cuius evidentiam est sciendum quod quando tota ratio analogi reperitur in altero de quibus praedicatur, sicut tota ratio entis absolute in Deo reperitur, tunc non erit praedicatum prius utroque, cum praedicatum non excedat subiectum. Cum vero tota ratio praedicati in neutro subiectorum est, necesse erit praedicatum prius esse et communius utroque subiecto, sicut tota ratio entis non salvatur in substantia quae est genus primum, cum ens divinum non includat. Et ideo ens genus non est, sed est de omnibus communiter praedicabile analogice.

Pages 67, 69, 131

44.1 De principio individuationis (authenticity uncertain) (undated)

. . . Omnis enim forma participat actum, qui est primus per essentiam; sed hoc analogice fit.

. . . Hoc autem non est quod illa potentia apprehendat materiam in se, cum ipsa non possit sciri nisi per analogiam ad formam.

Page 79

Analytic Index

to the Texts

Goodness

Imitation
of God by creature

Likeness, similitude (similarity?)

Matter and form

Metaphor

30. 1
33. 8, 9, 14, 15, 18, 22, 23, 27, 28, 29
34. 2, 4, 5

Proportionality

3. 1 (?)
4. 28, 35
5. 9, 15, 18
6. 2 (?)
7. 4, 7, 9
9. 6, 9, 11, 12, 35
11. 5
17. 35, 43, 111, 117
21. 1
25. 1
28. 1
33. 14, 22, 23, 27
34. 2 (?), 4

Substance and accident

2. 2
3. 1
4. 1, 2, 11, 17, 21, 23
5. 10, 16, 21
6. 1, 5, 6
8. 1
9. 9, 14, 15, 26

10. 1
14. 2, 20
15. 5, 7, 35, 38, 41, 42
17. 76, 100
18. 4
19. 1, 2
20. 1, 2, 4
22. 3, 7, 8
24. 6
25. 2, 4, 6, 7
28. 2
31. 1
33. 9, 10, 16, 17, 18, 19, 26
34. 1
37. 3
42. 1
43. 1

Wisdom

4. 2, 3, 11, 14, 29, 31, 33, 34, 35
9. 19, 21
14. 12, 30
15. 3
16. 1
17. 14, 16, 35, 40, 70
29. 2
32. 1
39. 7

Secondary Sources

There is no complete bibliography of writings on St. Thomas' doctrine of analogy. Both the historian and the student of St. Thomas would find such a bibliography very useful. The following list attempts to supply an adequate working bibliography. It contains three categories of works. First, it attempts to be exhaustive in listing all the books and scholarly articles dealing directly with St. Thomas' doctrine of analogy. Secondly, it indicates the treatment of analogy in the most important general expositions of Thomism, or Thomistic metaphysics. Thirdly, textbooks of Thomistic metaphysics are included when they modify or depart from the more traditional interpretations of analogy.

Abranches, Cassiano, S.J. "Ser e analogia." *Pensiamento,* XV (1959), 33-45.

Absil, Th. *Annotationes de esse,* Vol. 1, pp. 66-70. 3 vols. Haarlem: Gottmer, n. d.

Alverez-Menendez, S., O.P. "De diversitate et identitate analogiae juxta Cajetanum." *La ciencia tomista,* XLIX (1934), 310-29.

Anderson, James F. "The Basis of Metaphysical Analogy." *Downside Review,* LXVI (1948), 38-47.

——— *The Bond of Being,* pp. 93-103, 119-31, 156-66, 229-61, 295-311. St. Louis: B. Herder Book Company, 1949.

——— and others. "Some Basic Propositions concerning Metaphysical Analogy." *Review of Metaphysics,* V (1952), 465-72.

Balthasar, N. J. *L'abstraction métaphysique et l'analogie des êtres dans l'être,* pp. 23-112. Louvain: Warny, 1935.

——— *La méthode en métaphysique,* pp. 23-32, 56-58. Louvain: Institut Supérieur de Philosophie, 1943.

——— *Mon moi dans l'être,* pp. 194-218. Louvain: Institut Supérieur de Philosophie, 1946.

Barale, Paolo. "L'esse di Dio e l'esse della creatura secondo S. Tommaso." *Rivista rosminiana*, XLVII (1953), 166-84.

Barion, J. "Uber die Bedeutung der Analogie für die Metaphysik." *Philosophisches Jahrbuch*, XLIX (1936), 30-48.

Bauer, R. *Gotteserkenntnis und Gottesbeweise bei Kardinal Kajetan*, pp. 97-135. Regensburg: Pustet, 1955.

Bejze, Bohdan. "Zastosowanie analogii w dowodzeniu istnienia Boga." *Roczniki filozoficzne*, VI (1958), 149-73.

Bernard, R., O.P. Review of analogy literature. *Bulletin thomiste*, I (1924), 123-27.

Blanche, F. A., O.P. "L'analogie." *Revue de philosophie*, XXX (1923), 248-70.

———— "La notion d'analogie dans la philosophie de S. Thomas." *Revue des sciences philosophiques et théologiques*, X (1921), 169-93.

———— "Sur le sens de quelques locutions concernant l'analogie dans la langue de S. Thomas d'Aquin." *Revue des sciences philosophiques et théologiques*, X (1921), 52-59.

———— "Une théorie de l'analogie; éclaircissements et développments." *Revue de philosophie*, new series, III (1932), 37-78.

Bochenski, I. M., O.P. "On Analogy." *Thomist*, XI (1948), 424-47.

Boyle, Robert R., S.J. "The Nature of Metaphor." *Modern Schoolman*, XXXI (1954), 257-80.

———— "The Nature of Metaphor: Further Considerations." *Modern Schoolman*, XXXIV (1957), 283-98.

Brusotti, V. "L'analogia di attribuzione e la conoscenza della natura di Dio." *Rivista di filosofia neo-scolastica*, XXVII (1935), 31-66.

Cajetanus, Thomas de Vio. *The Analogy of Names and the Concept of Being*, translated by Edward Bushinski, C.S.Sp. and Henry Koren, C.S.Sp. Pittsburgh: Duquesne University Press, 1953.

———— *Commentaria in 'De ente et essentia,'* edited by M.-H. Laurent, O.P., pp. 31-38. Turin: Marietti, 1934.

———— *Commentaria in 'Summam theologiae.'* In *Opera omnia S. Thomae Aquinatis*, Ed. Leonine. Rome, 1888-.

———— *Scripta philosophica. III. De nominum analogia et de conceptu entis*, edited by N. Zammit, O.P. Rome: Angelicum, 1934.

Capreolus, Johannes. *Defensiones theologiae,* edited by Ceslaus Paban, O.P. and Thomas Pègues, O.P., dist. 1, q. 1, concl. 9, Vol. 1, pp. 125, 129-32, 141-44. 7 vols. Turin. Cattier, 1900.

Coccio, Agostino. "Vie vecchie e vie nuove per ascendere a Dio." *Rivista di filosofia neo-scolastica,* XL (1948), 227-48.

Copers, G. "De Analogie in de Metaphysica von Erich Przywara." *Tijdschrift voor philosophie,* XI (1949), 229-64.

Coreth, E., S.J. "Dialektik und Analogie des Seins." *Scholastik,* XXVI (1951), 57-86.

Daly, C. B. "The Knowableness of God." *Philosophical Studies,* IX (1959), 90-137.

De Finance, J., S.J., *Etre et agir,* pp. 119-61. Paris: Beauchesne, 1945.

Del Prado, N., O.P. *De veritate fundamentali philosophiae christianae,* p. 84. Fribourg: Paulusdruckerei, 1911.

Derisi, Octavio Nicolás. "Esencia y significación de la analogía en metafisicia." *La ciencia tomista,* LXXVI (1949), 298-312.

Desbuts, B. "La notion d'analogie d'après Saint Thomas d'Aquin." *Annales de philosophie chrétienne,* fourth series, I (tome 151, 1906), 377-86.

Descoqs, P., S.J. *Institutiones metaphysicae generalis,* Vol. 1, pp. 206-306. Paris: Beauchesne, 1925.

———— *Praelectiones theologiae naturalis,* Vol. 2, pp. 735-840. 2 vols. Paris: Beauchesne, 1935.

Emmet, Dorothy. *The Nature of Metaphysical Thinking,* pp. 169-88. London: The Macmillan Company, 1945.

———— "The Use of Analogy in Metaphysics." *Proceedings of the Aristotelian Society,* new series, XLI (1940-1941), 27-46.

Esdaille, B. W. "The Analogy of Being." *New Scholasticism,* XVI (1942), 331-64.

Fabro, C. *La nozione metafisica di partecipazione secondo S. Tommaso d'Aquino,* second edition, pp. 161-86, 189-212. Milan: Vita e Pensiero, 1950.

Farrer, Austin. *Finite and Infinite,* pp. 53-54. Westminster: Dacre Press, 1943.

Feckes, K. "Die Analogie in unserem Gotteskennen, ihr metaphysische und religiöse Bedeutung." In A Dyroff, editor, *Probleme der Gotteserkenntnis,* pp. 132-84. Münster: Aschendorff, 1928.

Flanagan, Sister Thomas Marguerite, C.S.J. "The Use of Analogy in the *Summa Contra Gentiles.*" *Modern Schoolman,* XXXV (1957), 21-37.

Foote, Edward, S.J. "Anatomy of Analogy." *Modern Schoolman,* XVIII (1940), 12-16.

Garcia López, J. "La analogía del ser." *La ciencia tomista,* LXXVI (1949), 607-25.

Gardair, J. "L'être divin." *Revue de philosophie,* VIII (1906), 599-626.

Gardeil, A., O.P. "Faculté de l'être ou faculté du divin?" *Revue néo-scolastique de philosophie,* XVII (1911), 90-100.

Garrigou-Lagrange,, Réginald, O.P. *Dieu, son existence et sa nature,* fifth edition, pp. 513-68, 780-82. Paris: Beauchesne, 1938.

———— *God, His Existence and His Nature,* translated by Dom Bede Rose, O.S.B., Vol. 2, pp. 16-32, 203-46, 453-55. 2 vols. St. Louis: B. Herder Book Company, 1934-1936.

———— *Reality,* translated by Patrick Cummins, O.S.B., pp. 87-95. St. Louis: B. Herder Book Company, 1950.

Gazzana, Adriano, S.J. "L'analogia in S. Tommaso e nel Gaetano." *Gregorianum,* XXIV (1943), 367-83.

Geiger, L.-B., O.P. *La participation dans la philosophie de S. Thomas d' Aquin,* pp. 51, 149, 265-66, 276, 370-72. Paris: Vrin, 1942.

———— Review of analogy literature. *Bulletin thomiste,* VII (1944), 355-58; IX (1955), 416-23.

Gilson, Etienne. "Cajétan et l'existence." *Tijdschrift voor philosophie,* XV (1953), 267-86.

———— *The Christian Philosophy of St. Thomas Aquinas,* translated by L. K. Shook, C.S.B., pp. 105, 135, 360-61. New York: Random House, 1956.

Goergen, A. *Kardinal Cajetans Lehre von der Analogie; ihr Verhältnis zu Thomas von Aquin.* Speyer: Pilger-Verlag, 1938.

Habbel, J. *Die Analogie zwischen Gott und Welt nach Thomas von Aquin.* Regensburg: Habbel, 1928.

Hart, Charles. *Thomistic Metaphysics,* pp. 27-51, 86-112, 178-79. New York: Prentice-Hall, 1959.

Hayen, André, S.J. "Analogia entis. Le méthode et l'épistémologie du P. Przywara." *Revue néo-scolastique de philosophie,* XXXVII (1934), 345-64.

Hayen, André, S.J. *L'intentionnel dans la philosophie de S. Thomas,* pp. 71-103. Bruxelles: L'Edition Universelle, 1942.

Hayner, Paul C. "Analogical Predication." *Journal of Philosophy,* LV (1958), 855-62.

Hegyi, Johannes, S.J. *Die Bedeutung des Seins bei den klassischen Kommentatoren des heiligen Thomas von Aquin—Capreolus—Silvester von Ferrara—Cajetan,* pp. 99-105, 138-41. Pullach bei München: Verlag Berchmanskolleg, 1959.

Hellin, José, S.J. *La analogía del ser y el conocimiento de Dios en Suárez,* pp. 55-118, 147-88, 230-58, 342-55 (Cajetan, pp, 147-61). Madrid: Editoria Nacional, 1947.

Henle, Robert J., S.J. *Saint Thomas and Platonism.* The Hague: Nijhoff, 1956.

Horgan, J. "L'abstraction de l'être." *Revue néo-scolastique de philosophie,* XLII (1939), 161-81.

———— "Aspects of Cajetan's Theory of Analogy." *Irish Ecclesiastical Record,* LXXI (1935), 113-35.

Huffer, E., S.J. "De analoge volmaaktheden in hun verhouding tot het ziin." *Bijdragen uitgegeven door de Philosophische en Theologische Faculteiten der Noord- en Zuit-Nederlandes Jezuieten,* (1947), 268-73.

Hugon, Edouard, O.P. *Les vingt-quatre thèses thomistes,* pp. 20-23. Paris: Téqui, 1937.

Jacques, J., S.C.J. "Abstraction et analogie." *Revue néo-scolastique de philosophie,* XXXVIII (1935), 530-35.

Joannes a S. Thoma, O.P. *Cursus philosophicus thomisticus. Ars logica seu de forma et materia ratiocinandi,* edited by Beatus Reiser, O.S.B., pars II, q. 13, aa. 3-5; q. 14, aa. 2, 3; Vol. 1, pp. 481-99, 504-13. 3 vols. Turin: Marietti, 1930.

John of St. Thomas, O.P. *The Material Logic of John of St. Thomas,* translated by Yves R. Simon, John J. Glanville, and G. Donald Hollenhorst, section 3, q. 13, aa. 3-5; q. 14, aa. 2, 3; pp. 152-83, 190-208. Chicago: The University of Chicago Press, 1955.

Jolivet, Régis. "A la recherche de Dieu." *Archives de philosophie,* VIII (1931), cahier 2, (133)-(219).

Kelly, Bernard. *The Metaphysical Background of Analogy.* Aquinas Paper, No. 29. London: Blackfriars, 1958.

Klubertanz, George P., S.J. *Introduction to the Philosophy of Being*, pp. 53-63, 101-03, 135-37, 170-74, 286-90. New York: Appleton-Century-Crofts, 1955.

———— "The Problem of the Analogy of Being." *Review of Metaphysics*, X (1957), 553-79.

Knox, Ronald A. "A Fragment." *Month*, new series, XXII (1959), 13-21.

———— " 'Proving God,' Another Approach." *Month*, new series, XXI (1959), 333-45, especially 340-45.

Krąpiec, Albert M., O.P. "Analysis formationis conceptus entis existentialiter considerati." *Divus Thomas* (Placentiae), Series III, LIX (1956), 348.

———— *Egzystencjalne podstawy transcendentalnej analogii bytu. Studium z zakresu podstaw metafizyki tomistycznej.* (mimeographed) Kráków, 1951.

———— "O rehabilitacje analogii bytowej." *Roczniki filozoficzne*, V, No. 4 (1957).

———— *Teoria analogii bytu.* Lublin: Katolickiego Uniw. Lubelskiego, in press, 1959.

Landry, B. "L'analogie de proportion chez S. Thomas." *Revue néoscolastique de philosophie*, XXIV (1922), 258-80.

———— "L'analogie de proportionalité chez S. Thomas." *Revue néoscolastique de philosophie*, XXIV (1922), 454-64.

———— *La notion d'analogie chez S. Bonaventure et S. Thomas d'Aquin.* Louvain, 1922.

Laurent, E., C.S.Sp. "Quelques réflexions sur l'analogie." *Acta pontificiae academiae S. Thomae*, V (1938), 169-84.

Le Blond, J. M., S.J. "L'analogie de la vérité." *Récherches de science religieuse*, XXXIV (1947), 129-41.

Leger, G., O.P. Review of analogy literature. *Bulletin thomiste*, VIII (1948), 572-79.

Leist, Fritz. "Analogia entis." *Studium generale*, VIII (1955), 671-78.

Le Rohellec, J., C.S.Sp. "Cognitio nostra analogica de Deo." *Divus Thomas* (Placentiae), Series III, IV (1927), 298-319.

———— "De fundamento metaphysico analogiae." *Divus Thomas* (Placentiae), Series III, III (1926), 79-101, 669-91.

———— *Problèmes philosophiques*, pp. 97-162. Paris: Téqui, 1931.

Lotz, Johannes, S.J. "Analogie und Chiffre." *Scholastik*, XV (1940), 39-56.

Lyttkens, Hampus. *The Analogy between God and the World: An Investigation of Its Background and Interpretation of Its Use by Thomas of Aquino.* Uppsala: Almqvist and Wiksells, 1952.

McInerny, Ralph. "The Logic of Analogy." *New Scholasticism*, XXXI (1957), 149-71.

Macintyre, A. "Analogy in Metaphysics." *Downside Review*, LXVIII (1950), 45-61.

McLean, George, O.M.I. "Symbol and Analogy: Tillich and Thomas." *Revue de l'Université d'Ottawa*, XXVIII (1958), 193*-233*.

Manser, G., O.P. *Das Wesen des Thomismus*, third edition, pp. 393-490. Fribourg: Paulusverlag, 1949.

———— "Die analoge Erkenntnis Gottes." *Divus Thomas* (Fribourg), Series III, VI (1928), 385-405.

Maquart, F. X. "Une nouvelle métaphysique." *Revue thomiste*, new series, IX (1926), 446-69.

Marc, André, S.J. *Dialectique de l'affimation*, pp. 293-338. Paris: Desclée de Brouwer, 1952.

———— "L'idée de l'être chez Saint Thomas et dans la scolastique postérieure." *Archives de philosophie*, X (1933), cahier 1.

———— "L'idée thomiste de l'être et les analogies d'attribution et de proportionalité." *Revue néo-scolastique de philosophie*, XXXV (1933), 157-89.

Maréchal, Joseph, S.J. *Le point de départ de la métaphysique*, Vol. 1, pp. 77-81; Vol. 5, pp. 424-37, 449-54. 5 vols. Paris: Alcan, 1923-1926.

Maritain, Jacques. *The Degrees of Knowledge*, translated by Gerald B. Phelan, pp. 418-21. New York: Charles Scribner's Sons, 1959.

———— *Distinguer pour unir, ou les degrés du savoir*, Annexe 2, "De l'analogie," pp. 821-26. Paris: Desclée de Brouwer, 1946.

Mascall, E. *Existence and Analogy.* New York: Longmans, Green and Company, 1949.

Masiello, Ralph. "The Analogy of Proportion in the Metaphysics of St. Thomas." *Modern Schoolman*, XXXV (1958), 91-105.

Mattiussi, Guido, S.J. *Le XXIV Tesi della filosofia di S. Tommaso d'Aquino*, second edition, pp. 40-44. Rome: Gregorian University Press, 1925.

Maurer, A., C.S.B. "St. Thomas and the Analogy of Genus." *New Scholasticism*, XXIX (1955), 127-44.

Meissner, William, S.J. "Some Notes on a Figure in St. Thomas." *New Scholasticism*, XXXI (1957), 68-84.

Meyer, H. *The Philosophy of St. Thomas Aquinas*, translated by F. Eckhoff, pp. 128-33. St. Louis: B. Herder Book Company, 1944.

Moore, Sebastian, O.S.B. "Analogy and the Free Mind." *Downside Review*, LXXVI (1958), 1-28.

Morard, Meinrad Stéphane, O.P. "Pour repenser la question de l'analogie." *Freiburger Zeitschrift für Philosophie und Theologie*, VI (1959), 145-62.

Moré-Pontgibaud, C., S.J. "Sur l'analogie des noms divins." *Récherches de science religieuse*, XIX (1929), 481-512; XX (1930), 193-223.

Munnynick, M. de, O.P. "L'analogie métaphysique." *Revue néo-scolastique de philosophie*, XXV (1923), 129-55.

Nemetz, Anthony. "The Meaning of Analogy." *Franciscan Studies*, XV (1955), 209-23.

O'Brien, Ignatius, O.P. "Analogy and Our Knowledge of God." *Philosophical Studies*, VI (1946), 91-104.

Owens, Joseph, C.Ss.R. *The Doctrine of Being in the Aristotelian 'Metaphysics,'* pp. 58-60. Toronto: Pontifical Institute of Mediaeval Studies, 1952.

Penido, M. T.-L. "Cajétan et notre connaissance analogique de Dieu." *Revue thomiste*, XXXIX (1934), 149-92.

———— Review of Balthasar. *Bulletin thomiste*, III (1926), 147-50.

———— *Le rôle de l'analogie en théologie dogmatique.* Paris: Vrin, 1931.

Phelan, Gerald. *St. Thomas and Analogy*, Aquinas Lecture, 1948. Milwaukee: Marquette University Press, 1948.

Philippe, T., O.P. Review of analogy literature. *Bulletin thomiste*, IV (1932), 504-09.

Pita, Enrique B., S.J. "El encuentro con Dios por la analogía." *Ciencia y fe*, IX (1953), 7-18.

Platzeck, E., O.F.M. "De conceptu analogiae respectu univocationis." *Antonianum*, XXIII (1948), 71-132.

Przywara, Erich, S.J. *Analogia Entis. Metaphysik.* München: Kösel und Pustet, 1932.

Przywara, Erich, S.J. "Die Reichweite der Analogie als katholischer Grundform." *Scholastik,* XV (1940), 339-63, 508-32.

———— *Polarity,* translated by A. C. Bouquet, pp. 29-62, 95-119. New York: Oxford University Press, 1935.

Raeymaeker, Louis de. *Philosophie de l'être,* second edition, pp. 43-74. Louvain: Institut Supérieur de Philosophie, 1947.

———— *The Philosophy of Being,* translated by Edmund H. Ziegelmeyer, S.J., pp. 33-60. St. Louis: B. Herder Book Company, 1954.

Ramirez, J., O.P. "De analogia secundum doctrinam aristotelico-thomisticam." *La ciencia tomista,* XIII (1921), 19-40, 195-214, 337-57; XIV (1922), 17-38.

Ramirez, S. M., O.P. "En torno a un famoso texto de santo Tomás sobre la analogía." *Sapientia,* VIII (1953), 166-92.

Reese, William L. "Analogy, Symbolism, and Linguistic Analysis." *Review of Metaphysics,* XIII (1960), 447-68.

Ross, James Francis. *A Critical Analysis of the Theory of Analogy of St. Thomas Aquinas.* (Brown University, 1958) Abstract in *Dissertation Abstracts,* XX (1959), 1045. Ann Arbor: University Microfilms, 1959.

Ryan, Columba, O.P. "God and Analogy." *Blackfriars,* XXV (1941), 137-43.

———— "The Reach of Analogical Argument." *Dominican Studies,* IV (1951), 102-18.

Santeler, Josef, S.J. "Die Lehre von der Analogie des Seins." *Zeitschrift für Katholische Theologie,* LV (1931), 1-43.

Schwartz, H. "Analogy in St. Thomas and Cajetan." *New Scholasticism,* XXVIII (1954), 127-44.

———— "Plato, Aristotle, St. Thomas and Univocity." *New Scholasticism,* XXVII (1953), 373-85.

Sertillanges, A.-D., O.P. "Agnosticisme ou anthropomorphisme." *Revue de philosophie,* VIII (1906), 129-65.

———— "La connaissance de Dieu." *Revue de philosophie,* IX (1907), 614-25.

———— *Foundations of Thomistic Philosophy,* translated by Godfrey Anstruther, O.P., pp. 77-92. London: Sands, 1931; Springfield: Templegate, n. d.

Sertillanges, A.-D., O.P. *Les grandes thèses de la philosophie thomiste,* pp. 67-80. Paris: Bloud et Gay, 1928.

———— *St. Thomas d'Aquin,* fourth edition, Vol. 1, pp. 176-90. 2 vols. Paris: Alcan, 1925.

Silvester Ferrariensis. *Commentaria in 'Summam contra gentiles.'* In *Opera omnia S. Thomae Aquinatis,* Ed. Leonine. Rome, 1888-.

Slattery, M. P. "Concerning Two Recent Studies in Analogy." *New Scholasticism,* XXXI (1957), 237-46.

Söhngen, Gottlieb. "Wesen und Akt in der scholastischen Lehre von der *Participatio* und *Analogia Entis.*" *Studium generale,* VIII (1955), 649-62.

Solages, Bruno de. *Dialogue sur l'analogie.* Paris: Aubier, 1946.

Suarez, Franciscus, S.J. *Disputationes metaphysicae.* In *Opera omnia,* disp. 2, Vol. 25, pp. 64-102; disp. 28, sec. 3, Vol. 26, pp. 13-21; disp. 30, sec. 15, Vol. 26, pp. 170-83; disp. 32, sec. 2, Vol. 26, pp. 319-29; disp. 39, sec. 3, Vol. 26, pp. 523-29. 28 vols. Paris: Vivès, 1877.

Toko, Kan'ei. "Essay on Analogia Entis of Thomas Aquinas." *Studies in Medieval Thought,* II (1959), 78-91 (in Japanese), 177-78 (English summary).

Valensin, Auguste. *A travers la métaphysique.* "Théorie de l'analogie," pp. 211-34. Paris: Beauchesne, 1925.

Van Leeuwen, A., S.J. "L'analogie de l'être. Genèse et contenu du concept d'analogie." *Revue néo-scolastique de philosophie,* XXXIX, (1936), 293-320.

———— "L'analogie de l'être. Précisions sur la nature de cette analogie." *Revue néo-scolastique de philosophie,* XXXIX (1936), 469-96.

Van Steenberghen, Fernand. "Le problème philosophique de l'existence de Dieu." *Revue philosophique de Louvain,* XLV (1947), 1-20, 141-68, 301-13.

Varangot, Oscar A., S.J. *Analogía de atribucion intrinseca y analogía del ente segun Santo Tomas.* "Excerpta e dissertatione . . . in Universitate Gregoriana." Buenos Aires: published by author, 1957.

Verhaeghe, M. "De metaphysische waarde der analogie bij Cajetanus." *Studia catholica* (Nijmegen), XXVI (1951), 1-21.

Walgrave, J. H., O.P. "Analogie en metaphysiek." *Tijdschrift voor philosophie*, XIII (1951), 79-110.

Wébert, J., O.P. "L'image dans l'oeuvre de S. Thomas." *Revue thomiste*, new series, IX (1926), 427-45.

Weigel, Gustave, S.J. "Contemporaneous Protestantism and Paul Tillich." *Theological Studies*, XI (1950), 177-202.

——— "The Theological Significance of Paul Tillich." *Gregorianum*, XXXVII (1956), 34-54.

White, Victor, O.P., and others. "The Knowledge of God." *Downside Review*, LXXVI (1958), 41-63.

Williams, C. J. F. "Existence and the Meaning of the Word 'God.'" *Downside Review*, LXXVII (1958-1959), 53-71.

Winance, Eleuthère, O.S.B. "Essence divine et connaissance humaine chez S. Thomas." *Revue philosophique de Louvain*, LV (1957), 171-215.

Witte, Ant. de, O.P. *Analogie*. Roermond-Maaseik: J. J. Romen en Zonen, 1946.

Zaragueta, J. "La analogía en la denominación de los seres esenciales." *Revista de filosofía*, IV (1945), 9-49.

315